THE PHENOMENON OF WELSHNESS II

or

'Is Wales too poor to be independent?'

By the same author:

The Phenomenon of Welshness:
   or, 'How many aircraft would an independent Wales have?'

The Welsh National Anthem – Hen Wlad Fy Nhadau

**Praise for The Phenomenon of Welshness: or,
'How Many aircraft carriers would an independent Wales have?'**

'Sion Jobbins [is] knowledgeable, witty, and a fierce patriot. The book reaches out to readers who yearn to know more about Wales, whether they are natives of Wales, or visitors from other countries.

> *Janet Watkins Masoner, NINNAU Publications,*
> *Newspaper of the North American Welsh*

'I have read your excellent book and I find myself in agreement with your arguments.'

> *Professor Kwesi Kwaa Prah, Director, Centre for Advanced*
> *Studies of African Society, Cape Town, South Africa*

'Enjoyed the read. Provocative. The world – and particularly the Welsh nation – needs idealists.'

> *Dai G. Morris, Worcester*

'Greatly enjoyed the *Phenomenon of Welshness,* which I've been recommending to people.'

> *Patrick McGuinness, author,* The Last Hundred Days,
> *winner of Wales Book of the year, 2012*

The Phenomenon of Welshness II

or
'Is Wales too poor to be independent?'

Siôn T. Jobbins

First published in 2013

© text: Siôn T. Jobbins

Published by Gwasg Carreg Gwalch 2013,
12 Iard yr Orsaf, Llanrwst, Wales LL26 0EH
tel: 01492 624031
fax: 01492 641502
email: books@carreg-gwalch.com
website: www.carreg-gwalch.com

Published with the financial support
of the Welsh Books Council

ISBN: 978-1-84527-465-8

Cover design: Welsh Books Council

Yn bell o flaen unrhyw gariad at wlad, iaith neu gred,
mae fy nghariad at fy mhlant:
Elliw, Gwenno ac Owain
(Hwmps, Wylyms a'r Hoj).

Mae'r llyfr yma iddynt hwy
am eu cwmni cariadus a chall dros gyfnod ysgrifennu'r llyfr hwn.

Contents

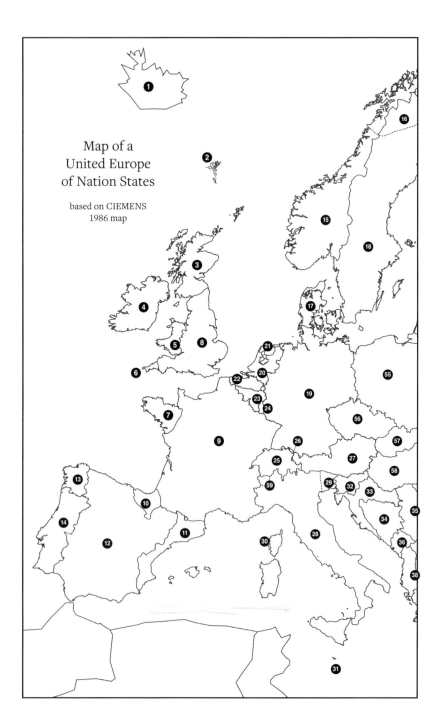

Map of a
United Europe
of Nation States

based on CIEMENS
1986 map

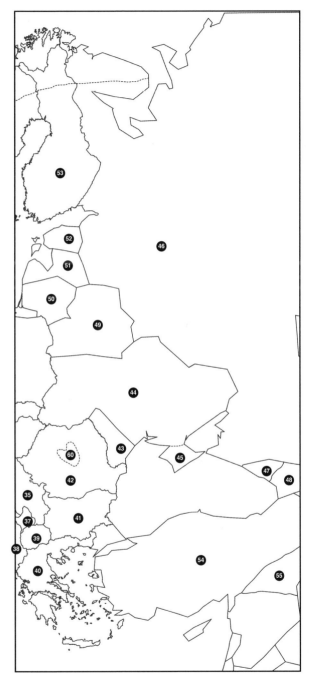

1. Iceland
2. Faroe Islands
3. Scotland
4. Ireland
5. Wales
6. Cornwall
7. Brittany
8. England
9. France
10. The Basque Country
11. The Catalonia
    Countries
12. Spain
13. Galicia
14. Portugal
15. Norway
16. Sami Territory
17. Denmark
18. Sweden
19. Germany
20. Netherlands
21. Friesland
22. Flanders
23. Walloonia
24. Luxembourg
25. Switzerland
26. Lichtenstein
27. Austria
28. Italy
29. Frialian territory
30. Corsica
31. Malta
32. Slovenia
33. Croatia
34. Bosnia Hertagovina
35. Serbia
36. Montenegro
37. Kosovo
38. Albania
39. Macedonia
40. Greece
41. Bulgaria
42. Romania
43. Moldova
44. Ukraine
45. Crimea
46. Russia
47. Abkhazia
48. Georgia
49. Belarus
50. Lithuania
51. Latvia
52. Estonia
53. Finland
54. Turkey
55. Kurdistan
56. Czech Republic
57. Slovakia
58. Hungary
59. Val d'Aosta
60. Hungarian-speaking
    region

Introduction

Congratulations! You've made a big choice to join a world-wide movement of great change. Or maybe you haven't and are just reading this page over the shoulder of the legitimate purchaser. In any case, welcome!

This is a book about Wales and about the choices people make. Their choice to create and imagine a different Wales, or their choice to go with the flow and accept being colonised. This is a book about people who've made Wales more diverse, more interesting and, frankly, kept it alive. You'll not have heard about many of them; I hadn't until I began questioning, researching and writing. It's a book about the little histories which gives us a bigger picture.

Many of the articles in the book concern the Welsh language, and I hope that won't turn off some readers. The more I wrote these articles, the more I realised that many Welsh people (and Welsh-speakers in particular) inhabit a world with footnotes. Footnotes to past events or political thoughts that they assume other people can also see and 'read'. But of course, others don't see these footnotes or are even unaware of them. This, I believe, helps explain some of the misunderstandings amongst the Welsh people themselves, and between Welsh people and those from outside. Very few books honestly explain why individuals make the choice to become active for Welsh self-government or the Welsh language, or what it actually means to be a nationalist. I hope this one does. As Welsh politics has been plagued by deliberate 'divide and rule' strategies I hope this book goes some way to explaining a side of Welsh life and philosophy which may not be clear to some.

Wales, I hope, is a warm house to people of different political persuasions, religions, sexuality and ethnicity. It's a house which should accommodate and celebrate all these diverse strands without losing what makes us unique: our language and our nationality.

This book is a sequel to *The Phenomenon of Welshness: or 'How many aircraft carriers would an independent Wales have?'* That book struck a chord with many Welsh people – both Welsh-speakers and non-Welsh-speakers – who were denied meaningful Welsh history at school and through the media. There has also been a generous response by people outside Wales too, such as Professor Kwesi Kwaa Prah of South Africa (who's standardising African languages), and Prof. Robert Phillipson, author of *Linguistic Imperialism*, and his wife, Tove Skutnabb-Kangas, in Denmark.

There are many international influences on this book, for Wales isn't just a small rain-soaked country; it's a world in itself. The efforts of the brave few to promote the national status of Wales are also mirrored in other countries. For to be Welsh – or more importantly, to empathise with Welshness – is to be a full world citizen; one foot in the global anglophone world and another in the shoes of the forgotten and hidden peoples.

If you are a Welsh person reading this on holiday in a foreign land then maybe you'd like to consider whether the history of your host country mirrors that of Wales. Do the people, or did they, have the same debates as us about identity, politics and language? Actually, the majority of European nations, and every state in Africa, America and Asia, have experienced what I'd call a 'Welsh history': that is, a history of the dominant nation and the colonised one; the historic nation and the non-historic one. To be Welsh is to care more about the demise of peoples and cultures than about states, regimes, and lines on maps. To be Welsh, I'd argue, is to be aware as much of the words quietly said in 'dialects', or not said at all, as of the loudly-proclaimed loud words from experts and those in authority. It's, hopefully, to cast a wry eye when anyone says a country is 'too poor' or 'too small' to be independent, or a language or culture 'not developed enough' or 'not modern enough' to have full status in education or on television.

For to be Welsh is to be about choice. As a Welshman I can choose between two routes. They are, essentially, the same two routes also taken by two different Corsicans. I can choose the Napoleon Bonaparte route and project my person and nationality to be part of the great big imperial identity. Or, choose the Pasquale Paoliani route. Paoliani? Not heard of him? He was a generation older than Napoleon and was Napoleon's early inspiration. Paoliani fought for Corsican independence and created a Corsican state with its own democratic constitution in 1755 – yes, thirty-two years before the more famous American constitution and thirty-four years before the French one. This is the choice every Welshman is offered: the Napoleon national complex – fame, power, aggrandisement on a big stage, or the Paoliani project – obscurity, powerless, ambition for your own nation, rather than conquest of others. Would the world be better for more Paolianis or more Napoleons? I choose Paoliani.

Napoleon or Paoliani? French or Corsican? Georgian or Russian? Catalan or Spanish? Welsh or British? It's not that there is virtue in obscurity, any more than in poverty. There is no more virtue in the small over the large either. But there is virtue in taking the hard route – if it is for the defence and promotion of a community that is marginalised by the larger community, to which you can also belong.

For, as we see the broad horizon of the future, millions of people make this choice every day, in Wales and in the other soon-to-be independent nations of Europe.

And not only in Europe either.

To be Welsh is to stand like John F. Kennedy beside the looming, forceful power of the Berlin Wall in 1963. As he said '*Ich bin ein Berliner*', the Welshman says: '*Rwyf Kurd*'; '*Rwyf Tibetiad*'; '*Rwyf Imazighen*', '*Rwyf Innuit*'. I am these people because their histories are mine.

But this book is as much about the future as it is about history.

Many of you will want to know if Wales is 'too poor to be independent'. I cannot give you a definitive answer, I'm afraid. But I can point you to the direction of the casualty rate of arguments which have been used by those who have been against independence for 'too poor' nations in the past. I can point to arguments against Welsh secession that have been proven wrong in the past. It's the same debate made by the same people. Would you buy a product from a salesman who was consistently wrong about his previous predictions? The economic question of whether Wales is 'too poor to be independent' is like those who said bilingual road signs would lead to more deaths on the road, or that raising your children bilingually will impair their education, or that Wales could not compete as an international rugby or football (or Olympic) team. These arguments are quack theories peddled to us by those with a political agenda. They were wrong on these matters, so why would they be right on the economy?

This is a book of hope. It's the story of a nation which, during its recent history, has had to reinvent itself several times. We are here because, although few in number, we've willed ourselves to live. This is about a People who wished to be a Nation. It's about what has been achieved through the power of dreams not dragoons.

In *Lanark*, a 1981 novel by the Scottish writer, Alistair Grey, there is an exchange between two characters, McAlpin and Thaw:

'Glasgow is a magnificent city,' said McAlpin. 'Why do we hardly ever notice that?'

'Because nobody imagines living here,' said Thaw.

McAlpin lit a cigarette and said, 'If you want to explain that I'll certainly listen'.

'Then think of Florence, Paris, London, New York [said Thaw]. Nobody visiting them for the first time is a stranger because he's already visited them in paintings, novels, history books and films. But if a city hasn't been used by an artist not even the inhabitants live there imaginatively. What is Glasgow to most of us? ... Imaginatively Glasgow exists as a music-hall song and a few bad novels. That's all we've given to the world outside. It's all we've given to ourselves.'

For Glasgow, see Cardiff or Wrexham. Since 1981 the Scots have successfully 'imagined' their cities and themselves, and we too in Wales can do the same.

Wales is interesting because many people have already chosen to live in Wales imaginatively. They've created, in English and in Welsh, new cultures and politics.

Despite this, some persist in portraying Wales as a backward, insular country. In this politically correct age we hold the distinction, with the Belgians, of being the nations that comedians are still allowed to make fun of. We are, with stories about royal pregnancies and surf-boarding dogs, the '... and finally' news item par excellence. For many, even some who live here, Wales is a joke and an 'intellectual Welshman' an oxymoron.

Be that as it may. I think Wales is a far more interesting and nuanced place than it is often given credit for and my example below will hopefully give one reason why I believe this.

Anyone familiar with Wales will be aware of its rich

Christian heritage and its influence on Welsh thought; likewise, the influence of socialism on Welsh thought. But there are other less well-recognised international influences on Wales too which show to me, at least, that Wales has its own window on the world, which I hope this book also demonstrates. One of those influences is the existentialist thought of Jean-Paul Sartre, Simone de Beauvoir and Paul Tillich that helped create the context for many of the events which are outlined in this and my first book.

Following the horrors of the Second World War and Auschwitz created by mass ideologies and beliefs, the existentialist philosophical perspective flourished. It concluded that a person must be true to their own spirit, personality or character rather than what labels, roles, stereotypes, definitions, or other preconceived categories the individual fitted. Human beings, through their own consciousness, had to create their own values and give their own life a meaning.

These writings, especially those of Tillich, who applied existentialism to Christian theology, influenced the philosopher and lay preacher J. R. Jones in the 1960s, who put some of these ideas in a Welsh context. He reasoned that for many people, speaking Welsh was to be true to one's own spirit. And yet, speaking Welsh, like any language, is a social affair. But if the number of Welsh-speakers was falling, he concluded that that affected the spirit, personality and character of the Welsh-speaker. How was a Welsh-speaker, then, to be true to his or her personality? And what was one to do to change the situation of the language?

To put it bluntly, those concerned about the fate of the language couldn't be happy and true to themselves if a part of their being was dying. They had put faith in other ideologies, definitions and rôles, but they hadn't succeeded in alleviating the very thing which undermined their potential happiness. The political became the personal. The demise of the Welsh language was not only a linguistic and political problem, it was a personal one.

The Welsh had been faithful to God. But idealistically and idly believing in God's providence of itself hadn't saved their language. They had faithfully fought pointless wars for the British state, even wars to save 'small nations'. But under the British state their language was losing ground, and that couldn't make them happy as Welsh-speakers or people who wished for status to their Welsh nationality.

Welsh people as individuals had made their own choice: to change their own reality to make themselves happier.

It was time for the Welsh to put their faith in themselves and not in other creeds or states. Existentialism swept across Europe, and its Welsh incarnation, drawing on other beliefs, traditions and post-War baby-boom, created the context for the rise of Welsh nationalism in the 1960s. It's that explosion of ideas and self-confidence of Welsh people that is the source of many of the articles in this book.

I've commented about the existential concern and unhappiness which was a contributing factor to the rise of the Welsh language rights movement of the 1960s. Allow me now to give a reason, again a little existential, why those who don't speak Welsh may wish to see the language grow and flourish in Wales. This also sounds a little soft and pretentious but may also help explain the support the language struggle has gratefully received from many of those who don't speak the language.

As well as the feeling of righting a historical wrong and of rolling back the colonial policies of the British state is there another less commented upon factor and powerful phenomenon in Welsh identity. Why, after all, would a non-Welsh speaker, or someone who isn't even Welsh, wish to see the language regain prestige? By doing do, aren't they supporting measures which will give those Welsh Speakers jobs and deny jobs to themselves and their own children? Aren't they like turkeys voting for Christmas?

Well, let me, maybe, suggest this reason and make a personal comparison.

As a white, straight man, by all calculable, measurable, scientific factors I should be against three of the great social and political changes since the Second World War: feminism and black and gay rights. All these movements presented a challenge, if not a threat to my job, status and world view. And yet, although there is much which depresses me about today's society – an economy built on rentier capitalism, and general shabbiness of buildings, clothing and appearance being some of them – I prefer this society to the 1950s say, when I as a straight, white man would be king of my castle. Maybe, despite the threats, the perceived diminishing of status, I still prefer to live in 2013 than 1953. Why? Because, I believe in many many ways today's society is fairer, richer and more interesting. Add to that the rolling back of historic injustice, like against the Welsh language and nation, and we maybe glimpse an inspiration for the phenomenon which has made Wales what it is today and what if could be tomorrow.

The revival of the Welsh language, like rights for women, gays and 'blacks', could make Wales a better, more interesting and happier place, or, at least, make a significant section of her population, beyond the native Welsh-speakers, happy.

Many people, including many of those in this book, have been infused by this existentialist thought, even though the vast majority of protagonists are unaware of it. This Welsh nationalist school of thought is also at the root of misunderstanding in the sometimes bitter debate in Wales, especially with the dominant British labour movement, on the Welsh language and what it means to be Welsh.

The 'Simon Glyn Affair' is touched on in the 'White is Not the Only Colour' article in this book, and in detail in my first volume. In this situation we see the two different ways of viewing the Welsh-language issue and the battle for its survival. Broadly speaking, the Labour movement seems to view the language issue as an ethnic one. That is, they view it as a fight for the rights (or 'favours', to use a more pejorative term) of a particular ethnic group – the Welsh-Speaker.

The nationalist perspective, held also by those who don't speak the language, views the struggle for Welsh as, yes, a struggle for language rights for speakers of the language, but also, crucially, for the language itself. That is, the language is a concept and vehicle for a unique history, culture and world-view integral to Wales that can be used by all. Gaining status for the Welsh language isn't, as many in the Labour movement seem to assume, aimed at enriching individual ethnic speakers. Gaining status for the language is there to enrich and promote the language itself. It is the Welsh language's enrichment and vitality that makes the Welsh-language supporter happy, not getting jobs for Welsh-speakers, or denying jobs to non-Welsh-speakers.

Some people may read this book hoping for a manifesto. I can't offer that. I'm neither a politician nor philosopher. My political views vary from left-wing to right-wing depending on the context and question. I come from the standpoint that Wales is a colonised nation coming to terms with its colonised past … and present. I make no apologies for that.

I hope this book lifts the lid on some of these footnotes and the choices people have made.

I'll not presume to tell you which choices to make in your

life or for Wales or your country. I'll only say that I've been inspired by many of the people I've written about in this book. In the light of the choices they've made and the colonised history of my nation, I've made a choice, in the spirit of Pasquale Paoliani, to walk tall as a full Welshman.

Enjoy the book, and enjoy life.

Siôn T. Jobbins
Aberystwyth
Summer 2013

Where indicated, these articles were previously published in *Cambria* magazine. I have kept changes to the minimum, because although the contents might appear dated quite soon after publication, they become more like historical documents as time goes on. The introductory paragraphs are intended to put the articles in the context of their period.

As in *Phenomenon of Welshness I*, I'd again like to thank, and to show my appreciation and respect for, Frances Jones-Davies and her husband Henry, who've edited and persevered with *Cambria* magazine. Without their vision and dedication, I and other writers would not have had the opportunity to share our ideas in such an attractive and influential magazine.

I'd like to thank Dr Gareth Popkins for his steadfast support and critical eye as he suggested corrections and changes to the articles over the years. I'd also like to thank Dr Jen Llywelyn, the book's editor.

People

Myrddin John:
Welsh Sporting Hero

My respect for the 'old warriors' is huge. Anyone who fought for the dignity of Wales and the Welsh language in the 1950s deserves a medal! A wonderful decade in many ways, but also a suffocating one for people who didn't want to, or couldn't, conform: Welsh nationalists, feminists, gays, ethnic minorities.

Myrddin John fought for Wales. And it was a fight! He believed in that little-used word, dignity. He fought for the dignity of Wales. With the London Olympics a very recent memory as I write, I wanted to remember and celebrate a man who'd stood for Welsh dignity.

The run-up to the 2012 London Olympic Games was a British nationalist festival. Oh no? Did you see any Olympic bunting or flags during the event? No, nor me; only red, white and blue bunting and Union Jacks. Of course, it wasn't called a 'nationalist event' (it never is); it was all 'patriotic' or 'uniting the nation'. But uniting which nation? Not Wales. We were 'uniting' (under the Union Jack, the flag which has no Welsh motif on it) into a nation that by its existence negates our nationality.

The Wales Sports Council debased itself as it celebrated the success of ethnically Welsh athletes: celebrating that Wales had no Team Cymru at the games. Shame on them. The political class which has accused Welsh nationalists of being 'ethnic' nationalists were telling us to support some TeamGB members because they were, erm, ethnically Welsh. I'm afraid I didn't celebrate nor cheer any member of TeamGB, and certainly not because they were Welsh.

How can I support a team which air-brushes my nation off the sporting map? How can I support the flying of the flag which caused genocide in Africa, America and Asia and Australia? The *flag whose supremacists' linguistic ideology gave us the 'Welsh Not' (when a plank was hung around the neck of a schoolchild as punishment for speaking Welsh) and every large and small humiliation my language has suffered? A flag which sent my grandfather's uncle, John Jobbins of Pontypool, to kill Zulus in Rorke's Drift – why? A flag to which every single councillor, MP or AM who has opposed Welsh national status or concession to the Welsh language (or Welsh national sporting teams) has shown allegiance.*

To support the Union Jack is to have no self-respect and dignity as a Welsh person. It's to place Wales as a sub-nation: conquered, humiliated, ignored, and invisible. I'll leave that to those with no respect for Wales, her history or future.

There's a James Griffiths Road and a Maes Gareth Edwards in Ammanford, and the obligatory Waterloo Road and Terrace. But not one street is dedicated to Myrddin John, the Aman Valley man who, in his chosen sport, won international recognition for Wales as an independent nation.

For forty years, Myrddin campaigned single-handedly to get Wales recognised as an independent nation in weightlifting. In 2004, against the odds, he succeeded. But now, as we get ready to be humiliated by enforced unity through sport in the London Olympic Games, you watch the British establishment elbow Wales and Myrddin off the winner's podium. Watch the Olympics succeed in the yomping footsteps of Edward I and the dry legalese of Henry VIII in disqualifying Wales. Where Myrddin campaigned for a free Wales; Team GB makes the Olympics a Wales-free zone.

Myrddin was born seventy-four years ago, the son of a collier. After National Service he became a PE teacher in his home town. He'd always enjoyed sport and was a keen rugby player, but through the local *Urdd* (Welsh-language youth movement) club, weightlifting was his passion and he soon became Welsh champion ten times and competed at weightlifting at the Imperial Games in Cardiff in 1958. But whereas most sportsmen just concentrate on the physical, Myrddin became political.

'I've always believed that Wales is a nation and that we shouldn't be beneath any other country. That kept me going, that gave me self-respect. There are ninety countries with a population less than Wales' competing in the Olympics, so why aren't we there? Why shouldn't a Welsh athlete, who'd be good enough to compete in the Olympics if he were from another small nation, not get the chance to compete for his own small nation because Wales is a part of Britain?' said Myrddin from his home in Ammanford.

Weightlifting has a long and illustrious history in Wales. The Welsh Weightlifting Federation was founded by Sid Frost in 1927 after he and others had been inspired by a display of physical prowess by the famous moustached German strongman, Herman Görner, at the Market Hall in Llanelli.

However, from the very beginning the British organisation, the British Amateur Weightlifters' Association, tried its best to strong-arm the Welsh association into submission. One tactic the BAWA used was to refuse to ratify British records broken by Welsh weightlifters unless they affiliated to the British Association.

It was in the 1954 Empire Games, then, that Welsh weightlifters first competed – and won medals – in the colours of their country. Since then, more medals have been won for Wales at Commonwealth Games in weightlifting than in any other sport.

As Myrddin said, the Welsh Federation gained

international recognition 'despite vigorous objections by the British Association'.

So how did Myrddin gain international recognition for Wales?

'Dyfal donc a dyrr y garreg' – continual striking breaks the stone – is the Welsh idiom Myrddin used to describe his strategy.

He held prominent positions in the Commonwealth Games, the International Olympic Committee and Welsh sports organisations. He organised competitions where people got to know him. He'd travel, he'd make speeches, always pressing the case for Wales – 'they were fed up of hearing me!' He'd canvass. He'd make the case based on Welsh nationality – the fact that Wales already had its own Weightlifting Federation and her own football and rugby teams, her own National Assembly, her own unique language.

Of course, people were polite towards the Welsh case (aren't they always?) but nothing was ever promised. Every Welsh bid was blocked by the Great British representative on the executive board. Essentially the IWF didn't care either way, although scare stories would sometimes be spread – black propaganda to the effect that if Wales gained representation then all the individual states in the USA would also want to be independent.

Although Myrddin could point to the existence of Welsh sporting institutions to strengthen his case, he received virtually no practical help from the Sports Council of Wales or the Welsh Commonwealth Games committee. It's a peculiarly Welsh case. In a world where sporting jingoism is the norm, Welsh authorities go out of their way not to be seen as being 'too Welshie'. Maybe it's because so many of those in charge of Welsh sport would actually be quite content were Wales to deselect itself and become a part of England ... sorry, Britain. The kind of mentality which leads kids to think that McDonald's is better than the village chippy because it's not local and it's bigger. Or, maybe it's a dog-in-the-manger-ism: content to have a national Welsh team but not actually knowing why.

In the end, Myrddin managed to get onto the all-important Board of the IWF as a Vice-President. He'd cornered the Great British Amateur Weightlifters Federation. At a meeting in the Westin Bellevue Dresden Hotel in Dresden on 27 March 2004, the IWF voted unanimously to welcoming Wales as the 170th member.

Following the heroic work by Myrddin, the Scots became independent in 2005 and the Northern Irish in 2006. But that wasn't the end of the story, nor were things that simple. Despite expectations that the English would also wish to be represented as a constituent nation, the English refused.

The English insisted on retaining the 'Great Britain' title. By doing so, they effectively played the trump card in the Olympics. Whilst Welsh athletes can compete in the Welsh colours in international weightlifting competitions, they can only represent Great Britain at the Olympics. Weightlifters are forced therefore to choose: if they choose to represent Wales they potentially forfeit their chance to compete at the Olympics. The existence of a Team GB effectively blocks the development of the Welsh weightlifting team and its chance of competing and winning abroad. It was check-mate to the British.

As is usually the case, Britain negates Wales. You can't have both.

So, are you ready to be patronised by the 'we're all in this together' Olympics now? Reminded with bunting and balloons, that somewhere in excess of £250m has been taken from the Welsh economy for us not to be represented as a nation? I for one hope that the London Olympics, like the 1980 Moscow games, will be the last circus of an empire. The last lap to create Homo Britannicus, as the Russians failed with Homo Sovieticus.

A Wales Olympic team is a valid possibility. With only 5 per cent of the UK population, we won 11 per cent of the UK medals at Beijing and 14 per cent of the Paralympic medals. At 0.05 of the world population we won ten times more than our international stature would expect. And there's the desire too. Brave Tom James of Wrexham, gold medal winner at rowing in 2008 Beijing, defied the Olympic ban by flying the Red Dragon.

So, what of this domino effect? This apocalyptical quagmire of 'giving' (it's always 'giving' isn't it, like giving pennies to starving, fly-infested black African kids) sporting independence to Wales? Would it open the floodgates to the other diacritic-writing, cousin-marrying lesser nations like the Welsh? Would it, as the whisperers at the IWF said, lead to a stampede of the fifty American states wanting independence too?

Well, let me give you my maximalist position. That is, my list of aspirant nations which should have a national team at the next Olympic Games. I'll suggest: the Celtic countries, Flanders, the Basque Country, Catalonia, Galicia, Corsica, Faroe Islands and Greenland. I don't know if the Friesians, Fruil or Sami conceive of themselves as aspirant nation states or not. So, let's give and take twelve nations.

Outside Europe I can't see any secessionist movements in South America, and only Quebec in the north. There could be a couple of secessionist movements in the Russian Federation – Abkhazia, Tartars and Chechens, and in Asia, the most famous being Kurds, Baluchis, Kashmiris, Uyghurs, Tibetians, Keren, Acenese, Kanaks and West Papua. Whilst there are many many more ethnic communities, many of these disputes are about ethnic communities split between states rather than creating new ones. Moreover, the *Zeitgeist* within the many ethnicities in booming India, China and South East Asia, like the effect of an expansive confident Victorian age on Wales, will be to dampen ideas of independence within the region for the next forty years.

In sub-Saharan Africa, whilst there are tensions, very few 'tribal' communities conceive of themselves as aspirant independent states. Again, like early modern Wales, the concept of a political nation seems mostly not to have surfaced with the Kikuyu, Wolof or Xhosa-speakers. There could, of course, be some new states created due to economic, ethnic, post-colonial or religious tension – mostly it seems to me along the Sahel. But I don't foresee a huge wave of new independent states spreading across Africa like there was in Europe post-1991.

So, most, though not all, of the aspirant Olympic states would come from Europe. We're talking of about thirty new states to add to the existing 190 IOC members. That's all – heavens, there are 650 MPs in the Westminster parliament! There wouldn't be a tsunami of states for at least two generations. And the USA? Well, there's no feeling of nationality or language or history to American rectangular states as there is to the historically-dimpled borders of Wales and Europe.

But back to Myrddin John. Why is he not known to all Welsh people? Why isn't he held up as a man to emulate: a guest-speaker at Assembly sponsored bow-tie events?

The Plaid Cymru MP for Myrddin's constituency, Jonathan Edwards, is a passionate campaigner for a Wales test cricket team (the governing body of the team commonly known as 'England' is officially 'the England and Wales Cricket Board', but you'd never know it). But why is he being sent out to bat for Wales by himself? Where's the Welsh Government's support? After all, a national team is a matter of national sporting pride, and also of promoting Welsh tourism, industry and services.

The Basque and Catalan governments actively support their national 'selection' teams and campaign for international recognition. National Basque, Catalan (and Breton) football teams have played international matches against the likes of Uruguay, Romania, Russia ... and Wales. However, they are unable to compete at tournaments because FIFA and UEFA don't recognise them as nations.

Wales is lucky. The founding of the Football Association of Wales in 1876, the translation of the Bible in 1588, and the Yes vote of 1997, are the Three Lucky Flukes in Welsh History. But we can't be complacent. What could be done to weightlifting could happen to our national football team. We could be on the slippery slope to dependency if the Olympic Team GB get their way. Myrddin John is wise to the politricks, and the son of the collier can hear the canary coughing.

'From my experience with the British and world authorities, the Football Association of Wales are right to be concerned about the moves to create a British football team for the Olympics. It's dangerous,' warned Myrddin.

There will be those who argue that a Welsh sporting identity can live with, or be under the umbrella of, a larger British sporting structure. The example given is the existence of the British and Irish Lions rugby team. Leaving aside that I'd prefer it to be called the Celtic and English Lions rugby side, so as to underline that it is no irredentist effort to undermine the true nations, this is a rare (probably only) instance. It succeeds because the Lions don't compete in any 'proper' competitions – they are in effect Harlem Globetrotters with cauliflower ears. In sports such as athletics and tennis, the existence of the British identity negates the Welsh one.

The middle-distance-staring London Olympic Games will highlight one thing more than any. In diametric opposition to the commitment, guts, and dedication of the athletes is the lack of ambition and bravery of the Welsh ruling class to fight for Wales. To gain the status which should be ours.

Our debt is great to our athletes. We should celebrate them. But we should also celebrate and honour Myrddin John and people like him who put Wales first, not second. Pity the land that does not celebrate its own heroes – only the heroes of its conquerors.

Cambria, vol. 13, no. 3, April 2012

Where Did All the Runny-nosed Kids Go?: the Strange Death of *Calennig*

My good colleague at the National Library, Dr Huw Walters, stormed towards me one lunchtime in the library's Pen Dinas café asking what I had against calennig*? Why, asked the immaculately-dressed Aman Valley man, had I implied that* calennig *singers were snobs? I said that was far from what I'd written. Of course, my mistake was to say 'snotty-nosed' kids in the title of the original article. My intention was to give the impression that the kids singing* calennig *did so in cold mid-winter Januaries ... and not that they were upper class snobs!*

That cleared, Huw was happy, and gave his warm appreciation of the article.

So, the title has been amended, thanks to Huw Walters.

Since writing the article I've thought a lot about its underlying theme, which is that we as a nation have been negligent of our unique culture and traditions.

As I see the million and a half people march for Catalan independence on 11 September 2012; the confident march for Scottish independence, and the powerful self-belief of the Basques and growing assertion of the Bretons, something struck me. Bagpipes.

What all these successful national movements seem to have in their unique traditions are bagpipes! In their bagpipes there's an almost primeval attraction, certainly a pre-modern, pre-industrial sound. That is, sounds, smells and traditions which predate the modern nation states which have tried assimilating us. It is as if the harsh sound of pipes, like the Jewish Shofar horn, reminds people, almost to the marrow of their bones, that their culture is older than a state that is just a fleeting line on a map. Our nations pre-date the establishment of the UK, Spain,

France, and the lines on maps in Africa and America. And if we pre-date them we can out-live them too.

If Wales is to survive as a national community then it needs to embrace the modern and the global. But it also needs to remind itself of its traditions and even revive some. It needs sounds, smells and events which pre-date the British state. We need to create sounds that are unique to us, sounds that create a cultural space where Wales is the universe. We owe this to the dignity of our forefathers – they were not idiots bereft of culture, poetry or ideas – and as our contribution to world culture and diversity.

Calennig is the ancient Welsh tradition of singing short verses of song usually to two or three known 'calennig' tunes on New Year's Day. It's usually sung by children, who are then given sweets or money in return for their effort.

Calennig is the diminutive of 'calan', a word whose root is in the Latin Kalendae, 'the called' – corresponding to the first days of each month of the Roman calendar. The concept of the 'first day' was adopted into Welsh to mean the first day of the year (Dydd Calan) and it survives in 'Calan Gaeaf' (the first day of winter – Hallowe'en in English). It is the same root as the word 'calendar'.

It's a New Year version of carol singing if you like … but without the Christianity or the morality or the variation in songs and tunes or the harmonies or the adults. OK, so it's not like carol singing at all, but it is hundreds of years old and is – or was – an accepted and much-loved tradition across Wales.

So how, may you ask, is an accepted tradition where – and this is the crucial bit – kids get sweets and money for not much work at all, dying out? What child doesn't like a face-full of chocolate? I'm intrigued by the case of the strange death of this tradition.

Now, I can understand that traditions die. But *calennig*? This is just baffling? More pagan than Christian, a totally financially, Mammon-driven tradition, which, with the exception of confirming if the occupant was alive (even if feigning momentarily deafness at the sound of the door-bell) had absolutely no boring worthy nor communal benefit at all. What better tradition for the Pompeiian celebonomics of late twentieth and early twenty-first centuries? That a minority of miserable grown-ups may not like *calennig* is one thing, but kids? It thrived through the Methodist Revivial, wars and TB. So why do old people in villages and towns up and down Wales now complain that no kids have been around to ask them for treats on New Year's Day?

Goronwy Edwards is a well-known and much-loved councillor in Aberystwyth. Born in 1934, he remembers singing *calennig* verses on New Year's Day in Penparcau, a large council estate a mile from the centre of Aber. Despite his Welsh name and his mother being a Welsh-speaker, Gron (or Grocsy as he's known to all) has lost his Welsh. It's partly a result of his mother remarrying an Englishman, and Gron's new stepfather 'didn't like Welsh being spoken at home', and partly the anglicised community which existed in Aberystwyth even before the War, unlike the villages merely two miles out of town. But Gron joyfully reels out a couple of verses of calennig remembered from his youth:

Calennig yn gyfan mae heddiw'n ddydd calan;
unwaith, dwywaith, tairgwaith.

Mi godws yn fore rhedeg yn ffyrnig i dŷ Mrs Jones
i ofyn calennig. Os gwelwch yn dda
ga' i swllt a chwech cheiniog?
Blwyddyn newydd dda i'r dime a'r geiniog.

[It's *calennig* day all day today;
once, twice, three times.

I woke early and ran excitedly to Mrs Jones' house
to ask for *calennig*. Please
may I have a shilling and sixpence?
Happy New Year to the halfpenny and the penny.]

So, even in Aberystwyth, which was quite anglicised and even despite the fact that Gron spoke mostly English with his peers, *calennig*, sung with Welsh verses, was still strong in the mid twentieth century.

Keith Morris, the well-known photographer, and photographic author of an *Aber – Essays on Aberystwyth* (Gomer Press, 2008), is also an Aber boy. Keith is a generation younger than Gron, born in 1958. Raised in the centre of Aberystwyth in terraced Cambrian Street, his father, Jack, was London-Welsh and ran a milk-round in the town. His mother, Mona, was from Aber and became a well-known councillor. Keith also remembers singing *calennig*, but, like Gron, stopped when he went to high school. He recalled:

> You'd have a patch, and our patch (my brother and friends) was Cambrian Street up to Northgate and Dan-y-Coed – essentially, my father's milk round and the people we knew. We'd expect sixpence but would sometimes be given a shilling, which was excellent.

Despite being fluent in Welsh, the verses he sang were much simpler than Grocsy's. It may be a fluke or it may show that by the 1960s and early 70s only the well-known 'standard' ubiquitous verse was known:

Blwyddyn newydd dda i chi ac i bawb sydd yn y tŷ,
Dyna yw'n dymuniad ni, blwyddyn newydd dda i chi!

[Happy New Year to you and to all in this house,
That is our wish, Happy New Year to you!]

It seems that Keith and his peers were the last generation of unbroken, 'organic' singers in Aberystwyth town. Keith's daughters, Ffion Jac (sixteen) and Sam Medeni (twelve) have never sung *calennig*.

Although *calennig* is still sung in different parts of Wales, it seems to have died out in Aberystwyth in the early 1970s. Why? Certainly, Aber itself has its own peculiar reasons. The Veniceisation of the town – the depopulation of established families to be substituted by a transient population of students – is one reason, making Aber a terra firma, rainier version of the Italian city. Without the established network of known families, kids wouldn't feel comfortable to knock on a door and sing *calennig*. And as both Goronwy and Keith noted, they would usually only sing to Welsh-speaking households.

So, a more transient population is probably a reason. And what was once peculiar to a university town like Aberystwyth has since become commonplace across Wales as more and more English people move into rural Wales: people who are ignorant of our traditions, possibly not part of the extended network of family, work and chapel which was once the hot-water bottle which warmed the bed of Welsh folk traditions.

To the changing nature of communities could be added the changing affluence of those societies. It sounds odd, but is *calennig*-singing the only tradition on earth ever to be killed off by pocket money?

Singing *calennig* was the pastime of a materially poorer society. Parents would be glad to see their kids run around the houses collecting *calennig* as it eased the burden on their possibly tight budgets (especially after Christmas). Wealthier families would give then as we may give to African kids today. But if the average child is today given £3 a week pocket money and has all creature comforts, why sing *calennig*? With one in five Welsh kids overweight and the Welsh Government giving £1.4m in 2009 towards a pilot programme to tackle the problem, then it hardly seems necessary that a nation of fatties needs any more sweets and chocolate – even if they could manage to run around the houses without pausing for breath.

The beauty of *calennig* was that, if nothing else, it was the tradition of the *caridyms*, the *rapscaliwns*, the *plant gefn stryd* and all the other words of the mild Methodist snobbery which pervaded Welsh life like the smell of mothballs until so recently. It wasn't self-conscious, it wasn't poetry, it wasn't 'culture', it was just a more elaborate form of begging. The kids weren't bad, they weren't always poor, but in Wales (like everywhere in Western Europe) until the 1960s, any kid was glad of a few more pennies and sweets. *Calennig* was on the cusp of what's called in Welsh, '*y pethe*' – literally, 'the things', the Welsh things people take interest in – *eisteddfodau*, *cymanfa ganu*, poetry, local history. It was a non-institutional, non-structured culture – a beautifully adult- and teacher-free culture.

But then, there are still poor kids in Wales today. A 2008 survey by Save the Children calculated that 96,000 children in Wales lived in 'extreme poverty' (most, though, no doubt, materially at least much better off than the average family before the 1950s). These kids may not get pocket money, so why aren't they singing *calennig*? After all, they may very well 'play' (threaten may be a better word) the horrible American import of 'trick or treat' during Hallowe'en. If asking or begging for money during *Calan Gaeaf* is OK, why not during *Dydd Calan*?

Is it that the kids who are most materially in need today, or indeed any kids, are less likely to be Welsh-speaking than in the past? Has the Welsh-language community lost a whole swathe of society, people who found the pull of Hollywood and Disneyland, '*pobol y carnifal*', more appealing than anything Welsh culture could offer? And even children of Welsh-speaking nationalist families don't seem to sing *calennig* either. Are parents today over-protective? Whatever the reason, there's a whole swathe of kids and their parents who are ignorant of *calennig*, not to mention the old ditties which kids would sing – couplets of insults which sound so harmless and quaint today.

I always feel uneasy when someone says, 'It's important to keep traditions alive'. It always feels to me like, 'Hey, Taff, conform to your stereotype', or the Saint Faganising of Welsh culture. After all, traditions, like people, change. And I'm not the only one who feels like this. Despite lazy stereotypes, the contemporary Welsh-language movement has a modernist philosophy rather than a conservative one: traditions and 'keeping traditions alive' haven't played as prominent a part in the movement as in other cultures, partly because the movement expresses the evolving Welsh society, and partly to prove to its adversaries that Welsh is a contemporary language. It's been a case of choosing a modern font rather than Celtic calligraphy; Welsh pop music rather than Welsh folk.

But I can't help thinking a part of us has died, that we've somehow neglected to nurture the little things, as St David would say; the things which made us a people. Who sings hymns in pubs or at international matches or on coach journeys any more? Do people still place flowers on graves on *Sul y Blodau* (Palm Sunday)? How long will it be before the names of the new groom and bride are not sprayed on the road leading to the chapel, or mothers stop lovingly making homemade Welsh cakes for their kids to take on a trip? Will people stop naming their houses with Welsh names proudly etched on elegant blue-grey slate because it's too old-fashioned?

Welsh-language culture can lose some traditions and create a few in their place. But when the Welsh language dies in a locality then bit by bit, it seems, a whole host of our unique traditions die out too and it seems there's very little to take their place. Or, rather, there are new cultures and pastimes in their place – but they're mostly things like Wii, Ninendo DX, the Internet, TV football or 'recipient pastimes': cultures we receive from others, which are not unique, nor Welsh, nor local.

The Welsh language is a medium of communication, but also a medium for transferring stories and songs, history and sense of place. It seems we're becoming a poor man's Guernsey, with our own state and assembly but little of our own culture woven into the fabric of our society. It's a route other nations like the Basques and Bretons have not taken when they celebrate the unique and the 'peasant' in music, food, sports and aesthetics as they create the new and the modern.

The effort to keep and promote the Welsh language has in many respects been hugely successful. So, if it's not too contrived an idea, should we now not be part of a new campaign, this time to keep and promote Welsh culture, and especially the little everyday cultures too? That would be something worth singing about.

Let's *calennig*!

Cambria, vol. 12, no. 3, November 2010

Eluned Morgan, Patagonia:
the Woman Who 'Walked like a Prince'

It's always tickled me that we say 'mamwlad' (motherland) and 'mamiaith' (mother language) in Welsh, but our national anthem is in deference to our fathers. 'Tadwlad' (fatherland) just doesn't exist in Welsh as a term.

Welsh women have had a hard time of it. For BBC Cymru employees 'Mrs Jones Llanrug' is the linguistically and socially conservative scarecrow used to ward off radical ideas or nasal mutationally-challenged presenters. 'Dame Wales', the embodiment of Welsh women, is less glamorous then France's Marianne and less intimidating than England's heroine Britannia.

And on top of this they've mostly put up with Welsh men.

Among this baggage, Eluned Morgan (of Patagonia) is a very attractive character. She was a woman who made her own history. There are many women like her in Welsh history: Cranogwen (1823–1916) of Llangrannog, who taught navigation, was editor of Y Frythones *[literal translation: the female Briton], and was a poet and preacher in an age dominated by men; or there's Gwenllian Morgan of Brecon who became Wales's first mayor in 1910. Eileen Beasley of Llangennech, the Welsh language's Rosa Parks, was another strong Welsh woman: during the 1950s she and her collier husband, Trefor, refused to pay their rates to Llanelli Rural Council until the demands were sent in Welsh or bilingually. For that the couple were taken to court sixteen times over the course of eight years by the Labour-run council and their possessions taken by the bailiffs. For years her husband and children, Elidyr and Delyth, lived with only their table, four chairs and their beds.*

Eluned Morgan's story appealed to me because it includes so many interesting strands: the Welsh colony of Patagonia, her strength in standing up for the Welsh language, and her failure in love. It is no coincidence that her confidence in standing her ground for the language came from her upbringing in Patagonia, where the Welsh created a state in which Welsh was the language of education, councils, courts and enterprise. It was also a colony which gave its women the same rights as men. The price of draping ourselves in the Union Jack was to denigrate our language and our women, all so that we could be proud to be part of a great empire, 'better together'.

In 1885, during the high summer of Victorian imperialism and with the 'Welsh Not' in force, a 15-year-old schoolgirl, Eluned Morgan, led a walk-out at her secondary school in protest against the colonial English-only rule at the school.

Eluned had been punished the previous day for speaking Welsh at the dinner table at Dr Williams' School, Dolgellau. She was ordered to stand outside as eighty of her schoolmates finished their lunch and stared at her.

'The arrogance of the English element had become unbearable, and the idiocy of the teachers in relation to things Welsh made my old Welsh blood boil over', she later recalled, in a letter she sent in April 1900 from her home in Patagonia to William George, a solicitor in Porthmadog in Wales.

Unlike the submissive, defeated Welsh of the Victorian Age – an age we as Welsh people should never celebrate in costume or deed because we were treated like colonials in our own country – Eluned Morgan stood her ground.

'Every Welsh girl in this room who has no shame of her country and language, come with me to the classroom!' she challenged in Welsh. Every Welsh girl in the school rose up and left the room, leaving about thirty English girls with the teachers. They marched to the head teacher's room as 'one big banner-waving crowd' to demand to be treated with respect in their own country. As Eluned wasn't fluent in English her friend, Winnie Ellis, spoke on her behalf.

Eluned recalled in the letter that there was 'serious disturbance' for a week, until in the end she called for 'Dr Jones' to help settle the dispute.

The Dr Jones in the letter 'became a great hero to me for ever after then'. He was none other than Dr Michael D. Jones, the leading force in the campaign to create a Welsh-speaking colony, *Y Wladfa*, in Patagonia, Argentina.

Eluned Morgan was no ordinary girl. She was born on board the *Myfanwy* in the Bay of Biscay on her parents' voyage to the new colony in 1870. She was christened Eluned Morgan – 'Morgan' because she was born at sea (môr being Welsh for 'sea'). Her father was Lewis Jones, one-time editor of *Y Punch Cymraeg*, a satirical magazine along the lines of the famous English-language namesake. He was also one of the leaders of the settlement movement, and the town of Trelew in Patagonia's Chibut province was named in his honour. (*tre* = town; *lew* as in Lewis)

In later years her best friend Winnie, who had spoken in English on her behalf, recalled meeting Eluned for the first time. 'She looked like the daughter of a king of some foreign land, big black eyes full of life, complexion the colour of gold, hair like the night and the walk of a prince.'

No, Eluned Morgan was no ordinary girl. She had, after all, been sent on her own to Wales on a month-long voyage to receive higher education. Her temperament and strength of character in defending the Welsh language was so very different from that of the cowed Welsh – a defeated attitude which is still alive and sulking today in the hearts of many Welsh men and women. She'd gained her confidence from being raised in a colony at the other side of the world where Welsh was the language of all aspects of life – society, education, state and religion – a situation we in Wales still haven't reached. The Welsh colony was the only colony in the world where the colonisers had more linguistic rights than in their homeland.

Her circle of friends was also very different from the majority of her compatriots. Her best friend, Winnie, was the sister of T. E. Ellis, who was later to become the MP for Meirionnydd and whose statue graces the main street in Bala. He was a leading light in the *Cymru Fydd* (Young Wales) movement, which campaigned for a parliament for Wales, but he tragically died too young, denying Wales a leader of courage and intellect to stand for her national rights.

The letter in which Eluned recalled the brave events at the school was written to William George. They are published in his son W. R. P. George's anthology of letters, *Gyfaill hoff* ... (Gomer, 1972). But William George was no ordinary solicitor either. He was the brother of David Lloyd George, then MP for Carnarvonshire, who later became the Prime Minister of the UK.

Her letters to William George and other leading personalities in late Victorian and pre-Great-War Wales are beautifully written, and give an insight to the personal hopes and aspirations of a woman who was destined to be – or thought herself destined to be – a major figure in Welsh life. In so many ways, the 'what ifs' of her personal life mirror the 'what ifs' of Welsh cultural and political life. Her letters are written in Welsh.

Between 1890 and 1918 Eluned crossed the Atlantic between Wales and Patagonia no fewer than six times. She worked for a while cataloguing Welsh manuscripts at the British Museum in London, and was later an assistant librarian at Cardiff, where she lived at 51 Hamilton Street.

Unlike other middle-class girls, she was no stranger to

rolling up her sleeves. The pioneering attitude of her father and the limited support in the colony meant she had to help shoulder the burden of being a leader. She was compelled to get her fingers 'dirty with ink' and become a press compositor, and in 1893 became editor of *Y Drafod*, the colony's journal. She 'grabbed the ears of some men' to get them to help revive the eisteddfod in the Wladfa in 1900.

She feared for the future of the Welsh colony. Months of heavy rain and flooding in 1899 destroyed many of the Welsh homesteads, forcing the settlers to live in tents. The floods also made the Argentine authorities move their military barracks from Rawson to Gaiman, in the Welsh-speaking heartland of the colony. This Hispanised the area. In 1900 the Argentinean government (in an echo of the similar policy in the UK) made Spanish the sole language of instruction in education.

Eluned tried, but failed, to set up a Welsh-medium secondary school in Gaiman. This would have been the first secondary Welsh-medium school in the world – we had to wait until 1956 for Glan Clwyd at Rhyl to be opened in Wales. It was in the secular schools in Patagonia, not in Wales, that the first modern educational textbooks in Welsh were written, such as *Gwerslyvr i Ddysgu Darllen at Wasanaeth Ysgolion y Wladva* [Coursebook for Teaching Reading, for Use in the Colony] by R. J. Berwyn (who, along with Eluned's father, was imprisoned by the Argentine authorities in 1882–3 for their part in the campaign to defend the rights of the Welsh). It was these *Gwladfawyr*, teaching mathematics which adapted the Welsh counting system from the classical one based on twenties (for instance, forty being '*deugain*' – two twenties) to the decimal one (*pedwar deg* – four tens).

Eluned's long letters to William George are full of frustrated longing for his company. She calls them '*oases yng nghanol crasdiroedd bywyd'* (oases among life's parched lands). They include references to politics and literature. She compliments him on his articles to *Cymru Fydd*'s periodicals, *Young Wales* and *Ysbryd yr Oes*, especially his article in praise of the Hungarians for fighting for their linguistic rights first in their struggle with the Austrians (the Hungarian nationalist leader, Kossuth, like the Italian, Mazzini, were favourites of the early Welsh nationalist movement). They discuss the Boer War (David Lloyd George was an opponent of the war). In her letter to William in 1899 she writes, in Welsh, that 'John Bull can sometimes be a terrible tyrant at times and very unjust – the whole cry of our hearts here [*Y Wladfa*] is with the brave oppressed Boers – we are brothers under the same oppression'. She notes how she's translated Ruskin's *Sesame and Lilies* into Welsh and asks him to send her copies of *Anna Karenina* by Tolstoy and *The Children of the Ghetto* by Zangwill – two books she's read about but couldn't get hold of in Patagonia.

She hints for William to send her a photo of himself, and on receiving a photo says suggestively, 'only treasures enter my cell'. She chastises him for reading her letters aloud to his family and later says she wants him to burn their letters rather than let the 'cold eyes of the world' see them. But despite the beautiful, lovingly-written letters and the hints, Eluned was to be disappointed. Her love was unrequited. She had expected (or hoped) she would meet William again at the National Eisteddfod at Llanelli in 1903. He didn't turn up, choosing instead to go on a cruise to the Scottish islands. He was no doubt aware that in the convention and expectation of the age, to be with her so publicly at the Eisteddfod would effectively have meant an intention to marry.

Although Eluned lived to 1938 I can't help feeling a small part of her also died when she returned to Patagonia in 1918.

Wales was being anglicised, steamrollered by the British 'Better together' nationalism of the First World War. Likewise, Spanish was gaining ground in *Y Wladfa*. Did she daydream about how different life could have been? She could have been sister-in-law to the Prime Minister, possibly casually advising him about the topography and politics of Palestine (where she had travelled) as he set out for Versailles. Where once she was the centre of attention for men, she was now a spinster, encouraging the children she never had, through her books, to speak Welsh with pride.

But Eluned Morgan cannot and should not be forgotten. She published four books which went to several reprints: *Dringo'r Andes* (climbing the Andes, 1904), *Gwymon y Môr* (an account of the voyage from Wales to Patagonia, 1909); *Plant yr Haul* (1915) about the Incas, and *Ar Dir a Môr*, an account of her visit to Palestine (1913), which is a frustrating read because of its obsessive reference to Biblical topography but no reference at all to the Hebrew revival which was going on under her nose.

Her life is a parable for us of how things don't turn out for even the most attractive and talented of people. But she's also a shining example of an independent, patriotic and strong woman.

She's not, of course, the only schoolchild to lead a protest against language policy. In another time and another continent, at Soweto in South Africa in 1976 brave young black children were killed for protesting against making Afrikaans a medium of education at their school.

During the same period, Welsh children were leading their own language protests, but unlike in South Africa, protests to be taught in their own language and not English. Eluned would be proud of people like Eifion Lloyd Jones, who led a language protest at her high school in Porthmadog in the early 1970s. She would smile in support of the late author, Eirug Wyn, who, as a 17-year-old learning to drive a car, single-handedly defied the law, slapped a self-made 'D' plate (for '*dysgwr*' – learner) on the window, and broke the Highway Code to gain status for the Welsh language. There are a number of principled young people who've followed in their footsteps.

Eluned's particular kind of Welsh female nationalism can be traced to the backlash among a small segment of intellectuals in Welsh society to the Government Report into Education in Wales in 1847 (known as 'the Treachery of the Blue Books'). Eluned Morgan is interesting because in her person she personifies two particular strong strands of the reaction to the Blue Books.

One reaction was to found a 'New Wales' across the sea, far from the tsunami of the British state's policy of turning Wales into a compliant, English-speaking province. This was the strategy decided upon by Eluned's father and Michael D. Jones in founding the Welsh-speaking colony in Patagonia in 1865.

Another more general reaction, which also tied into mid-Victorian ideas of morality, was to defend the moral honour of Wales, and especially her women. This particular, maybe peculiar reaction came about because one of the main accusations of the Blue Books against the Welsh concerned the supposed loose morals of her women. The Welsh folk custom of 'bundling' whereby an unmarried couple were allowed to spend time together in bed (but with a sheet dividing them) before marriage was particularly held up as an example of lax Welsh morals. The Welsh, even Welsh patriots, decided to go out of their way to prove to the English that they were a holy and moral nation.

So, the defence of the Welsh language and of Welsh female morals for many people became one and the same. One reaction to the Blue Books was *Y Gymraes* [The

Welshwoman], which was published in Cardiff in 1850. It was edited by Ieuan Gwynedd, a minister, early modern nationalist and former editor of the London-based *The Standard of Freedom*. *Y Gymraes* was the first publication for women in Welsh. It sold around 2,000–3,000 copies, not an insubstantial number when one considers (as Siân Rhiannon Williams notes) that in 1844, out of 3,224 women, only 29 per cent could sign their name (rather than draw a cross) on their marriage certificates. One must also remember that newspapers would be read out aloud to rooms full of illiterate people. Although supported by the magnificent Charlotte Guest (*Gwenynen Gwent*) of Abergavenny, the publication failed.

Why? Among the myriad of reasons, Siân Rhiannon gave a very telling fact in her article in *Our Mother's Land – Chapters in Welsh Women's History, 1830-1939*: the majority of people who bought *Y Gymraes* were not women, but men! That is, the magazines tended to be written *by men* for what they thought women should do. It hardly spoke to the newly-emerging Welsh-speaking working class. The bustling, sweaty, grimy Welsh-speaking town of Merthyr Tydfil, with its 10,000 women, sold only 108 copies of *Y Gymraes*! Surprisingly enough, women didn't want to be preached to, or to read articles on house-keeping and how they should behave.

The Welsh-language activists of the nineteenth century made a big tactical error. They decided to align the Welsh language with the defence of Christian morals. By doing so, for perfectly good and honest religious reasons, they painted themselves into a corner. They began equating the Welsh language with a particularly idealised form of society and women.

With time, Welsh women, especially Welsh-speakers, came to be seen by some as more conservative and less assertive in their fight for women's rights. In an echo of the attitude of the Blue Books, many early English feminists also believed that the Welsh language and culture held women back. They saw English as being the progressive language and vehicle this time from the enlightened and progressive politics of the Suffragettes.

It's true that, for many, the Suffragette movement was seen as an English phenomenon. The Suffragettes attracted many women from wealthy, middle-class backgrounds – the very class that was thinner on the ground within Welsh-speaking Wales. It was an issue of culture and class. As Kay Cook and Neil Evans note in *Our Mother's Land*: 'Wales was slow in taking up the issues [of women's votes] because its women, in general, lacked economic power'. The Suffragette movement in the north of Wales, for instance, tended to congregate around the most anglicised towns and networks, such as the new Victorian sea-side resorts like Llandudno, where the first branch in Wales was launched. Thousands of Welsh women spoke no English, or very little of the language, and the Suffragette literature was translated, digested and distributed through the Welsh-language temperance movements.

There was also the added twist that the Suffragette campaign became more radical just as the Liberals gained power. This led to attacks on the most prominent Welshman of his age, David Lloyd George. Welsh men and women didn't take kindly to the Suffragettes attacking their national icon –and that at their national festival, the National Eisteddfod.

But the sometimes ambivalent attitudes towards the Suffragettes shouldn't be seen necessarily as Welsh people being hostile to women's rights. To try and address the point that Welshness and women's rights were compatible, Welsh Suffragettes marched in traditional Welsh costume at the Women's Coronation Procession in 1911. This inadvertently gave a modern spin and helped breathe new life to the costumes promoted (if not invented) by Augustus Hall, the sponsor of *Y Gymraes*.

But Welsh women weren't just receivers of ideas: they also formulated them within their culture and language. The Welsh colony in Patagonia, Eluned Morgan's homeland, gave women the vote in their internal matters in 1865, on an equal footing as men from the outset – possibly the first modern society in the world to do so. The Welsh Women's section of the Liberal Party combined Welsh patriotism with women's rights. The campaigns of *Cymru Fydd*, of which Eluned was an ardent supporter, had the women's right to vote as a central tenet of a Welsh parliament. It was the redneck disruption by Anglophone supremacists like John Birt against creating a National Welsh Liberal Federation at the famous meeting in Newport in 1896, which effectively brought the end to *Cymru Fydd*. His colonialist views against 'the domination of Welsh ideas' meant we never saw a Welsh parliament that could have included votes for women.

A woman of Eluned's middle-class background, were she English or anglophone, could have been expected to be a leading light in the Suffragette movement. But she was Welsh, and her energies, like the energies of thousands of Welsh women then and today, were directed towards defending and promoting Welsh – a crusade which couldn't be left to others. Eluned's strand of Welsh female activity, then, was different to the Suffragettes'.

Eluned's 'political' commitment combined love of the Welsh language and Christian Nonconformist values. It also included pacifism and nationalism. She famously fell out with her childhood hero, O. M. Edwards, one-time MP, school reformer and editor of *Cymru*, the magazine that published many of Eluned's articles from Patagonia, when, in 1916, he used the pages of *Cymru* to call on Welsh boys to enlist for the imperialist British war.

This Welsh dimension to women's history seems rarely articulated, appreciated, or studied, and is largely ignored by the mainstream feminist movement. But it has pedigree and character. It can be seen as a silver thread which ties Eluned's 1885 Dolgellau school walk-out with that of another famous walk-out which took place in Meirionnydd eighty-two years later. In that year, 1967, the members of the Women's Institute at Parc, a tiny village outside Bala, walked out of the 'national' WI (really, 'Englandandwales', as Scotland has its women's movement) because they were told to take the minutes of their meetings in English. This brave stance led to a split, and to the foundation of *Merched y Wawr*, the Welsh-language women's movement.

Like Eluned, *Merched y Wawr* has the defence and promotion of Welsh at its standard and is drinks deep from the well of Nonconformist and pacifist Welsh traditions. It's also no coincidence that it was the women of Meirionnydd, the county of Michael D. Jones, O. M. Edwards and T. E. Ellis (and Eluned's walk-out) who made this radical break.

So, what of Eluned Morgan? Reading her erudite and yearning letters to William George still strikes a deep melancholic chord with me, and with many more, I'm sure. Her heroism, as a 15-year-old girl, in defying the might of the British Empire and the English language, is as inspiring for today's Wales as ever. Her Welsh nationalism and principled pacifism, even at the price of falling out with her hero and good family friend, is especially prescient as we approach the centenary of that British 'better together' imperial ethnic war. Her internationalism, intellect and fluency in three languages is a role model for any woman.

As we celebrate the annual World Women's Day on 8 March we in Wales, both male and female, would do well to remember Eluned. Why not a memorial in her memory, maybe at the City Library in Cardiff or the site of Dr

Williams's school in Dolgellau – the present-day Coleg Meirion Dwyfor? Or honour her with a competition in her name for young Welsh women? She's as worthy as other better-known women from outside Wales. She's certainly more worthy of public recognition than that other woman, Queen Victoria, in whose name millions were killed and thousands of Welsh-speakers, like Eluned, were humiliated. Whilst Victoria's miserable, blood-stained name disfigures our streets and parks, Eluned Morgan is unknown.

If we were to follow in the footsteps of the girl from the pampas, then we would all 'walk like a prince'.

Cambria, vol. 13, no. 4, October 2012

Y Ddraig Binc:
Welsh Gays Come Out of the Closet

It may be simply that there is less to do in Aberystwyth than in Cardiff.

Is that the reason why Aberystwyth, despite its small size, has played such a disproportionately large part in Welsh political and cultural life? People are almost forced to do something and create their own culture rather than consume it. After all, Cardiff, Swansea and Bangor have their own universities but it's Aberystwyth which keeps popping up in the indexes of Welsh history.

Whatever the reason, at the beginning of the 1992 I found myself back in Aberystwyth, my Alma Mater, after a few years in Cardiff. I was at the National Eisteddfod in that year and remember the incident mentioned, but it was only after beginning work with Berwyn Rowland's public relations company that I began to meet the gay circle in Aberystwyth.

Working for Berwyn I came to know and like the people active in Cylch. They were witty and interesting. It may be the nostalgia of old age, but it was also a busy and exciting time in Aberystwyth. Berwyn's company organised the annual Welsh International Film Festival in the town; a bilingual radio station, Radio Ceredigion, was just beginning, and Cynog Dafis became Ceredigion's MP on a Plaid Cymru-Green Party ticket.

Cylch was another component of a cosmopolitan Welsh-speaking scene where one could meet Welsh-speaking Norwegians, Basques, Catalans, Galicians and, of course, Germans, Bretons and English people in the town's pubs and parties. I would often find myself being the only first-language Welshman in a Welsh conversation of four or five people. It was all a truly liberating and beautiful time.

So, on a personal level, I'm grateful to the Cylch people and I admire their guts.

At the 1992 Eisteddfod in Aberystwyth an anonymous person shat in the stand of *Cylch*, the Welsh gay rights movement. Yes, you read that correctly: someone shat in the stand to show their hatred of *Cylch*'s presence at Wales' premiere cultural event.

There really is something animal-like about defecating your disapproval of a whole section of society. The crass act ranks you there with the beast, defining your territory like a hyena with the most basic of body functions.

But there it was. On an August morning members of the Welsh-language gay and lesbian society, *Cylch* (circle), opened up their canvas stall to find that someone had defecated in their stand. Maybe it was a dare or joke. Hilarious.

What had Welsh Lesbian and Gay Society done to deserve such hatred?

Well, exist.

Cylch was formed in Aberystwyth in 1991. The 1992 Eisteddfod was the first time that *Cylch* had rented a stall at the festival. It is to the credit of the Eisteddfod, so often wrongly accused of being conservative, that they allowed *Cylch* to have a stall.

One of the leading lights of the Welsh-language gay society was Richard Crowe, a softly-spoken translator originally from Bournemouth. Richard came to Aberystwyth as a student in 1978, ostensibly to study German and French. As he was fascinated with the Welsh soap opera, *Pobol y Cwm*, which in those pre-S4C days was broadcast across the UK on BBC2, he chose Welsh as the third subject option. By the end of the first year he'd decided to drop German and French and concentrate on Welsh.

Speaking from his home in Cardiff, Richard recalled that he wasn't 'out' as a gay man whilst at university and stayed 'in the closet' until he was about thirty years old. 'I was of course aware that I was gay at university,' he said, 'but I would have rather have died than come out! There were some people who were more honest but the atmosphere wasn't positive towards gay people. You knew you'd be the butt of jokes and humiliated.'

The change in Richard's confidence happened during the 1980s, and it was at Aberystwyth in 1990 that *Cylch* was founded. The university town was as close to a hotbed of political gay activism as Wales will ever see. Centred on the town's unique cultural blend of the university, Welsh institutions, radical Welsh language politics and the annual International Film Festival Aber, it was, for a time, dubbed by some 'the Gay Capital of Wales'.

The founding of *Cylch* was due to the meeting of minds of a cohort of exceptionally brave and driven people: Dafydd Frayling, George Jones and Berwyn Rowlands.

In 1991 *Cylch* published its first issue of *Y Ddraig Binc* (The Pink Dragon) newsletter – Wales's first dedicated gay and lesbian publication. In case anyone hadn't understood the nature of the publication by the heavy hint in the title, the front cover sported a cartoon figure coming out of the closet with the heading '*Dewch allan dan ruo*' (come out roaring).

The first issue was more an amateur fanzine than a magazine. It included a variety of articles written in an idiomatic Welsh which often transcribed common English words into the Welsh language's elastic spelling system. Page two included a humorous quiz,'*Ydych chi'n siwr eich bod chi'n strêt?*' ('Are you sure you're straight?').

Among the questions it asked was whether the reader enjoyed listening to Joan Armatrading, and if its female readership preferred wearing comfortable flat shoes to stilettoes. Question 7 underlined why this new gay movement made some members of the Welsh public feel uncomfortable. It asked provocatively: 'A male rugby match is: a) light entertainment for the whole family; b) a ritual to promote male bonding; c) your only option if you're in the closet.'

An article in that first issue by the lesbian Danu November questioned another iconic Welsh institution. November – who seemed for a while to be the only Welsh-speaking lesbian in Wales, such was the regularity of her appearances on the Welsh language media – asked provocatively if participants in the Rebecca Riots had included lesbians. You may know about the anti-toll-gate riots that swept across parts of Wales in the 1830 and 1840s in which men hid their identity by dressing as women and blackening their faces. Her observation was based on instances such as the attack at Llanfihangel-ar-Arth in 1837, when a policeman, giving witness, noted that one of the rioters had hands 'as soft as a female's'. November notes that some of the actions of the Rebecca rioters, such as those in Newcastle Emlyn in 1843, included attacks on men who were known to beat their wives. She believed that some of these proto-feminists would have been lesbians. Who knows?

The issue also tellingly uses Cymdeithas yr Iaith's slogan, 'Rhaid i Bopeth Newid' (everything must change).

The reference to Cymdeithas yr Iaith's slogans was not a coincidence. One of the most notable aspects of this gay and lesbian rights movement was that virtually all its leaders had been active with Cymdeithas yr Iaith. They transferred many of the arguments and tactics used by Cymdeithas to campaign for respect and status for Welsh-speaking lesbians and gays.

Following the Coal Miners' Strike of 1984–85 Cymdeithas yr Iaith developed a progressively left-wing critique of the issues undermining the Welsh language. In common with Plaid Cymru it actively sought to create alliances with other self-proclaimed progressive groups, from CND to the Sandinista cause in Nicaragua, anti-

Apartheid campaigners, greens and feminist groups. The campaign to support gay and lesbian rights was one obvious grouping among this 'rainbow' coalition of the left. This strategy and the debate about recognising gay rights weren't without opposition. For many Cymdeithas yr Iaith members the society seemed to be taking its eye off the ball, by campaigning for 'trendy lefty' ideas rather than concentrating on the language.

Cylch members, however, unlike previous half-hearted British and anglophile gay right groups, understood the importance of placing gay rights at the heart of the same argument as that for language rights. For them, it was one and the same struggle. What use was saving the language, if gay people who spoke Welsh felt the language didn't belong to them and didn't recognise their Welshness?

Another striking feature of *Cylch* was that so many of its pioneering members were Welsh people from English-speaking backgrounds or were (as in Richard Crowe, Grant Vidgen and Danu November's case) English. Berwyn Rowlands, the son of a builder from a council estate in Llangoed, Anglesey, was one of the few native Welsh-speakers to play a prominent part in *Cylch*. He also later founded the Iris Prize gay film festival in Cardiff.

Richard Crowe, who speaks fluent Welsh, concedes:

> It was easier for people who were not from a native Welsh-speaking background to play a public part simply because our families didn't live in Wales or couldn't speak Welsh. If they did appear on the media a lot of the native Welsh-speakers would also tend to highlight the softer social side and importance of Cylch rather than make the hard, political case

Richard's interest in the Welsh language led him to study

Hebrew and publish a book on the Hebrew language revival.

'The fact is there were really only about three or four active members of *Cylch* who would go on all the TV and radio programmes. That's all you need to make a big difference!' Richard's contribution varied from writing articles on gay literature for Welsh literary journals, to letter-writing to the press and occasional media appearances.

'We'd write letters to the press, like the weekly, *Y Faner*, usually under pseudonyms. The media was also interested in the new movement and issues and, either in the name of balance or just to create a story, would find homophobic people to argue against us. However, after a while one got fed up of appearing on the media to debate with bigots. I remember once appearing on a programme on S4C and some doctor said that homosexuality was an 'abnormality' which needed to be 'cured'. I was gobsmacked. After that I just got a little bored of arguing with these people,' Richard added.

Like all political movements *Cylch* wanted – needed – to prove the provenance of their politics. That is, to give some historic legitimacy which would tie into Welsh history. That first issue of *Y Ddraig Binc* included an ancient Greek poem by Sappho that had been published in Welsh in *Y Traethodydd* in 1878. The poem is about a woman's love for another woman. (However, *Y Traethodydd* asked the reader to understand that the female author wrote the poem from a man's perspective!)

The need to prove the authenticity of new political concepts within minoritised communities is an extra struggle for social movements such as gay and women's rights. As many of the ideas have been formulated in a metropolitan environment, in different language and different cultural contexts, the new movement can be seen as an alien threat to members of the minoritised community, which already feels under siege. In this respect, members of *Cylch* or the gay community were under extra stress: not only the personal dilemma of their own sexuality, but also possibly a nebulous feeling of betraying their own cultural background.

That's why it was important for *Cylch* to place itself at the heart of the conscious symbol of Welshness, the National Eisteddfod.

Cylch also deserve credit for making Welsh a language for gay culture. It's one thing to be an ethnic Welsh gay person and be 'out and proud' in the English language and culture. It calls for extra personal and political resources and vision to win that cultural zone for Welshness. *Cylch* members took the Pasquale Paoliani course, not the Napoleon Bonaparte one.

In his book on Britishness, *Prydeindod* (Gwasg y Dryw, 1966), the philosopher J. R. Jones describes the malign effect of Britishness on the Welsh-speaker. He draws an image of a young girl from the thoroughly Welsh-speaking countryside going to work in a more anglicised town like Carmarthen. He outlines that the political strength of British ideology has created a new cultural context which humiliates and alienates her from her language. Britishness had made her feel her language has no place in the new milieu. The words he uses are prescient in their similarity to those used by gay people: [the Welsh language] becomes 'a skeleton in her cupboard' ... Truthfully, in some context with her friends, she'd prefer the ground to swallow her up rather than for her to speak Welsh.

But of course, gay people weren't new to Welsh life. Maybe the earliest reference to homosexuality can be found in the Laws of Hywel Dda from a thousand years ago. In one version of the laws, reference is made to *'gŵr a gydio mewn gŵr'* (man who holds onto man) from which the contemporary word for homosexuality, *gwrwgydiwr*, derives. It's made in the context of sections of society which can't be used as witnesses ... among the other non-dependable people are the blind and deaf. An old reference but maybe not the positive image some may have hoped for!

The winner of the 1924 Crown at the Pontypool National Eisteddfod was Prosser Rhys, a 23-year-old editor of *Y Faner* from Aberystwyth with his poem, *Atgof* (reminiscence). The poems reference to the '*llanc penfelen*' (blond-haired lad) caused great controversy and he was referred to as the Welsh Oscar Wilde by one critic. A recent biography by Alan Llwyd of the early twentieth-century Welsh novelist Kate Roberts points to lesbian tendencies she may have had. However, it was not until the 1980s that the first openly gay Welsh writers, Aled Islwyn and later Mihangel Morgan (again, a person who'd learnt Welsh), found their voice.

There are of course numerous Welsh slang terms for gay or effeminate men, which suggests strongly that Welsh society wasn't as naïve as some wished it to be. The modern word for gay is '*hoyw*', which is a *calque* (a literal translation) of gay. Like 'gay', it was an underused word for happiness, used mostly in poetry. The word gained wide publicity in the late 1980s as 'Ricky Hoyw' – an old cheesy rock star Alvin Stardust-type comic character created by Dewi Pws in his popular show, 'Torri Gwynt'.

The term '*hoyw*' was rarely, if ever, used in Siôn Eirian's hard-hitting and brutal play about gay men in German concentration camps, *Wastad ar y Tu Fâs* (always on the outside), in 1986.

In English, the raucous 1978 rugby film, *Grand Slam*, feature the quintessential Valleys queen, Maldwyn Pugh, played by Siôn Prosser. The camp Valleys gay is a common feature in Welsh stage repertoire and every 'Cecil' in Welsh literature seems to be a highly-strung gay drama queen, such as that in Islwyn Ffowc Elis's 1955 novel on intellectual decadence, *Ffenestri Tua'r Gwyll*. In his readable autobiography (*Fy Ffordd fy Hun* (2010); *A Rebel's Story*

(2012), Gwasg Carreg Gwalch) the Tory, Felix Aubel, recalls his up-bringing in the 1950s Cynon Valley when three men would hold 'Bible-reading sessions' above his parents' shop.

By 1995 the success of *Cylch* seemed such that one of its bravest and most tenacious campaigners, Dafydd Frayling, published a poem to his lover, Rheinallt Huws, in '*Tu Chwith*' entitled '*Rydym Bellach yn Ystradebau, Rheins*' (we're clichés now, Rheins).

We've discussed attitudes towards homosexuality by Welsh-speakers. But there was also a reaction from non Welsh-speakers. Surprisingly, some gay people, whilst wishing rights for their sexuality, viewed Welsh culture and language with suspicion or incomprehension. Richard Crowe recalls that there could be hostility at Aberystwyth's 'gay pub', The Fountain in Trefechan, towards gays who spoke Welsh – by other gay people.

'People would question us. "Why are you so concerned about this Welsh language?" They'd imply there was a wide world out there, so why waste time on the Welsh language', recalled Richard.

Despite opposition or incomprehension from within and without the Welsh-speaking community, the people of *Cylch* wanted to be both gay *and* Welsh. They didn't want to deny one or the other – many of them had done enough denying in their life already. Was there an unspoken assumption among some gay people that the Welsh language was, by definition, too backward to accommodate a modern expression of open homosexuality?

But the existence of the language created *Cylch* and forced its members to create publications and campaigns that wouldn't have happened if there was no language issue. This was a great help to Welsh-speakers, but also, maybe, people who felt themselves Welsh but didn't speak the language, and had been forced to put up with the 'Maldwyn Novello Pugh' comic caricatures of gay Welsh men.

As we've seen, the language of Welsh-language rights could be easily translated and understood when put in a gay rights context. That context wasn't so handy for English-speaking society in Wales.

Maybe then it isn't a surprise that the first openly gay person in the rugby world came from the heart of Welsh-language culture. The international rugby referee, Nigel Owens, was well known to viewers of S4C for compèring on the middle-of-the-road show, *Noson Lawen*. (Think English variety meets German *Schlagermusik* and you have *Noson Lawen*.) In his autobiography, *Hanner Amser* (Y Lolfa, 2008), Owens recalls how his inability to deal with his homosexuality led him to attempt suicide. Such has been the support and admiration for him since the book's publication that he was appointed President of the Welsh Young Farmers! Maybe Welsh people supported him because they'd seen how he had supported Welsh-language culture in the past.

Owens's brave admission was followed in December 2009 by the Wales international rugby player, Gareth 'Alfie' Thomas, Wales's most capped player, announcing that he was also gay – something that would have been totally impossible in 1991. Wales truly has changed; Wales was even leading the way. In 2003 Adam Price, of Plaid Cymru became Wales's first openly gay MP.

Looking back at the 1992 Eisteddfod, Richard Crowe recalls that people would avoid visiting the stall. People were 'suspicious' of us – a suspicion which *Y Ddraig Binc* alludes to and satirises in its Summer 1994 issue with an article which begins: 'My name is Dafydd Frayling, you can bet I'm a member of the Secret Police who's come here to Wales to destroy the national movement.'

It would be grossly naïve to believe that there is no homophobia or suspicion of gay and lesbian people in Wales. Maybe it's good to say that people are more accepting.

For my part, we see thousands leave Wales every year; I don't want to be responsible for seeing more people leave Wales because they don't believe that Wales offers them a home. People can find many reasons for hating other people, but being a man who loves another man, or a woman who loves another woman, isn't a reason in my book. As a nationalist, I'm glad the gay rights people in *Cylch* have shown us that the Welsh language and Welshness is a culture that can accommodate many different people and different voices. A pink dragon isn't a paler shade of the red one.

Past Studies

Flying the Flag:
the Boring Story of the Red Dragon

Nothing 'just happens', and I wanted to find out when our flag was actually designed and made an official flag. I also wanted to find out the political context and to get to the root of how decisions are made. Maybe my intention when writing this article was to show to Welsh people that we can decide our own identity if we are willing to commit some time and energy to making it happen. During my campaign for a Welsh Top Level Domain – the .cymru bid – with Maredudd ap Gwyndaf, I learnt to recognise that very often things don't happen, because, simply, no one person has gone to the effort to initiate change. It's as simple (and boring) as that.

I knew, as we all do, that the Red Dragon was an ancient emblem of Wales, but I was also partly aware of the 'Welsh Office' flag, having caught a glimpse of it in some old photos.

In many respects, the campaign to have the Red Dragon made the official flag is more romantic and heroic for me than any story of dragons fighting under the castle of Dinas Emrys. Heroic, because we need to recognise the majesty of writing letters, petitions and lobbying politicians and bureaucrats. Mythology is great, but, like waiting for the Messiah, it lets us off the hook. It allows us the luxury of believing that 'stuff happens' when, in fact, nothing happens without human endeavour.

The exciting part of our life is that we can actually force change. If we are not all great politicians or world-known celebrities, we are all the authors of the graffiti of our nation. The Red Dragon is truly a nation's flag. It is a flag we as a people willed into existence, and we gave it legitimacy.

The Red Dragon. It's one of the most distinctive flags in the world. Its origin is shrouded in the mists of time in legends of Roman legions, Merlin's Prophesy, Cadwaladr ap Cadwallon, Tudors ... and a bog standard Member's question at the House of Commons in London on a cold February in 1959.

Yes, that's it, the red dragon has been around for the fatter side of two millennia, but it has been the official flag of our country only since 1959. More rock and roll than bow and arrow. The modern history of the Welsh flag, or rather a flag for Wales, is as interesting as anything cloaked in antiquity.

In 1953 Wales was presented with a new flag. A flag drawn by committee if ever there was one – and a committee without style, and without love for Wales, at that. It seems it was part of the nascent Welsh Office, what was then the Ministry for Housing and Local Authority and Welsh Affairs, to give some kind of mealy-mouthed recognition to Wales. It was a rather scrawny red dragon with a ribbon around it bearing the motto '*y ddraig goch ddyry gychwyn*' (the red dragon takes the lead) with a representation of the crown on top. It was set on the familiar horizontal white and green background of our present flag.

The prime minister, Winston Churchill, despised the badge's design. According to the Cabinet minutes of the meeting in 1953, he called it an 'odious design expressing nothing but spite, malice, ill-will and monstrosity. Words ("Red Dragon takes the lead") are untrue and unduly flattering to Bevan.' (Aneurin Bevan, that is, the Welsh Labour MP).

Like Churchill, but for different reasons, Lord Elystan Morgan, a young trainee lawyer in Cardiganshire at the time, didn't like the flag either. This man, who was later to become the Labour MP for the county, remembers the embarrassment of seeing the flag flying:

The flag was so laughable that people wouldn't use it. It wasn't popular. It looked undignified. I was a young lawyer working in Cardiganshire County Council and I remember my boss, Eric Carson, Clerk to Cardiganshire County Council, referring to the rather bedraggled dragon as 'that one balled lamb'.

The sexual reference to the flag wasn't out of context either. Unknown to the queen, the motto '*y ddraig goch ddyry gychwyn*' was a very unfortunate one indeed. Rather than being an 'unduly flattering' motto as Churchill thought, it was in fact the first line of a couplet by Deio ab Ieuan Ddu (1450–80) in celebration of a bull fornicating. The second line is '*ar ucha'r llall ar ochr llwyn*' (above the other, next to a bush). The '*ddraig goch*' then was but a name of a bull and it only 'took the lead' as far as fathering a new herd! The bull must have been a large beast to gain its 'dragon' nickname. It was probably more brown in colour than red – 'coch' was commonly used in Welsh for what we would today call brown.

Although the new flag was flown from official buildings and occasional public displays, it was the traditional flag that was mostly used by the public. That flag is an adaptation of the Royal Badge created in 1807 – itself based on older designs and traditions. It depicted a red dragon placed on a green mound on a white field. But from old photographs and paintings it seems the flag was rarely used in the nineteenth century. Why? I'm not sure. Maybe Britishness was so strong within Wales that not even Iolo Morganwg, 'Mad Ned' to his friends and enemies, was mad enough to think of Wales as a constitutional nation state. It's as if to fly the Red Dragon flag would be to presume that Wales could be a nation state – a thought too dangerous or too abstract for the Welsh of the time? Perhaps, in the same way that most African 'tribes' or linguistic communities today – the Zulu, Kikuyu, Xhosa –

don't have their own flag, the eighteenth and early nineteenth century Welsh people saw themselves more as a 'tribe' than a nation?

Following the First World War, and especially the Second World War, the Red Dragon flag slowly gained in popularity. But as the barrister and former Archdruid, Robyn Lewis (to whom I'm indebted for his article on this subject in the April 2009 edition of *Llanw Llŷn* papur bro) notes, even in the 1950s it was quite rare to see the Red Dragon flown at all:

> I remember going to university in Aberystwyth in 1952 at the time of the competition to choose a capital city for Wales. There were five contenders: Cardiff, Caernarfon, Wrexham, Swansea and Aberystwyth. There were so many Union Jacks flying in Aberystwyth that I thought to myself you'd think Aberystwyth was competing to become the capital of England.

The 1950s was in many ways the last Victorian decade – a peculiar time of subtle change amidst waning conservatism.

Supporters of the Welsh language increasingly realized that Welsh couldn't be saved through quiet favours by nice people. Wales seemed to be losing out culturally to the nuclear age bright lights of Anglo-American modernity and politically to a British establishment indifferent to Welsh deference.

Increasingly there were tensions and sides to be taken. In 1957, Islwyn Ffowc Elis's *Wythnos yng Nghymru Fydd* [a week in the future Wales] summed up the private and public choice many Welsh people were starting to contemplate. It was the Welsh-version of Theodore Herzl's 1902 dream of a Jewish homeland, *Altneuland*, offering the reader a choice of a Welsh utopia and dystopia.

The small Welsh nationalist movement supported the independence campaign in Africa and was encouraged by it. It almost seemed that Wales was, tortoise-like, gaining status in tandem with the hopeful young, clean-shaven African states.

In 1955, at one of the most anglicised periods in its history, Cardiff was made capital of Wales. On 24 April 1956 a petition with 250,000 names was handed in to Westminster by the all-party Parliament for Wales campaign. In 1956 Ysgol Glan Clwyd in Rhyl became the first-ever Welsh-medium high school, and in 1958 Cardiff held the Empire Games. And as a backdrop to all this was the threat of the drowning of Tryweryn to provide water for Liverpool – where people in multi-layered clothes of multicoloured shades of brown and grey marched in protest through the cold, blitz-damaged streets of Liverpool behind the defiant Red Dragon.

It was in this climate that in July 1958, in preparation for the public proclamation of the National Eisteddfod being held in Caernarfon the following year, the fate of the future of the national flag was discussed. The Gorsedd of Bard's proclamation ceremony was to be located within the walls of Caernarfon Castle – the castle built by Edward I following his defeat of Llywelyn in 1282. In his book *Atgofion Hen Arwyddfardd*, Dilwyn Miles recalls that the *Cofiadur* (registrar of the Gorsedd), Cynan, failed to get confirmation that the traditional Red Dragon flag would be flown at Caernarfon Castle on the day of the proclamation rather than the official 'Welsh Office' flag. Cynan believed that the dragon with the ribbon was 'too limp [tila] to be seen if flown from the top of the building and the motto was unreadable, not to say too undignified and laughable to be the National Flag of Wales'.

Maybe Cynan remembered also that at the National

Eisteddfod in Pwllheli in 1955 activists took down the Union Jack from the top of the Pavilion, and he was keen not to see a similar event repeat itself at Caernarfon. Whatever the reason, it was decided that the only flag the Gorsedd would recognise was the traditional one, and with that the Gorsedd called on all the institutions and public bodies in Wales to follow their lead.

The Gorsedd received unanimous messages of support (with the exception of Newport council), which inspired political action. On 23 February 1959 the Conservative MP for Barry, Raymond Gower, tabled a question on the Welsh flag. In response, Henry Brook, Conservative MP for Hampstead, Minister of Housing and Local Government and Minister of Welsh Affairs, announced in March 1959 that the queen had given her seal of approval on the traditional Red Dragon, and the 'Welsh Office' flag was to be consigned to the further end of the *cwtch-dan-stâr* (cupboard under the stairs) of history.

There's no doubting the popularity of the Red Dragon. It's flown from public building, schools and increasingly homes. But the issue of the national flag isn't totally resolved either.

Whilst I'm against any laws forbidding the defamation of a flag (as the USA) I'd like an authority, the Assembly, to standardise the flag itself and remind flag-producers of the correct design and colouring. Others, however, have questioned if it is even the right flag for Wales.

The writer and *Cambria* contributor Meic Stephens, in the heady post-devolution Yes vote, wanted to adopt a new national flag. Writing in the December 1998 issue of *Planet* magazine, Meic, whilst wishing to keep the Red Dragon for 'ceremonial purposes', proposed 'for our body politic ... for all official purposes of an embryonic Welsh state, we surely need a tricolour'.

Meic felt the *Draig Goch* reminded him of 'our distant origins and our status, for more than a thousand years, as a 'non-historic people'. He's right. To a large extent the flags of non-nation states do tend to be more elaborate and unorthodox – a vexillogicial version of a colourful national folk costume as opposed to a diplomat's pinstriped suit of the tricolour. He designed a Welsh tricolour, the *Trilliw*, of green, white and red, to the unusual and unique proportions of 1:1:4. I haven't heard of the *Trilliw* since then, but it was a point that needed to be raised.

I'd keep the *Draig Goch* as the national flag, but I'd like to make a suggestion to add to our other national flags, those of Glyndŵr and Dewi – a maritime flag.

The combination of red and green is an unfortunate one and goes against the recognised first rule of heraldic design as succinctly expressed (ironically) by the Welshman Humphrey Llwyd in 1558, the rule of tincture: 'metal should not be put on metal, nor colour on colour'. That is, yellow should not be placed on white and a colour like red should not be placed on another colour such as green, as happens with our flag, because the colours become a dark blur beyond a certain distance. In view of the confusion with the colouring, and in light of the fact that since April 2010 the Assembly has responsibility over the maritime economy in an extended jurisdiction that borders Irish waters, and that so many private boats already fly the *Draig Goch*, it's time we adopted a maritime flag for Wales. This maritime flag would be the white field and red dragon, but the green half of the current flag lowered to touch the bottom of the claws of the dragon. By doing so the flag would avoid the issue of red on green and so be easily recognisable at sea and would confirm us as a maritime nation.

There's a nice turn in the dragon's tail to the 'one-balled lamb' flag of the government. In July 2009, fifty years after the unfortunate flag was given the boot, the Assembly issued a new Badge of Wales. It's based on a similar design to the Welsh Office badge and is stamped on all new laws passed by the Assembly. However, the Presiding Officer, Dafydd Elis Thomas, saw well that the new Royal Badge has on it the crest of the House of Gwynedd – the quartered lion passant (as opposed to Glyndŵr's lion rampant) and looks very majestic and fitting for an Assembly becoming a parliament. He's also placed a more appropriate line from the national anthem, '*pleidiol wyf i'm gwlad*', in the ribbon.

Wales has changed a lot since Cynan's single-minded campaign to get the traditional red dragon flag recognised as the only flag of Wales. From a nationalist perspective, the arguments and complexes about Wales and Welsh identity, so succinctly captured in the flag campaign of 1958, must appear like the 1950s do to present-day feminists or Afro-Americans – a scared nation only slowly gaining confidence. This little battle was an important symbolic one highlighting the quiet disquiet many felt at the way Wales was treated. To me, Cynan's decision also proves that one person can make a difference, and that once in a lifetime we owe it to ourselves and our nation to make a stand.

Flags are a country's Freudian slips. The Welsh Office flag was a put-down flag, a flag that by its very design was meant to convey subservience and tidy, conservative governance. The Red Dragon is a more confident and democratic flag. It was officially made the flag of Wales in March 1959 by the queen. But its legitimacy rests in the Welsh people's love and affection for it, for it was the queen, through Cynan and the Gorsedd of the Bard's campaign, who bent to the will of the Welsh people. The flag is ours: let's fly it high and often.

Cambria, vol. 12, no. 2, October 2010

The Day we Stopped Singing
'God Save the Queen':
the 'Forgetting' of an Anthem

I am old enough, just, to remember Welsh rugby teams having to sing 'God Save the Queen' at our international matches. If you're too young to remember, I suggest you grab a copy of the raucous 1976 rugby film, Grandslam, *which gives it a fleeting mention.*

Writing this article was like trying to work out a puzzle. When did we stop singing 'God Save the Queen'? And more particularly, why did we stop singing ... and then vote 'No' to devolution in 1979?

The more I read of the events and the period, the more amazed that we stopped singing 'God Save the Queen' at all. Maybe the question is, why are we still *not singing it?*

Writing the article reminded me of the put-down by the lowest-common-denominator type politicians. The type which says that such and such a campaign – be it women's rights, ecology, Welsh language – has never been raised on the doorstep. Or that these minority and marginal subjects are of no interest to 'ordinary people' and are never at the top of any political agenda. My guess is that if you were to take an opinion poll of people's political concerns in any decade you'd see education, health, and law and order at the top every time. However, we remember the 1960s as a period of great change for the rights of women, black people, the Welsh language, to name a few. That is, big social political and cultural changes often do not register in opinion polls or a particular vote. Instead they disseminate through society, gradually. Maybe that's what happened with the 'forgetting' of 'God Save the Queen'.

Did you see the TV report about the day a little peasant people snubbed a glorious Crown? Did you read the paper the day the Welsh stopped singing 'God Save the Queen'?

Me neither. But it happened. The question is when, how ... and why wasn't the revolution on the television? It's funny how significant movements in Welsh society don't get reported on the news, whilst weather reports that it will rain (again!) in Wales, do.

There was a time when 'God Save the Queen' was Wales's national anthem, or was played in conjunction with '*Mae Hen Wlad fy Nhadau*' – you may remember it yourself. So, when did that stop and a little part of Britishness die?

The change happened gradually. The tradition for decades at Wales's international football matches was to play both '*Hen Wlad fy Nhadau*' and 'God Save the Queen'. But a significant change was made for the Wales v Austria game on 19 November 1975. For it was at that match, for the first time, that it was decided not to play 'God Save the Queen' before the match.

Why this game? Well, Phil Stead, author of *Red Dragons* (Y Lolfa, 2012), a book on the history of Welsh football, explained that it was billed as the most crucial game in the recent history of Welsh football. Maybe the organisers felt Wales needed the full backing of the crowd at Wrexham – implying, maybe, that singing 'GStQ' didn't go down too well with all Welsh fans. Whatever the reason, Wales won the match.

But the British anthem was still played at the Wales v Hungary match on 1976 and at the game with West Germany on 6 October 1976: in that game, the programme notes that 'God Save the Queen' would be played at the conclusion of the game and the players would stay on the field. This compromise arrangement was decided possibly because it had been expected that the queen would be in attendance as Patron of the Football Association of Wales in its centenary year.

But 'GStQ' was on its wobbly last legs and into extra time. The Wales v Czechoslovakia game on 30 March 1977, just five months later and yes, in the queen's jubilee year, was the first international where 'God Save the Queen' would officially not be played. If the past is a foreign country, then today playing the British royal anthem is, like Czechoslovakia, a distant memory of a faraway land.

Trawls through the newspapers of the time make no reference to this symbolic event. It's implicit only in the game's programme. So, 30 March 1977 can be officially noted as the day a tradition died. It's a headstone date – if not a headline one.

But it didn't go totally unnoticed – not by the English FA at least. At Wembley in 1977, the England officials refused to play 'Hen Wlad fy Nhadau' during that year's 'Home International' football match against Wales.

Phil Stead believes the English act was in reaction to Wales's decision not to play 'the Queen' during their aforementioned match with Czechoslovakia. In any case, the Welsh players, led by John Mahoney and Terry Yorath, bravely remained in line in defiant protest after the rendition of 'God Save the Queen' despite the English officials' panic as they tried to usher the team away. As Phil noted, 'They only broke the line once they felt their point was made'.

The change in national anthems at Wales' football matches followed, and was probably encouraged by a surprising similar set of events on the rugby field.

Professor Gareth Williams, author of numerous seminal books on Welsh rugby and society, says the dual anthem issue came to a head in rugby in 1974: 'the year of the fuss', as he called it.

In that year it was decided not to play 'the Queen' as one

of Wales's dual anthems in Cardiff, and rather sing only 'Hen Wlad fy Nhadau'. In 1974 when Wales played England at Twickenham the English Rugby union retaliated against the perceived snub and decided not to play 'Hen Wlad fy Nhadau' at all. However, whilst the band didn't play the Welsh anthem, the Welsh crowd sang the anthem as an act of defiance.

So, what was going on? Was this a resurgent, nationalist Wales, awoken, like Arthur by the sound of the bell? Well, the 1960s and 1970s did certainly see a rise in a politicised Welsh identity. But it wasn't that simple – it never is. For every two steps towards Welsh nationality there was one step back.

During 1977 there was much talk of the Kilbrandon Report on devolution for Wales and Scotland. There's a melancholic feeling to reading the passionate letters and optimistic inky pamphlets discussing the dreamed-of 100-member Assembly in Cardiff's Mount Stuart Square. It's melancholic because we know that it was – that time, anyway – all to end in a crushing defeat for devolution.

The 1970s are famous for the iconic pulling-down of monolingual English road signs so vividly captured by the protest songs and photos of the long-haired radicals. However, how many today also remember that Barry Jones MP, Labour's Undersecretary for State at the Welsh Office, refused to attend the official opening of the new Llanelltud road near Dolgellau in protest against Gwynedd County Council's decision to place Welsh above the English on the road signs?

Here's another snippet chosen from many. On 4 November 1975, a fortnight before the Austria game, two nationalists, Iestyn Garlick (who makes the announcements at the Millennium Stadium) and Gethin Clwyd were arrested for daubing anti-royalist slogans on Caernarfon castle in preparation for the queen's visit. But as we know from the queen's jubilee in 1977, Wales looked as if it had been squeezed through a tube of toothpaste and come out all red, white and blue.

In this bipolar political atmosphere, how on earth did the Welsh people decide to stop singing 'God Save the Queen'? ... and how did such conservative and royalist institutions as the FAW and WRU agree to it?

There's little written evidence of booing 'God Save the Queen', but although the TV and radio commentators would try to ignore it, it certainly happened. The booing was nationalistic, but there was also an element of good-natured chiding of the opposition. It was pantomime politics. After all, the least Welsh of songs was meant to be sung at a time when it was expected that the fans would be at their *most* Welsh!

Gareth Williams suggested it might also have been the banality of the apolitical that killed the anthem. When Wales played there could be three anthems – 'Hen Wlad fy Nhadau', 'God Save the Queen', plus the anthem of the opposing side. For many it just added unnecessary tedium and delay to the kick-off. It wasn't only politics which got rid of the anthem, then: the empire was conquered by the low boredom threshold of the players and fans.

'Maybe by the 1970s,' as Gareth Williams recalls, 'more than anything else 'God Save the Queen' seemed an embarrassment.'

But why wasn't dropping 'God Save the Queen' – the UK state anthem after all – not opposed more vigorously by the British establishment? And if a people stopped singing 'God Save the Queen', why didn't they vote 'Yes' for a Welsh Assembly in the 1979 referendum? In fact, the more I think of it the more amazed I am that the Wales of the 1970s decided not to sing 'GStQ' at all.

Maybe we can begin answering the first question by explaining that news programmes report the 'news' – or rather, what they believe is news, which is 'events'. What the news doesn't do so well is report underlying trends. This may explained why the revolution wasn't televised.

It wasn't an 'event' and so it wasn't 'news'. It was what I'd call 'a forgetting'.

The Welsh 'forgot' to sing the anthem in the same way many of them 'forgot' the Welsh language in a previous generation. It was a conscious decision unconsciously done. A very Welsh process if ever there was one.

If it weren't for the 'event' of the census charting the decline of Welsh, then the decline of Welsh wouldn't be 'news', it would have been a 'process'. And 'processes' (as the Bretons know because the French census has no question on the language people speak), aren't 'news' items, and so are denied a rallying point. The same may be sure of 'GStQ'.

Mundanely, I'd also add that 'GStQ' is not a very affectionate anthem. The words feel ill-fitting, even for many people who are far away from Welsh nationalism. It's a cold anthem. It's turgid, too, except for the ascending notes leading to the fourth line. It's hardly endeared itself even to the English in the way that the democratic 'Hen Wlad fy Nhadau' has endeared itself to the Welsh. Its most redeeming feature is that it's so short.

How different would history have been had the British anthem been like the truly majestic anthem of the Soviet Union, or rousing like that of South Africa, or even like the darkly sinister but beautiful (in a 'Llef' kind of way) Montenegrin anthem? What if its verses were about people and places, not pampered monarchs? The lesson – if you're going to conquer a country, pick a decent tune.

And what of the moral authority of the British state that it did not insist that 'the Queen' was sung? Is it a coincidence that the 'forgetting' happened 105 days after the British state asked for a bail-out by the IMF, when spiteful thin new flat-roofed architecture disfigured the landscape, when food was as bland as magnolia woodchip wallpaper? What was there to celebrate? And in any case, to be anti-establishment was the intellectual orthodoxy.

Another factor is that there was no obvious or genuine connection between Welsh sport and the English royal family. Like the (Royal) National Eisteddfod of Wales, but unlike the Royal Welsh Agricultural Show, it could 'forget' its royal link because people didn't feel the royal affinity and interest was genuine or relevant.

What of the second puzzle? The contradictory situation of a stateless nation asserting its identity by not playing the dominant state's anthem, but then perversely voting against having its own Assembly? A unique case of neither having your cake nor eating it!

Well, maybe it was that the devolution vote came too early? Rather than being an exclamation mark at the end of a process of national assertiveness, as one would expect, the fact is, the 'forgetting' to sing 'GStQ', was, for most Welsh people, the opening paragraph. As it was a process, a foot-draggingly slow process, then maybe the confidence of the British-Welsh establishment was such that dropping 'GStQ' was not seen as a big deal. It was allowed to happen. Or maybe the booing de-normalised the banal nationalism of the British anthem and created too much hassle and embarrassment for those in authority. Revolution by institutional lethargy.

Wales had to wait twenty years from the dropping of 'GStQ' to voting 'Yes' for an Assembly. A generation. A generation for many of the baby-booming 'booers' of Wales to see their own kids coming to voting age. Is there a 20-year cycle in a political or cultural process? There are those who believe so. One, among many, is the economist, Fred Harrison. As an economist of the 'Georgist' school, his belief is that the comparatively light taxation of land value (as opposed to labour or goods) leads to predictable cycles of property bubbles, with the boom and bust consequences we are now living through. Fred Harrison warned back in 1987 about the 2008 sub-prime mortgage crisis. Well, it took twenty-one years after the Prague Spring and May 68 for the Berlin Wall to collapse, and twenty years from the Croat Spring to Croat independence.

So, here's an intriguing question. If there is a twenty-odd year cycle for cultural, economic or political process, then what will Wales be like in twenty years' time? But that's the unknown unknown, for the question may be 'twenty years from when'?

For that, maybe, we need not only watch the news and read about the 'events', but we need to keep our senses open to the processes and the forgettings. You can be sure of one thing. The processes probably won't be on the news, and they won't be over until a fat fan in the terraces stops singing.

Cambria, vol. 12, no. 4, May 2011

Adfer:
the Rise and Fall of a Movement

In the 1970s a radical language movement, Adfer *(restore) was founded to defend Welsh in those areas where it was still widely spoken –* the Fro Gymraeg.

I was too young to remember Adfer *in its heyday, but I knew of the movement. If* Adfer *was discussed at all in the Welsh-speaking community in Cardiff of which I was a member, it was with loathing. After all, this was the movement that believed that Welsh-speakers shouldn't be in Cardiff, but rather working in Dyfed or Gwynedd, strengthening the* Fro Gymraeg.

By the time I entered university in 1986 the movement had effectively died, though the more unthinking students from the west would make sarcastic pseudo-Adfer comments about the 'yuppies' from Cardiff.

Funnily enough, I never felt any ill-feeling towards Adfer. *I tended to feel that many of those from Cardiff, or who had recently settled in the city, protested just a little too much. Arguments about 'freedom to live where you wished' or being 'as Welsh as people in Caernarfon' seemed just a little too forced. Why not be honest and say that they enjoyed the restaurants, clubs and anonymity which a city like Cardiff offers? And it's maybe on that simple, almost unthinking level that* Adfer *failed – people like cities, and Wales had one.*

Adfer *was essentially right in its insistence that language communites need heartlands. The loss of a Welsh-speaking heartland affects a language – it denies it the breadth of class, interest, ethnic diversity and experience. The Welsh language now is a thinnner language. Even in the brave new world of the internet and virtual communities, the lack of use of Welsh online as a medium of communication is down to the loss of territorial communities.*

After some bitter decades there is some opportunity if not to fulfil Adfer*'s dream, then at least to make the obvious decision in language strategy of recognising different geographical landscapes of the Welsh language. Section 44(2) (b) of the 2011 Welsh Language Act states: 'A compliance notice may require a person to comply with a particular standard ... (b) in some area or areas, but not in other areas'. Maybe we can now have policies which strengthen the language where it is strongest, and not just go for the lowest common denominator when it comes to language planning.*

Maybe now, forty years after Emyr Llywelyn's articles, we can have a discussion which doesn't come down to insulting people or getting out a measuring tape to determine people's Welshness. It's about language, not nationality.

History is written by the victors. That's why many readers will not have heard of *Adfer*, a radical language movement which had a short, terrier-like life in the 1970 and early 80s. The name translates as 'restore' in English. It was a movement that wished to restore Welsh to its rightful place as the only official language of every council and public service, and make Welsh essential in the part of Wales in which it was still a majority language.

During the course of a decade *Adfer*'s boldness, honesty and assertiveness for the Welsh language created a schism and bitterness within Welsh nationalism which still leaves an unpleasant after-taste thirty years later. Its successes are still with us, but as we take a look at *Adfer*'s rise and demise we may ponder: was it a movement which came too late or too early, and was its critique of the Welsh language wrong or just unpopular?

For a binocular view of the period when 'revolution' was a word used without ironic inverted commas, and anti-colonial wars were fought on the streets of Belfast, Biafra and Vietnam, click on to YouTube and listen to Tecwyn Ifan sing 'Y Dref Wen', the movement's unofficial anthem. The words for this haunting song are based on the early pre-medieval poetry called Canu Cynddylan and Heledd. It's poetry from the period when the Welsh were being forced west by the Anglo-Saxons and Cynddylan's court, Y Dref Wen, had been laid waste and burnt. The line 'awn i ail-godi bro, awn i ail-godi'r to' (we'll go and restore the land, we'll go and restore the roof) became the melodic manifestation of Adfer as it aimed to consolidate and build the Welsh language in the areas in which it was still spoken by over 50 per cent of the population – Y Fro Gymraeg.

During its hey-day in the mid 1970s Adfer's can-do community pilosophy succeeded in attracting young activists and students. Adfer members came together to rebuild houses for local people and campaigned against holiday homes. Its members were at the vanguard of setting up the all important papurau bro (community monthly newspapers) and in asserting Welsh as the language of administration and public use in Welsh communities. They were the leading lights of creating UMCB and UMCA, the Welsh-language student unions in Bangor and Aberystwyth, which came into regular conflict with the English educational system. Its philosophy of locating Welsh institutions in the Welsh-speaking areas helped strengthen the rural economy with jobs which would otherwise have been located in Cardiff.

The term Y Fro Gymraeg ('Welsh-speaking land') was coined by Owain Owain, an erudite nuclear physicist who invented Cymdeithas yr Iaith Gymraeg's distinctive dragon's tongue logo, as well as the term 'Gwledydd Prydain' (the 'Countries of Britain'), which elevates Wales's distinctiveness and undermines the banal nationalist terminology of Britain being a unified nation. He used the term *Y Fro Gymraeg*, with a map outlining the *Fro*, in the January 1964 issue of the Cymdeithas' magazine, *Tafod y Ddraig*, which he also founded and edited. The *Fro* is based on the areas according to the 1961 census where over 50 per cent of the population spoke Welsh. These included the whole of Gwynedd, Ceredigion and Carmarthenshire, north Pembrokeshire, Denbighshire beyond the coastal strip, a northern arch of Montgomeryshire right to the border with England, and parts of western Glamorgan. He notes: 'If we win the *Fro Gymraeg*, we can win Wales, if we don't win the *Fro Gymraeg*, we cannot win Wales' [for the language].

However, the movement which aimed to make the concept of the *Fro Gymraeg* a reality was *Adfer* and, in particular, the founder and leading theorist of the movement, Emyr Llywelyn. A small, intense man, Emyr Llywelyn (or Emyr Llew, as he's widely known) has given a life-time's dedication to the Welsh language, and through his active political career embodies many of the different strands of Welsh nationalism. Emyr Llywelyn was raised in Pont-garreg, central Ceredigion. His father was the famous poet and children's author, T. Llew Jones. Emyr, however, was a more political animal. He began his political life campaigning in the 1959 General Election for Dyfrig Thomas, an Aberystwyth student friend and Plaid candidate.

However, Emyr Llywelyn became disenchanted with Plaid Cymru and constitutional politics. As he describes in an article, the Welsh language was dependent on begging for the votes of the 'Alf Garnetts of this world' (Alf Garnett was a popular reactionary fictional television character of the time). As he told me from his home in Ffostrasol near Llandysul in Ceredigion: 'We were dependent on the votes of an electorate who were totally opposed to, or uninterested in, the fate of the language. It was totally false to believe you could save the language in an election every four years.'

The late 1950s was a frustrating and heartbreaking time for supporters of the language. It was becoming patently obvious that Welsh was losing ground quickly. For a mostly cowed and indifferent Welsh-speaking population enjoying new-found electric appliances, and boosted in their British pride by 'international socialism' and the new Elizabethan age, Welsh was a language for the old dusty chapel and the boring old days. With Plaid Cymru's inability to take an effective stand against the drowning of Tryweryn, young nationalists were looking for other avenues to save the language. Saunders Lewis's historic '*Tynged yr Iaith*' lecture in 1962 gave the intellectual go-ahead that many needed. Lewis argued that the language was more important than a parliament and that it was only through revolutionary means that it could be saved. It didn't have the luxury of waiting for a Welsh parliament or Plaid Cymru's next deposit-losing Westminster election.

On 10 February 1963 Emyr, with two other nationalists, Owain Williams and John Albert Jones of MAC (*Mudiad Amddiffyn Cymru* – 'movement for the defence of Wales') blew up the transformer at the Tryweryn's construction site. Llywelyn was caught and spent a year in gaol, during which time he was force-fed to break a hunger-strike. As he recently told me his home in Ffostrasol, 'We went to Tryweryn and acted by night because they, the politicians, didn't go by day.'

Emyr Llywelyn came out of gaol a different man. He decided against continuing the line of protest he had taken in Tryweryn and returned to play an active part in Cymdeithas yr Iaith. It's difficult today to recall the hatred and venom which Cymdeithas yr Iaith drew from the press, British nationalist politicians and 'respectable' Welsh people. Those campaigning for bilingual signs or Welsh-medium education would casually be called Nazis or racists by opponents. Cymdeithas yr Iaith's protests could become very nasty affairs, with policemen manhandling protesters; the situation in Wales (as Emyr Llew's actions proved) could have gone in either direction – direct violent action or direct non-violent action:

> We had a situation where you couldn't be sure that any protest wouldn't turn violent. I'm very proud therefore that under my Chairmanship of Cymdeithas yr Iaith that we voted and decided on the policy of non-violent direct action. The way you do something is as important as the objective. The language wasn't worth anyone getting killed for. It wasn't a sign of weakness – we would have been playing into the hand of the British state had we decided on violent action. The state has a monopoly of violence and a movement can't beat that.

Emyr Llew was a leading member of an unprecedented generation of talented 'organic intellectuals' aiming to dismantle the British state and the Britishness that had, over the centuries caused the demise of the Welsh language. His most important articles were published in '*Adfer a'r Fro Gymraeg*' (1976), a shooting star of an anthology which is as fearlessly brave and honest as it is challenging and, for some, insulting.

By the 1970s Llywelyn had become a teacher, teaching in Port Talbot and then Aberaeron, and also father to three young children. His intellectual journey which ended with a split from Cymdeithas yr Iaith is outlined succinctly and honestly in his article of March 1970, titled '*Adfer*'. In it he noted that the Welsh-speakers as a minority have three options: accept integration and give into the pressure of the dominant English language and Britishness; protest and try and force the enemy to create favourable conditions for the minority by self-sacrificial protesting and 'destructive protest', which, he said, was Cymdeithas yr Iaith's path; or a third option, which Llywelyn suggested hadn't yet been tried. This was to 'turn our back on the hostile environment (*amgylchfyd gelyniaethus*), cut it out by the power of our will. Create a new independent environment totally apart from the environment which suffocates and kills'. He accused Plaid Cymru and Cymdeithas yr Iaith of asking her enemies to give the Welsh language her rights:

> They believe that they must give their whole time and resources to force the English Government to recognise the problem and accept responsibility to sort out the problem. But when you ask someone for something you recognise that the power to give, or not to give, lies with that person or body ... Instead of protesting that the authorities close Ysgol Bryncroes we should go and build and support our own school. Instead of complaining that the Cambrian News is anti-Welsh we should start our own paper.

Llywelyn warned against his audience putting faith in political movements. He said:

> Every political movement crumbles, dies and vanishes. That's the fate of Plaid Cymru, that will be the fate of this movement [Cymdeithas yr Iaith] – but the Police, Law, Educational System which is the English Government in Wales will continue like the rock of ages; the English civil service in Wales will continue. Even were we to see self-government they will continue to be Anglocentric – that's the experience of India, that's the experience of Ireland.

He asked, therefore:

> What can we create which will be permanent?' His
> answer was: 'Only a Welsh-speaking society with its
> own independent institutions. Only this can
> guarantee our continuation as a people. We can begin
> to create this society now, we need not wait for the day
> of a Welsh Parliament until we begin to live a full,
> dignified, free, Welsh-speaking life.

He then outlined the importance of percentages of Welsh-
language speakers – and this is where the concept of the *Fro
Gymraeg* is given political meat. Emyr Llywelyn's belief was
that the Welsh language had to consolidate in those areas in
which it was still a community language and where it could
create independent Welsh institutions. It was linguistic
scorched-earth politics.

It is at this point that the split with Cymdeithas yr Iaith
and the Plaid Cymru hierarchy began. He told his readers:

> Welsh will never live whilst its speakers are scattered
> across the suburbia of anglicised cities. Extinction
> awaits your Welshness and your children's in Penarth,
> Ely, Cyncoed, Eglwyswen, Rhiwbina, Swansea, Neath,
> Aberafan and yes, even the towns of Cardigan and
> Aberystwyth. Wherever the Welsh-speakers are less
> than 50 per cent you are an integrated, vanishing
> element. Within two generations it will not be possible
> to recognise your descendants from the non-Welsh
> speaking descendants around you.

He argues: 'I am totally certain that we will not see the revival
of Welsh as a community language in Glamorgan in my
lifetime, but, it's a totally practical dream to turn the counties

of the west Welsh-speaking within twenty years.' This, in a sentence, is *Adfer*'s position, and the answer to halting and then reversing the continual decline of the Welsh language.

By August 1970 Llywelyn had developed his ideas further and sought to outline what he hoped would be guidelines or suggestions which would enable Welsh-speakers to 'reject false British providence'. They varied from dropping the anglicised forms of their surnames, such as Jones, Davies, Evans – 'your names will be a symbol of a new majesty' – to adopting a distinctive dress, as the Norwegians had adopted their cap to confirm their nationality during the Nazi occupation. The aim was to create a counter-culture which would empower at least a dedicated, politicised minority to withstand the pressure to conform to banal British nationalism.

Leaving aside some idiosyncratic suggestions, there is very little in Emyr Llywelyn's writing so far with which most language campaigners, or indeed professional language planners, would have disagreed at this stage. Welsh-speakers in Cardiff may have found his chilling prediction of language assimilation disheartening, but not totally unreasonable. After all, the percentage of Welsh-speakers in the city had declined from 27.9 per cent in 1891 to 2 per cent in 1961, and in a city of 250,000 people there was but one Welsh-medium junior school, Bryntaf, at which I was a chubby-cheeked pupil.

Census returns are, to Welsh-language activists, the equivalent of the doctor telling the patient he has terminal cancer. We all know the end result. With this in mind, Emyr Llywelyn's articles from 1974 took a more desperate turn as he was no doubt disheartened by another depressing set of census returns, with the percentage of Welsh-speakers falling again from 26 per cent in 1961 to 20.8 per cent in 1971 across Wales. Those with eyes could see bilingual signs being erected; those with ears noticed, what the poet Grahame Davies calls the 'audible minority', was become quieter.

Adfer and Emyr Llew then grabbed the one trump card the Welsh language still had. That card was that speaking Welsh gives the speaker the undeniable ability to claim that he or she is Welsh in a way that the non-Welsh-speaking person can't. That is, to speak Welsh is the true essence of Welshness. This was a defensive course of action. After all, Welsh was a minority language with only the minimum of official status and no legal compulsion to learn it. Nobody had to learn Welsh. If now that a consensus was being created that one need not speak Welsh to be considered a full Welshman either, Llywelyn reasoned, then there was no emotional reason to speak it. The language was being undermined from all sides.

Although Llywelyn says that to be known as a 'nationalist' will in the future to be an '*adferwr*', the movement was in many ways a very un-nationalist one. That is, the concern of Emyr Llywelyn and *Adfer* wasn't with the concept of nationality but with the reality of a spoken language. The purpose of campaigning for a Welsh Parliament was to have a vehicle which would defend and promote Welsh in the same way as Westminster had defended and promoted English. As the likelihood of a Welsh Parliament seemed distant and the language had no time to waste, Emyr Llywelyn had little time or concern for campaigning for a parliament and by definition in creating a sense of Welsh national identity which could be mobilised to call for that parliament. This, of course, was in direct conflict with Plaid Cymru, which was very much about 'nation-building', and wished its concept of Welsh nationality to be as wide and warm as possible for different manifestations of Welshness, be they Welsh-speaking or not.

And this is where it became a bare-knuckle fist fight about

what is Wales, and what is a Welsh person. In his August 1974 article, *'Adfer Enaid y Cymro'* (restoring the soul of the Welshman), Emyr Llywelyn tried to win back for the Welsh language the prestige he saw it losing on every front. In hindsight this article became a joker in the pack and not a trump card for the movement.

Emyr Llywelyn began by saying that to speak Welsh is to *be* Welsh (*Cymro*). This is, of course, a 'given' with most nationalities – an Englishman can't be an Englishman unless he speaks English, likewise a Frenchman or German. But it's not so simple in a colonised nation. If a person who speaks Welsh is a *Cymro* – then it follows that a person who doesn't speak Welsh is not a *Cymro*. Llywelyn went further and stated that the non-Welsh speaker isn't even *'di-Gymraeg'* (this means 'non-Welsh speaking', and not 'non-Welsh' as is sometimes assumed) but rather 'cyn-Gymraeg' (formerly Welsh-speaking) or a 'Welshman' (he uses the English term). 'Our great task,' he wrote, 'is to make them *Cymry* again'.

He went further and noted that because Welsh, like all languages, is a communal phenomenon, then those who lived in non-Welsh speaking communities couldn't be fully Welsh either. They were a *'Cymro Anghyflawn'* (Incomplete *Cymro*). Of course, a Welsh-speaker who lives in a community where Welsh is the community language, and can live his life fully in Welsh, is a *'Cymro Cyflawn'*.

With characteristic honesty and directness (Emyr Llywelyn's *Adfer* does what it says on the tin), he wrote:

> Those of you who live outside the *Fro Gymraeg* will naturally feel very aggrieved with me for saying this, but rather ... be honest with yourself and admit that what I say is true. Face the truth – a *Cymro* without a Welsh-speaking community is a *Cymro Anghyflawn*.

Do not fool yourself that you and your children will be fully Welsh outside the Fro Gymraeg.

As you can imagine, that went down like a rat sandwich with most Welsh-speakers outside Gwynedd and Dyfed, with the Plaid Cymru hierarchy and rank and file who were trying to nation-build, and with many in the *Fro Gymraeg* as well.

Llywelyn continued the rest of the article outlining a dozen or so ways an *Adferwr* should lead his life to create and strengthen the *Fro Gymraeg*, from setting up businesses in the *Fro* to organising a local theatre group or creating a papur bro. He also forcefully added:

> the fact that I say that it is the influx of English people into our communities which is decimating our communities does not give me, or anyone else, the right to hate English people. Nationalism based on hatred of English people is not worthy to pass on to our children.

Emyr Llywelyn's articles, and his split with Cymdeithas yr Iaith (though many continued to be members of both), created great bitterness – on both sides. Emyr Llywelyn suffered more than anyone, and he and his family came under great strain and attack. Many nationalists from outside the *Fro*, both Welsh-speaking and non-Welsh speaking, felt insulted, and angered, too, by his articles, and the low-level insults by *adferwyr* towards their Welshness. It was maybe Dafydd Iwan's editorial in *Tafod y Ddraig* of September 1974 which is most balanced. Trying to offer a conciliatory and optimistic note, Dafydd Iwan finishes his editorial by saying 'Let's hold hands, we'll form a strong chain from Anglesey to Monmouth, from Flint to Pembroke – and joyfully, with hope in each another we'll be Welsh people!'

However, by the early 1980s the movement that had been formed to restore the Welsh-speaking areas was in decline and effectively dead. So, what went wrong?

Adfer was the logical conclusion of a growing assertiveness within Welsh-speaking society to demand her rights. But this confidence came at the very time when the very fabric of the *Fro Gymraeg* was also anglicising. The advent of holiday homes and later the mass movement of English people into the *Fro* meant that Welsh-speaking communities lost their coherence, strength and primacy.

Among these and other reasons I'd also like to offer a more prosaic reason for *Adfer*'s failure –the need for the political vitamins of success to ward off political despair. People need hope to live to fight another day; they also have lives to live.

In the post-1979 dog days the Welsh language movement was desperate for any positive sign of growth for the language. Unfortunately, Emyr Llew's critique almost made it difficult to enjoy many of those successes. A rare rugby win by the national side was no comfort, as *Adfer* weren't concerned about nation-building, and especially, one guesses, success celebrated by false 80-minute patriots at the Arms Park. The one great hope of the decade, the launch of S4C in 1982, was a ray of warm sunshine – but so many of the jobs were located in Cardiff, and so added to the haemorrhage of young people from the *Fro*. The opening of a Welsh-medium school in the south-east wasn't something to celebrate; it was a diversion from the crisis of Welsh-medium education in the *Fro*. The opening of *Clwb Ifor Bach*, a Welsh-medium club in Cardiff built on subscription, wasn't a glimmer of hope: it was a playground for the children of the *crach* (wealthy snobs), and an artificial, unsustainable, Welsh-speaking society.

In his articles Emyr Llew envisioned how the *Fro*

Gymraeg could be the '*pair y dadeni*' (the famous 'cauldron of rebirth' in the *Mabinogi*, where the dead Welsh soldiers fighting the Irish are thrown into the cauldron and are then miraculously reborn to fight again). The strengthened Fro in the west would help reclaim the east. But during the 1980s the irony was that it was the east which in many respects strengthened the west. With the wilting of the Welsh-speaking communities in the west it was in the east that Welsh-language campaigners looked for hopeful signs to boost their morale.

Unfortunately, *Adfer*'s philosophy seemed not to allow its members to relish or celebrate in these little victories. It was the east too which offered the young Welsh-speaker the opportunity of living a Welsh-life in a city in Wales – it made Wales and the Welsh language seem bigger. Maybe, for many people, *Adfer*'s critique, while holding many truths was just too depressing, too difficult.

Adfer didn't 'win', but was it 'wrong'? Certainly its decision to prioritise strengthening the language where it was still the community language was correct. Llywelyn was aware of the situation in other countries. In 1963, following years of campaigning by the Dutch speakers, the Belgian state was organised into two distinct monolingual language communities. By doing so it halted the threat to the Dutch language in Flanders. Likewise, in the 1960s as the percentage of French-speaking communities across the Canadian provinces of Ontario, Newfoundland and New Brunswick declined dramatically, the French-speakers in Quebec took the 'adfer' position – possibly to the detriment of the French communities outside Quebec but certainly not to the language in the province. *Adfer* were also aware of the distinct Irish-speaking areas in Ireland called the *Gaeltacht*, where Irish was made the only official language in 1956.

Although these haven't been great successes, Welsh would have started from a stronger position than Irish and crucially covered a significant and continuous territory. The thought of a Welsh *Gaeltacht* didn't appeal to many Welsh-speakers and was seen as too restrictive by others. But then isn't the whole of the UK one big English-speaking *Gaeltacht*?

The mainstream Welsh national and language movement seems almost unique in underplaying the essential importance of defending geographic areas where Welsh was already the majority language.

In his August 1975 article, '*Dinasyddiaeth a'r Fro Gymraeg*' (Citizenship and the *Fro Gymraeg*) Llywelyn outlined that all institutions in the Fro would be Welsh, including the council and public services and that television and radio would be based in the polity, rather than in Cardiff. Had S4C, Radio Cymru, the Welsh Language Board and myriad other Welsh institutions been located in, let's say, Aberystwyth, it would have strengthened the Welsh language in the *Fro* immeasurably. It would essentially have created a compact mostly Welsh-speaking city, and by default would also have gone a long way to rebalancing the Welsh economy in what is now poor Objective One areas, spreading the wealth from Cardiff and the south-east.

And as we are discussing Objective One areas, isn't this the other great irony of the opposition to *Adfer*? Is it not peculiar that whilst many are vocal against creating a designated 'Welsh-speaking area' and of 'dividing Wales' they support dividing the country to create other designated areas? Businesses and politicians actively campaigned for Wales to be 'divided' into Objective One areas (which includes most of the *Fro Gymraeg* and Valleys) and discriminate against businesses which are just a mile from its border. Or what of the strict planning regulations of the National Parks, which are also another line on the map? The twenty-two different unitary authorities set different rules and priorities and limited taxation too. No problems there. So, why was a *Fro Gymraeg* so difficult for people?

Adfer didn't split Wales in two. It was already split. People knew in 1970 which towns and villages were Welsh-speaking and which weren't. People knew you could walk into a shop in Dolgellau and naturally speak Welsh with the assistant, but not do the same in Newtown. It was something Welsh-speakers knew in their mental map. Emyr Llywelyn wished to solidify what was that linguistic reality before it was too late. *Adfer* wished to make that social reality a legal reality.

But despite Tecwyn Ifan's call to *'ail-adfer bro'* [reclaim the land], Ac Eraill's 1973 song *'Tua'r Gorllewin'* [to the West] and Edward H. Dafis's 1974 rock anthem *'Yn y Fro'*, Emyr Llywelyn's Zionistic challenge for young people to settle the land fell mostly on deaf ears. Like in Israel, only a handful of dedicated pioneers would make a conscious decision to move. To continue the Jewish comparison, only some 25,000 Jews emigrated to Palestine during the first Aliyah between 1882 and 1903. During the same period, some two million Jews emigrated from Eastern Europe to the USA, Britain and other states. People live where they can find work. The *Fro Gymraeg*, without the numbers to create its own 'independent Welsh institutions' and without the backing of the state to lure them there, was left battling by itself against the tsunami of British capitalism.

Adfer's legacy wasn't a total failure, and many of its can-do attitudes could appeal to left-wing co-operative sentiment on the left or Tory 'big society' on the right. Its emphasis on building indigenous Welsh instutitions is one which should have great resonance at a time when the British state can cut S4C's budget by 36 per cent, and organisations in Wales are dependent on the political whims of their paymasters in the

Assembly government, unable, or unwilling, to articulate an independent Welsh aesthetic or prognosis.

Adfer's philosophy didn't completely die either. The Welsh language and human rights movement Cymuned was formed in 2001 in direct response to the Blair-Brown bling-economics housing boom. It used many of *Adfer*'s arguments for strengthening what was left of the Welsh-speaking areas. With the National Assembly in place, and with it Plaid Cymru's fear of 'splitting Wales' gone, Wales could have given some recognition towards strengthening the Welsh language where it was strongest. However, Cymuned, like *Adfer*, was attacked as much by Plaid Cymru as by Labour. For Labour's membership it seemed that a part of Wales where English wouldn't be the dominant language was beyond the Pale. Plaid Cymru, on the other hand, were still fighting the arguments of the 1970s based on supposed slights towards non-Welsh speakers, though Cymuned avoided denigrating people who couldn't speak Welsh, except to point out that they didn't want their communities to become English-speaking. It all became a little bizarre when I remember hearing Plaid Cymru members who'd learnt Welsh say they were no less Welsh now than when they didn't speak Welsh. Which is fine, but did beg the question of why they had learnt Welsh in the first place. To follow this argument to its logical conclusion one could say that Wales would be just as Welsh if it had no one speaking Welsh. England, would no doubt, be 'just as English' if nobody spoke English.

Adfer lost to the nation builders. It lost because it was perceived to be making an already small community even smaller. Now that we have our Assembly that has decided, in the name of 'bilingualism', that there will be no monolingual Welsh-speaking communities, it's up to us all to question if there should be any monolingual English-speaking communities. As the state has decided against the Belgian or Swiss model of defined monolingual language communities within Wales, the state should now deliver on the assumption that every Welsh citizen should be expected to have some basic knowledge of Welsh. Bilingualism should mean being able to walk tall like a *Cymro Cyflawn* in every part of Wales.

Published in summarised form in
Cambria, vol. 13, no. 5, Summer 2013

Cofiwn:
Once were Princes

During my early teen years, my father was a member of Cofiwn [we will remember]. Maybe it's for that reason that the historical movement made a great impact on me.

I attended the 1982 Cilmeri rally to commemorate the death of the last Prince of Wales, Llywelyn ap Gruffudd: a great colourful affair. It's against that benchmark that I've compared all subsequent nationalist rallies. And they've all fallen short on iconography, colour and pomp.

There's a segment of the national movement in Wales which finds flags and pomp a little distasteful; a little lacking in intellect; maybe a little beneath them. However, I believe in following best practice. The masters of pomp are the British – and they've successfully managed to create a state and draw the affection and service of many people to it, partly through ceremonial splendour and pageant.

Some may find this anti-intellectual; that it appeals to the basest of human interest. But then, there comes a point when a movement has to go with the flow of human nature. If we can accept that a natural part of humanity is for some people to be gay, or not believe in a divine being, they why can't the same people recognise that enjoyment, and a need for ceremony and colour, is also a natural part of human existence? Maybe that part of the Welsh national movement which now shies away from, or is disdainful of, pomp or ceremony should go with the grain of human life, and not, like Puritans, go against it.

Or maybe they do, but are themselves embarrassed to see fellow Welsh people unashamedly fly flags and celebrate past victories, for the simple reason that deep down they have accepted Wales's subservient role. That maybe, drawing 'too much' attention to ourselves is a bad thing?

Of course, arguments are made that celebrating past history is not relevant to the politics of funding the schools and hospitals of today. But that is to deny a people the basic right of the dignity of their own identity and culture – a right which exists to all people. And make no bones about it, when the British state, in its dying years, will wish to remind people of its future glory it will reach to its glorious (to some) past. The British left wing will be more than happy to hitch a ride on the medieval dressing up and ceremonies of flags and uniforms for royal weddings and funerals when it suits them, and even denigrate Celtic nationalists for not taking part.

All of us who identify with Wales – of whatever background – can be proud that this country once had princes who, despite their many faults, made laws, treaties and sponsored the arts. Since the medieval Age of the Princes, Wales has yet to reattain that height of sophistication.

In 1983 the peasants took over the colonial castle. Some 600 sans-culotte 'historians' managed to lock the gates of Caernarfon castle, thereby stopping tourists getting in or out of Edward the Conqueror's garrison.

The protest was part of their '*Sarhâd 83*' (Insult 83) campaign against the Tourist Board's 'Wales Festival of Castles', a festival they saw as a celebration of the conquest of Wales.

The protesters in their jeans and jumpers were the footsoldiers of *Cofiwn* – a radical historical society almost forgotten today, but one Wales would do well to revive. Radical historical society? Wait a minute! Wouldn't that be like a radical campanology society? Why would you have a radical historical society?

Cofiwn, the wonderfully concise way of saying in Welsh 'we will remember', was a nationalist historical society. It was founded in 1972 by Gethin ap Gruffydd of Bridgend and the late Tony Lewis of Cwmbrân.

One of the leading members was Siân Ifan, a small, determined, chatty woman who still wears the long flowing hair of a 1970s radical.

As you may have guessed, *Cofiwn* wasn't a cosy, dozy, tweed-jacketed historical society. The fact that Gethin ap Gruffydd (Keith Griffiths) had been jailed for nine months on charges of being part of the organisation of the Free Wales Army may give a clue to its ethos and politics. Both ap Gruffydd and Lewis, who were inspired by Irish republicanism, had founded many patriotic movements in the 1960s, including the Patriotic Front. However, *Cofiwn* was the most successful, most mainstream and least fractious.

The political dimension of *Cofiwn* was confirmed by mass arrests on Palm Sunday 1980: sixty-five nationalists were arrested across Wales, including the twenty members of *Cofiwn*'s governing body.

Gethin ap Gruffydd chose the ivy as the movement's symbol. It was in commemoration of the crown of ivy which Edward I's troops placed on Llywelyn the Last's head, on a pike on the Tower of London. Working from a shed in her home in Ystumtuen on the badlands behind Aberystwyth, Siân churned out posters, T-shirts, flags and badges for the movement.

The movement had several hundred members, each paying £1 annual subscription, with branches across Wales. Eminent historians such as Dr John Davies and Prof. Hywel Teifi Edwards would give talks on Welsh history for *Cofiwn*, educating the duffle-coat-wearing members in under-heated halls.

Cofiwn raised money to lay stones to commemorate Glyndŵr's battle at Hyddgen above Aberystwyth, for

Llywelyn the Last at Abbey Cwm Hir and Llywelyn the Great in Aberffraw in Anglesey. In Merthyr Tydfil it held annual processions to remember Dic Penderyn and Lewsyn yr Heliwr, the first martyrs of the Welsh working class after the Riot of 1831.

Its most successful event was the 700th anniversary at Cilmeri of the death of Llywelyn ap Gruffudd, the last Prince of Wales. Events were held every month throughout 1982 commemorating dates in Llywelyn's life. On a bright, clean snow-capped Radnorshire day on 11 December 1982, some 2,000 participated in the procession, including a republican marching band from Scotland. A wreath of ivy was placed at the foot of the majestic *maen-hir* which was placed there by a previous nationalist group in 1956. Following the 'No' vote in the 1979 Devolution Referendum, *Cofiwn* understood that parades were needed to raise the spirit of the bedraggled troops, not just plodding along churning out party-political policies which would never be implemented.

But despite its impressive achievements in 1984, a year following the successful closure of Caernarfon Castle, *Cofiwn* came to an end. So, why was that?

'There were many reasons,' explained Siân, who now lives in Swansea and is active in another historical agitprop movement, Embassy Glyndŵr. 'From infiltration or fear of infiltration by the Special Branch, to people prioritising their careers over politics. There was also the strain. The movement never had enough money, and there's only so many years you can fund events from your own pocket,' recalls Siân who's also writing a book about the history of the movement.

Maybe, like fragile eco-systems, the lifespans for radical political movements are inevitably limited. Maybe we should just accept that for radical cultural movements like *Cofiwn*, a dozen years or so is the natural lifespan in such heightened intellectual and emotional activity?

But, was there a historic legacy for this historical society?

Certainly the banners of the Welsh Princes which *Cofiwn* did so much to propagate – the four lions of Llywelyn and Glyndŵr, so exotic and unexpected in the 1980s – are now commonplace. Some also still sport the ivy on their lapels on 11 December, Llywelyn's Day. Welsh history is also now more widely taught and understood, but there's no place for complacency.

As Siân notes, it's interesting that Cadw, the Welsh Historical Agency, was formed in 1984. Of course, Cadw, unlike *Cofiwn* (from *'cofio'* to remember) didn't use the concise, active version of the verb to keep – that would be *'Cadwn'* (we shall keep) … a little too close, too active, and too political, maybe?

Cofiwn's experience and legacy also rouses the deeper question, 'What's the point of history?'

Cofiwn's appeal was that it was so honest. History there to promote a political agenda. That was the point of it – though you're not meant to say so in polite 'apolitical' circles, of course. *Cofiwn* also understood which history to promote – the history of our princes. This was tut-tutted by some sophisticated academics or politicians, for, after all, to celebrate the history of Welsh princes seemed too uncouth and, well, positively medieval.

In Chapter V of *The Prince*, 'Concerning the way to Govern Cities or Principalities which lived under their own Laws before they were Annexed', Niccolò Machiavelli outlines three ways to govern: 'The first is to ruin them, the next is to reside there in person, the third is to permit them to live under their own laws, drawing a tribute and establishing within it an oligarchy which will keep it friendly to you.'

Cofiwn's mission was to undermine the intellectual power which gave this 'oligarchy' legitimacy. They understood that they had to do this because of what this intellectual oligarchy, the 'deep state' as it called in Turkey, had achieved. In the words of the Kenyan anti-colonialist, Nguni Wa Thiong'o in his seminal book *Decolonising the Mind*, the process of colonial education:

> annihilates a people's belief in their names, in their languages, in their environment, in their heritage of struggle, in their unity, in their capacities and ultimately in themselves. It makes them see their past as one wasteland of non-achievement, and it makes them want to distance themselves from that wasteland. It makes them want to identify with that which is furthest removed from themselves.

Cofiwn wanted to prove that Wales wasn't 'one wasteland of non-achievement'. It wanted to prove that we once wrote laws, made treaties, won battles, built castles and ports and sponsored the arts – that we once were a nation – and it was only through again becoming a nation state could Wales defend itself politically, economically and culturally. That was the point of history. Everything else is an anorak full of facts for a pub quiz.

Cofiwn's genius was to understand the psychology of individuals and the psychology of belonging.

Any self-help book will tell the reader that if they wish to be a successful business person they first have to think of themselves as a successful business person and act like one. *Cofiwn* did the same for Wales.

If Wales was to become an independent nation it first had to think and act like one. To do that it had to put on its psychological suit of armour. To paraphrase the seminal 1994 Maori film, *Once were Warriors: Cofiwn*'s slogan would be 'Once were Princes'.

I have no doubt that I come from an unbroken line of damp-footed peasants who've toiled the bare hills of Brycheiniog and the windy vales of Llŷn since the last Ice Age. So why would I not be for promoting the history of our downtrodden, of the working class, my family's history? Why not build a movement for our nation-state around the glorious battles and struggles of the nineteenth-century 'gwerin' (working classes)? Why did Cofiwn seem mostly to promote the history of princes and the 'crachach' (gentry)?

It's because promoting the history of the downtrodden, the dominant Welsh historiography and political narrative, hasn't worked and doesn't work for Wales. It doesn't arm us with the psychology, with the confidence, to be a nation-state, and without being a nation-state we can't defend our interests as Welsh people – whatever our class. As Saunders Lewis wrote in his famous letter to the *Western Mail* on 26 February, on the eve of the 1979 Referendum:

> May I point out the probable consequence of a No majority. There will follow a general election. There may be a change of government. The first task of the Westminster Parliament will be to reduce and master inflation. In Wales there are coalmines that work at a loss; there are steelworks that are judged to be superfluous; there are valleys convenient for submersion. And there will be no Welsh defence.

A nation which wishes to exercise power itself can't always wear the hair-shirt of the powerless. To take the route of the downtrodden is constantly to take the contradictory view where being poor or weak is, by virtue, good. It's to share in the optimism of the defeated which afflicts Wales – the quarter glass is half full, where, as long as we're not physically certified stone-cold, marble-dead in the morgue, then, 'Well, boys, it could be worse'.

Likewise in the current economic quagmire it's not the socialist 'down-trodden' historical narrative which will defend Wales. Commemorating the history of Rebecca, of Tryweryn, of the General Strike of 1926, of the Miners' Strike of 1984, is all very well and good ... and cosy because it only reinforces the narrative that we as a nation can't take power. It doesn't breed rebels, it breeds conservatives. In contrast, the 'conservative' historiography of Welsh princes does breed rebels. Why? Because it challenges the legitimacy of the British state and British capitalism.

It's all very well for British left-wingers to sneer at a Welsh historiography which celebrates our princes. They'll call it the history of the *'crachach'*, which ignores the 'ordinary Welsh people'. But they're like those radical chic Trotskyists who preach revolution knowing full well that if push comes to shove Daddy will bail them out. Likewise, if political push comes to shove the British left will go running to the British establishment – military, monarchy and mother tongue – to shore up the state they wish to defend against the nationalists.

It's not that the history of Princes should be the only history studied or promoted – far from it. But it should be the frame of our house – as it is in all free countries.

For, as *Cofiwn* and Saunders understood, it's the exceptionalism of civic nationalism – with its history as ballast – which gives strength to a polity and people to stand among nations and stand up to international capital.

It was the very so-called 'internationalism' of socialism which partly created the cultural muzak which allowed international capital to fleece the defenceless. It is civic nationalism that gives a people legitimacy to be different. It is civic nationalism that arms politicians not to be herded into 'being international' and be cowed by capital like stumbling somnambulists. Civic nationalism gives strength not to follow the crowd in an economic rerun of the famous 1963 'Obedience to Authority' Milgram test, where people were asked to follow the crowd and inflict pain on other humans as part of an experiment to see how far they would go.

In 2011 it's good that we thank Gethin ap Gruffydd, Tony Lewis and Siân Ifan, and remember the jeans-and-jumpers historians of *Cofiwn*.

Cambria, vol. 12, no. 6, November 2011

Prints, Programmes and Portals

Don't Mention Mohammed:
Pulping Copies of *Y Llan*

Another in the 'will this damage my career and reputation?' file.
But as a failed politician who now has no political ambition at
all, I'm free to speak my mind.

My intention here is not to attack the Muslim community.
My main attack is on the intellectual laziness and cowardice of
the Welsh political class whose over-reaction was the cringe
factor at its worse, masquerading as defending the right of
Muslims not to be offended.

It is, of course, important to remember that at the time of the
writing of the article the attack on the Twin Towers was still
comparatively fresh in people's mind and that the 7 July 2005
attacks on London had happened only a year earlier. However,
one would have expected the secular state to stand for its own
morality rather than cowering. As I re-read the article years
later, I'm still speechless at the unfairness and ridiculousness at
the response to Meurig Llwyd Williams' article. I'm glad to say
that many people approached me after the original publication
of my own article to support my view.

What do you do if you see someone being mugged on the
street? Well, if you're the Welsh Establishment you just walk
on by, and even go back and give the poor man another good
kicking just to make sure he's down.

That's what happened when Meurig Llwyd Williams
made the muggable mistake of writing what seems to have
been an intelligent, ecumenical article about the
commonality of the world's monotheistic faiths in the
Church in Wales's Welsh-language periodical, *Y Llan*. As its
editor he also understood that a picture is worth a thousand

words, so Meurig Llwyd included an image (I won't use 'cartoon' which has a pejorative infantile feel) which had appeared in the French daily *France Soir*. The image shows Christ, Mohammed and Buddha perched on a cloud with Christ telling Mohammed '*Paid â chwyno ... rydym i gyd yn cael ein gwawdlunio yma*' ('don't complain ... we've all been caricatured here' – although, the word 'gwawdlunio' implies something stronger than caricature, closer to mocking-image). And that was it.

Meurig Llwyd, who is also the Venerable Archdeacon of Bangor, had tried, it seems, to include an intelligent critique and a balanced argument on interfaith commonality. It was an outstretched hand of fellowship, believer to believer in a secular world. But *Y Llan*, under his editorship, had committed the crime of publishing an image of Mohammed. For that the Archdeacon was given a bell to hang around his neck, clanking and tolling his political uncleanness for all to hear. Meurig Llwyd's treatment by the Church in Wales would have been no worse, and probably better, had he been an apologist for the Palestinian suicide bombers of Tel Aviv's cafés. He was sacked as editor.

He found to his own cost what can and can't be debated in Wales, and who sets the boundaries of that debate.

Y Llan's publication of an 'image' of Mohammed came hot on the heels of the controversy of the publication of cartoons (and I use the more pejorative word here) in the Danish daily, *Jyllands-Posten*. Although originally published in September 2005 it was a full four months before the combustion of aggrandised effrontery on the part of some members of the Islamic worldwide community hit the global media. In February 2006 the editor of *Gair Rhydd*, the Cardiff student magazine, was sacked for publishing the Danish cartoons and the paper's 8,000 print run pulped – ironic considering the paper's title ('free word' in Welsh).

And it seems that *Y Llan*, a publication with a print run of 500 copies sent to that most threatening and dangerous of constituencies, the *bara brith*-munching, tea-sipping Welsh clergy and its parishioners, was also reprimanded – by itself! The Church in Wales, under the authority of no less a figure than its own Archbishop, Barry Morgan, believed the images to be so offensive that the newsletter was pulped and subscribers asked to return their copies.

Along with thousands of others I haven't been allowed to make my own judgment on the article, but I assumed that at least a copy would be at hand at the National Library of Wales. However, so diligent (or paranoid) was the Church in destroying any last copy of the edition, that even the one sent to the National Library, our citadel of conscience, was called in. So there we have it: a reader at the Library can order and see a copy of *The Protocols of the Elders of Zion* or even *Fiesta's Readers' Wives Special* (two publications I have never ordered, I hasten to add) but not *Y Llan*. Was the March 2006 edition of *Y Llan* such a threat to civil society and morality that even the copy sent to the National Library had to be withdrawn? That edition has now been airbrushed from history. Even the historians of the future won't be able to read it.

Surely if English Law can differentiate between murder and manslaughter, then the Church in Wales could differentiate between an article and a cartoon that aimed to mock Islam and one that didn't? Couldn't Muslims in Wales and beyond appreciate the difference? Couldn't Saleem Kidwai of the Muslim Council of Wales understand this too, and take a more intelligent view by accepting Meurig Llwyd's article for what it was?

The argument that Mohammed can't be depicted doesn't stand up to scrutiny either, as there is a long tradition of portraying him in Islamic culture – just as, incidentally, there is a tradition in Christianity that stands against idolatry and the worship of images of saints and biblical figures. It is called Puritanism. The offending Danish cartoons had even been published by the Egyptian newspaper, *al-Fagr*, in October, and by a Jordanian weekly – both Arabic newspapers in Islamic states – before *Y Llan* even went to press.

There are good moral and practical reasons to show sensitivity towards the Muslim community in Wales, as a minority can always be susceptible to scapegoatism. There is also a need to educate the public of the majority culture about the subtleties of the minority. But withdrawing every copy of *Y Llan* demonstrated the cringe factor at its worst.

Do we really think that some evil men are hunched in the slums of Baghdad or the coffee houses of Cairo or even the mosques of Cardiff cursing and plotting against the editor of *Y Llan* because of this offending cartoon, as they struggle to master the voiceless alveolar lateral fricative – 'll' – of its title? And if so, should not we, the media, the Church, the state and the police in a free democracy, be defending the editor of *Y Llan* for his right to free speech rather than slapping him down like an errant dog? Is Western liberal democracy so shallow that it cowers before bigots and murderers and those who threaten murder? Or are the majority of decent Muslims as represented by the Muslim Council of Wales too afraid or disrespectful of Western liberal democracy to accept its traditions too?

In a democracy one has the right both to be satirical and to be satirised. Our Muslim co-citizens have to accept that, as do their Christian and Jewish brothers and sisters. The image of Mohammed was published in a Christian magazine aimed at a mainly Christian readership. Does not the religious, theological press have the freedom to discuss issues on its own terms which may be outside the realm of the secular, or is Christianity more a secular life-style than a theological journey? Beyond the natural law of common decency and an avoidance of provoking violence, the publication surely had no reason to take into account a Muslim view any more than the secular, the Jewish or the Catholic one. The depiction of Mohammed isn't against Islamic law, nor even every Islamic practice or tradition, and there was certainly no malice in the piece (from what I've read or heard in interviews) nor was there any intention to offend. In fact it was the opposite. So, why was it that virtually the whole of Welsh civil society crossed to the other side?

The Welsh press was (once again) conspicuous in withholding its support for those who go against the political grain. The only publication to give any support to Meurig Llwyd Williams's position was the Welsh-language monthly *Barn*. *Bwrw Golwg*, BBC Radio Cymru's Sunday morning religious affairs programme – incidentally the station's most interesting current affairs programme – didn't do the affair proper justice: in the interests of not creating a fuss it was too deferential in its questioning of both the editor himself and the Church in Wales.

The issue became an embarrassment to the political establishment too. Between the Assembly, Westminster, and the European Parliament Wales has 104 elected, fully-paid representatives. Not a single one stood up for Meurig Llwyd Williams or made an effort to give some balance to the affair. It is inconceivable that not even 1 per cent of the Welsh population thought, 'Hey, come on boys, let's put this in perspective', and that not one elected representative was willing to give that constituency a voice. Shame on them!

Plaid Cymru, a party that confuses silence with statesmanship and statesmanship with cowardice, made no comment on the affair. A party jam-packed with preachers and lay-preachers and led at the time by not one, but two sons of preachers (Ieuan Wyn Jones and Dafydd Iwan), had absolutely nothing to say about the sacking of the editor of a religious magazine for preaching the plurality which is presumed in a secular state.

The Labour Welsh Assembly Equality Minister Jane Hutt said publishing the cartoons was 'extraordinarily inappropriate' adding, 'I'm glad to hear that the editor has resigned.'

Let's pause and rewind. That a government minister, in a democracy, states she's 'glad', that an editor has resigned over an editorial about plurality and the strength of the secular state is truly shocking. 'Glad'. Not even the treaclier, and more insincere 'unfortunate', but 'glad'. And nobody – not the Church in Wales, not the opposition parties, neither the press nor media, absolutely nobody bats an eyelid. That is scary.

How is it that publishing an image with no intention to slander is 'extraordinarily inappropriate', but the same politicians do not oppose the staging of *Jerry Springer the Opera*, which some Christians also see as 'extraordinarily inappropriate'? Does the Minister for Equality also call for the reintroduction of the Blasphemy Law too? So why is offending one sector of a religious community acceptable but offending another is not? Is the secular state above religious law, or are we drifting to the 'millet' system of the Ottoman Empire, where different religious communities were answerable to their own different religious laws?

Or is it that for those political parties whose intellectual traditions are rooted in the Enlightenment there is one thing that scares them more than moral abyss or racism? It's the same thing that strikes the fear into the hearts of the mainstream Secular Christians (if the 'non-evangelical' Christians in Wales can be so labelled). The fear in their all-too rational hearts is fear of the Irrational. Is it the fear of the Irrational Muslim, and a deep, deep echo of Saladin's sword on Christian necks – is that their deepest fear? Is that not a reverse racism – the racism of the coward as he imagines the Different and the Other to be uncontrollable and irrational? The Other which is beyond the constraints of the Enlightenment and Western 'morality' and so cannot be understood? Are they in awe of the Other, the Irrational's hard-rock certainty of its own faith and mission? Perhaps the Evangelical Christian's biggest mistake is not that they are not extreme, but that they are not extreme enough? Not extreme enough in the sense that the more extreme nationalists of the IRA and Sinn Féin enjoy cups of tea in Downing Street whilst pacifist Welsh nationalists are reported to the police for 'race hate' by the same political party that delighted in the banishment of Meurig Llwyd?

Had the Minister and the politicians actually read the article or seen the image? Is there not an underlying presumption by some that an article in Welsh, a covert and, by extension, suspect language, would be by definition 'anti-cosmopolitan' and 'reactionary' in nature? That kind of contempt for the 'non-cosmopolitan' languages is in the tradition of genocidal theories and policies from the French Revolution, to Communism and Stalin.

Meurig Llwyd's experience is part of a growing trend since devolution where the author of some mildly provocative but commonsense comments, insipid by standards of the London dailies, is humiliated by the Welsh political Establishment. The author then internalises the Establishment's prejudice and feels 'it's best for all concerned' if he says nothing and doesn't defend his position. So, in this creeping climate of self-censorship and in the name of 'equality', rather than fight for his good name, intellectual position and, yes, faith, Meurig Llwyd hid behind his sofa – much to his discredit. He did this, no doubt, with the wise, paternalistic and patronising hand of the Church in

Wales as they, erm, guided him through his humiliation and character assassination.

The whole *Llan* episode – the treatment of Meurig Llwyd, his unwillingness to fight his corner, the sneering of the political class and the cowardice of the Church in Wales – was depressing in its predictability. The Church in Wales, of course, is perfectly right to foster good relations with the country's Muslims, but in an effort not to offend the Islamic community and to appear decisive the Archbishop of Wales, Barry Morgan, managed the impossible. In my opinion he made his Church appear weak and servile, while demonstrating that he had neither a theological conviction nor a conviction in the founding tenets of the secular state.

The Archbishop recently announced his chairmanship of *Cymru Yfory* – Tomorrow's Wales, a cross-party, non-partisan campaign for the implementation of the Richard Report on further powers to the National Assembly. I wish him, and the campaign, well. But what use will more power and democracy be to the Assembly if our self-censorship means we won't use it and speak our minds? Why bother publishing a religious, theological publication like *Y Llan* if you have no theological critique? What use is the Church in Wales if it values being nice as being more important than belief?

After generations of 'inappropriate' debate, in 1922 the Anglican Church in Wales was disestablished from the state. It gave the Anglican Church in Wales the freedom to believe and act as it wished, beyond the control of the state, but not above it. In March 2006 another faith, Islam, gained the freedom to believe and act as it wished beyond the control of the state – and above it.

Cambria, vol. 8, no. 3, August-September 2006

White is Not the Only Colour:
Wales' Multi-ethnic Screen

The early years of the new millennium were a difficult and humiliating time for the Welsh language movement. Following the Conservative Party's New Welsh Language Act in 1993 the movement went, by and large, into hibernation. Added to this was the self-imposed decision not to make Welsh a political campaign in the lead-up to the Devolution referendum in 1997. Following that successful Yes vote a feeling of creating a 'new Wales' built on 'consensus' and 'equality' flowed across the political class like a sedative. There was an unwritten pact in the first election for the Assembly, too, not to make the Welsh language a political football.

And then came the Seimon Glyn Affair in February 2001. An Affair where a little-known Plaid Cymru councillor in Gwynedd called for monitoring of the number of English people moving into Pen Llŷn, and for efforts to linguistically integrate the new arrivals and give local people (in one of the UK's areas of lowest incomes) a chance to buy or rent housing. His comments – totally innocuous if put in an English context – were seized upon with gusto by the Labour party.

Taunts of racism were casually chucked about. People from the powerful, populous, rich state language were, by the British Left, placed into the same category as poor Pakistani immigrants. Welsh-language activists, almost to a person peaceful and law-abiding (unlike the former IRA members who were at the same time courted by the Labour government), were treated as if they were members of the Ku Klux Klan.

Labour's dank hypocricy was underlined over the coming years as Labour politician after Labour politician stepped up to defend the English language (but not Welsh). By May 2006 even Labour's Gordon Brown, later Prime Minister, said:

I think people who come into this country, who are part of our community, should play by the rules. I think learning English is part of that. I think that understanding British history is part of that. That's why I want to see changes in the curriculum. I think being more explicit as a country about what we value about being British is a very essential element of how we are part of the modern world. I would insist on large numbers of people who have refused to learn our language that they must do so.

For the Labour party, concern for English as a community language was policy; concern about Welsh as a community language was racist. Right concern; wrong language.

In this heated atmosphere, Plaid Cymru's leadership had a breakdown. The platitudes of 'consensus' and 'equality' were just those: platitudes. The curse of 'racism' – probably the worst insult imaginable in Tony Blair's Britain – was used to refer to almost any Welsh-language event. Even the National Eisteddfod was called a 'festival of hate' by the Labour-supporting agitprop daily newspaper, the Welsh Mirror.

After a decade lacking in meaningful honest and robust intellectual debate, the Welsh language movement, and more particularly the Plaid Cymru leadership, had not delivered the philosophy or even words to express their concern for Welsh as a community language. Plaid effectively accepted the British left-wing narrative. They lost the intellectual battle. It's a mistake the national and language movement must never make again. In a desperate effort to appear radical, a significant section of the Welsh nationalist movement spent their time and energy opposing the war in Iraq. All well and good – but it did make me think. What would Wales be like now if the brave people who pulled down English-only road signs, or opposed the Investiture of an English prince as 'Prince of Wales' in 1969, had decided to channel their time and radicalism to opposing the Vietnam War?

In this atmosphere I wanted to show what all nationalists knew was true; that Welsh could also be, and had been, a multinational language, and that Welsh was a language open to all. If Welsh was a 'white language' it was because the British state, and the supporters of that state (many of whom were in the Labour party now attacking Plaid), had, by and large, inhibited making Welsh a civic language with rights. These rights would have enforced Welsh and by doing so integrated people of different backgrounds into the language community. That is, the more 'extreme' the language laws are, the more status a language has and so the more multi-ethnic it is. Accusations that Welsh-language zealots wanted to create Welsh-speaking 'Gaeltacht' (Irish-speaking areas, the word used in this case disparagingly as 'language ghettos') where Welsh would be the prime language of administration, education and use, were used as an insult. But isn't the whole of the UK one big English-speaking Gaeltacht? It is only through a deliberate policy of 'forcing' everyone to speak English, controlling immigration and giving language rights to the indigenous English-speaking population that English has been able to retain her status and now integrate people from different backgrounds in England and Wales.

My message was simple, give us the tools, the status and we'll make Welsh, too, a multi-ethnic language; a multi-ethnicity which will enrich Welsh, and the Welsh-speaking community. We want to see non-white people speaking Welsh. But to do that we need geographic communities that can integrate people from non-Welsh-speaking backgrounds

Freddie Grant probably wins the prize. He could possibly go down in history as the first black person to appear in an indigenous Welsh film. I'm using these evasive words – probably, possibly – because frankly it's quite a difficult job, not so much to pin-point the person, but to decide on the criteria.

The black singer and human rights activist Paul Robeson appeared in 1940 in the emotionally Welsh film *Proud Valley*. It strikes a chord with many Welsh people. But then, the film was shot in Stoke and alas, despite the best intentions of many people, Robeson wasn't, erm, Welsh.

Speaking to the good people at the National Screen and Sound Archive in Aberystwyth I was told a black person appears in film footage of the Machynlleth National Eisteddfod of 1937, but was later diligently phoned up and told they'd been mistaken, although, an Indian woman does appear in a film from the 1952 National Eisteddfod at Aberystwyth. The person apparently was on a visit to Wales organised by the British and Foreign Bible Society to see the grave of Mary Jones, the woman who, as a young girl, walked barefoot the 24 miles across the mountains from Llanfihangel-y-Pennant to Bala to buy a Bible from Thomas Charles. The story, it seemed, was as well known to Sunday School children in India as it was in Wales.

So, we're back to Freddie Grant, who appears in a film called *Yr Etifeddiaeth* in Welsh and *The Heritage* in English. The film was made in 1949 by John Roberts Williams (the editor of the weekly newspaper *Y Cymro*) and the photographer Geoff Charles. As a fervent Welshman, Roberts Williams was frustrated that unlike other small European countries Wales lacked the national film institutions which would validate Welsh culture, language and community, and so decided to film *Yr Etifeddiaeth* off his own bat. Working tirelessly between 1947 and 1949, the two amateur film-makers pieced together a delightful portrait of the life of Pen Llŷn and Eifionydd, narrated by the Super-Gog voice of the Archdruid, Cynan. Amongst the scenes of white-foreheaded sheep-shearing farmers and happy young maidens running late to choir practice appears a rather shy-looking Freddie Grant.

Freddie Grant was a young black boy from Liverpool who was evacuated to Eifionydd (the commote between Porthmadog and Pwllheli in Gwynedd) during the Second World War. Within months the young Scouser had been immersed into the local community, speaking Welsh, no doubt with the clear muscular accent of Gwynedd. And it is for this reason that he is in *Yr Etifeddiaeth*. Freddie appears alongside images and commentary about the Irish and English workers who flocked to the quarries of Trefor and Llithfaen on the north Llŷn coast who were assimilated within a generation into the vast Welsh-speaking hinterland that was nineteenth- and early twentieth-century Caernarfonshire. We don't know precisely what became of Freddie Grant, although the staff in the Archive believed he eventually returned to Liverpool.

Between John Robert William's pioneering work and the late 1960s very little footage survives that shows any black or Asian ethnic minority communities in Wales. In truth, disappointingly little survives of any Welsh community at all up until that time – white or black.

Of course, *Tiger Bay* is undoubtedly the most well-known film located in Wales' famously ethnically mixed area. Although, unfortunately, all the main protagonists in this 1959 film by J. Lee Thompson are white. (By the way, the name Tiger Bay, according to some, comes from the description given by Portuguese sea-farers to the choppy waters leading into Bute Dock, '*a bahia de los tigres*'.)

The veil isn't therefore lifted on Wales' black community until 1968, with the film *After Many a Summer – the Changing Face of Tiger Bay*. This fifty-seven minute black-and-white film recalls the history of one of Wales' most interesting communities, the multi-ethnic, multi-lingual ghetto that was Tiger Bay and which is now the heartless Slough-by-sea called Cardiff Bay. Spurred on by the demolition of the old decrepit back-to-back streets of the area for the decrepit new flats of Wilsonian Britain, the directors, Harley Jones and Chris Bellinger, strove to catch a piece of history on film before it was consigned to the dustbin. Another 1976 Arts Council-financed film, *A Home from Home*, reflects upon Yousaf Ali, a Muslim immigrant from Pakistan, living in Newport. And that seems to be it – unless of course, readers know better ...

So what of now – how big is this very diverse community? According to the 2001 census the whole ethnic minority population of Wales stood at around 42,000 people, which was 1.5 per cent of the Welsh population, as opposed to 7.1 per cent of the whole UK population and almost 10 per cent of the English population. The percentage in the northern counties was even smaller – less than 1 per cent – mostly workers and families based around the main hospitals in Bangor, St Asaph and Wrexham. The difference in the size of the English and Welsh ethnic communities will raise interesting questions if quotas are used to promote the profile of the ethnic minority communities – will the context be the Welsh one or British?

On television, once one subtracts sports or news coverage that includes black or Asian people, then there really isn't much left, especially, and ironically, in English. That's a mirror of the reality of Welsh demography and the dearth of hours produced in English from Wales. BBC Wales's Tiger Bay was a brave attempt at creating a soap opera, but for numerous reasons it flopped. Putting the charming Nigel Walker, simultaneously Wales's fastest and clumsiest rugby player, to front rugby coverage was still a somewhat ground-breaking decision by the BBC in the mid 1990s. As one English columnist noted, whilst the Welsh viewers were somewhat intrigued by having a black face present a rugby programme, English viewers were intrigued by seeing a black person speak with a Welsh accent. Nigel Walker is now the Head of Sports at BBC Wales and we do now have a black newscaster, the ever-dapper Jason Mohammad. There hasn't been a black newscaster in Welsh yet ... although Jason, I understand, does speak Welsh ...

The relationship between the ethnic minority communities and Wales should be an interesting one – a fusion of cultures, languages and *Weltanschauung* which has yet to blossom fully. After all, wasn't the campaign to ensure that place names were spelt 'Caernarfon' (not 'Carnarvon') and 'Ceredigion' (not 'Cardiganshire') the same as the one to call the Indian city 'Mumbai' and not 'Bombay', and the African country 'Zambia' rather than 'Northern Rhodesia'?

Both the Welsh-speaking and Asian communities in particular have much in common – a concern that one's language is not being passed on to the next generation, and the importance of religion to the community's identity. Linguistic politics isn't alien to the Asian communities – the fifth track on my Bhangra Beatz CD is '*Meri Maa Boli Punjabi*' ('My mother-tongue language of Punjabi') by Balbir Bittu, which extols the young listener to speak Punjabi – a sort of Dafydd Iwan sings *bhangra*, if you like. And isn't the mosque and temple central to Muslim and Sikh identity, as was the chapel to Welsh identity – obviously for religious reasons, but also because it's the one place within a larger dominant culture that their language and culture is given a status and normality which it doesn't have outside? Between our macaronic meals in Cardiff's Queen Street's McDonald's and the diglossic dialogues of our sit-coms we speak the same language.

And yet in Wales some personalities have used the cover of promoting multi-culturalism as a stick to beat the Welsh language and Welsh constitutional aspirations and to promote instead a new British nationalism. Is there anything more ironic or nauseating than being preached to about the importance of multi-ethnicity by a white monoglot English-speaker? A member of the one ethnic community which, by virtue of its skin colour and the commercial and political power of its language, has resolutely refused to integrate into any indigenous community in the world – from North America to Australia, via Africa and South Asia; the one ethnic community that has made the minimal cultural, political or linguistic concession and whose biggest sacrifice is savouring spicy dishes, listening to exciting new music and tolerating somebody else (but not themselves) speaking another language.

We in Wales are gradually creating through our media a Welsh civic nationality which also takes into account our historical legacy and the amazing complexes of this big little country. Radio Cymru has had two black presenters – the effervescent Ali Yassine, the Cardiffian who speaks Welsh like a Cofi, who presented a motor-mouthed world music programme some years ago (which should get another go), and the London-raised Bev Lennon. For over a decade Radio Wales has broadcast the soft voice of Annand Jasani on *A Voice for All*. Sharif Shahwan, who started on Radio Ceredigion, now co-presents the world music slot with Rez Jamal, and Nadira Tudor does telly and radio. Of course, whilst having black people present radio programmes is good there is something ticklish about making a virtue of the colour of your presenter's skin on a medium no one can view. Had it not been for the big PR I'd have been none the wiser that Bev was black.

At times it seems S4C takes Andy Warhol's dictum a little too literally as there isn't a single Welsh-speaking member of the ethnic minority community who hasn't been on the channel. From Catryn Ramasut (whose father runs the Thai House restaurant in Cardiff) on the young people's soap,

Xtra, to Jeff Diamond, the black actor with the soft Carmarthenshire accent in the Cardiff-based big-shouldered, deep-sighing 1980s soap opera, *Dinas*. The daily soap, *Pobol y Cwm*, recently had two Welsh-speaking black brothers in the series – two characters which would have seemed totally incredible ten years ago now seem no more unlikely than the eye-brow raising number of Gogs in this quintessential 'Sioni South' village. But, for me, possibly the two most moving and thought-provoking programmes on S4C were two programmes dealing with Islam.

One was on *Taro 9*, BBC 's documentary series for S4C. In the wake of the September 11th attack the presenter interviewed two young Pakistani women from Caernarfon about their experiences. Speaking as a Welsh-speaker, a language which has for too long been an ethnic language, for me seeing and hearing two normal girls in their saris speak like two *Cofis Dre* (Caernarfon townies) was still a moving experience and must resemble a Sindhi speaker hear a white Welsh person speak their language with a strong Karachi accent.

The other great little series was *Dyddiadur Ramadan*, presented by Ali Yassine. These short ten-minute diaries on S4C documented the religious fasting month of some of Wales's admittedly small Welsh-speaking Muslim population. We need more stuff like this on S4C and BBC Wales.

There is no future in the twenty-first century for a white-only Welsh culture – be it in Welsh or English. It would just die of boredom. The ethnic minorities are an integral part of creating an exciting new Wales; white media producers need to embrace that. Some members of the ethnic minorities are embracing Welsh culture and language as well and others need not be afraid of it. But we can take it further – *bhangra* songs in Punjabi about nights out in Newport or Bangor;

film scripts in Welsh and English by black writers; a black Chief Executive of S4C – why not? Contrary to the accepted wisdom, the creation of independent Welsh institutions doesn't militate against the ethnic minorities in Wales, but actually promotes and validates their identity – *Yr Etifeddiaeth*, S4C, Radio Cymru, BBC Wales confirm that.

Seeing Welsh black and Asian faces on the Welsh media is as important to white Welsh people (and especially to the Welsh language) as it is to the ethnic minority population. Not to see those faces is to stigmatize Welsh identity as a purely ethnic one – and that's a cultural and linguistic cul-de-sac.

Keep smiling, Freddie Grant.

Cambria, vol. 5, no. 3, Winter 2002/03

*For more on the Simon Glyn Affair' please read the chapter 'Beyond the Pale' (p. 158) in *The Phenomenon of Welshness, or 'How many aircraft carriers would an independent Wales have?'* (published 2011).

Celtic Film Festival I:
Aberystwyth 2000

These are two articles from two different years of the same event, the Celtic Film and TV Festival, when they were held in Wales.

I've included them because they give some sense of place and time. The 2000 article reflects the happiness and optimism of the post 1997 Referendum and the first Assembly elections in 1999, and in general the Blair/Brown economic boom. In hindsight the reference to the Irish discussing property prices is particularly prescient. Though I can't claim any credit for foreseeing the crash which would afflict Ireland I remember an Irish delegate discussing property prices with me at the bar of the Marine Hotel on Aberystwyth's promenade. That has probably stuck with me because he seemed such a wide-boy, and it still seems a rather peculiar thing to have been discussing at what I believed to be a mainly cultural event.

Likewise the 2005 article and my conversation with another very different Irish delegate now seems prescient as he questioned the sales of the Irish language daily, Lá. His cynicism was shared by the Assembly as they declined to support the venture to launch the Welsh-language daily, Y Byd (see the article 'What's the point of Wales?' in The Phenomenon of Welshness *(2011)).*

Sometimes we need to listen to the little conversations, not the grand speeches, to understand what's really happening.

I've always nurtured imperialist aspirations for Wales. You've heard of Pax Romana: well, here's Pax Cambria. For a short week in April the vision came true as Aberystwyth welcomed delegates to a sun-kissed imperial city from the furthest parts of the Celtic countries.

Broad-vowelled Scots, confident Irish men talking of the

sky-high price of property in the booming cities of Dublin and Galway, Bretons discussing and dancing, the hardy Cornish fighting their corner and the Welsh from the cities of Caernarfon and Cardiff carrying the accents of our land and talk of digital television and the new Assembly. They were all convened for the twenty first Celtic Film and Television Festival, which was held at the newly painted and hoovered Arts Centre on Penglais Hill, with its beautiful, breath-taking vista of the city of Aberystwyth and the sparkling Celtic Sea, *Mare Nostrum*.

Like a wandering Gogynfeirdd poet, the Celtic Film and Television Festival is an event without a permanent house but with many homes. Last year it was in the northern lands at Stornoway on the Isle of Lewis, before then in Tra Lí on the west coast of Erin. In 2001 it will be at Falmouth in Cornwall. In 2000, in the 600th anniversary of Owain Glyn Dwˆr's proclamation as Prince of Wales, Aberystwyth hung out its brightest colours and welcomed 400 delegates to show their wares, trade, form alliances and be merry. The assembly was a resounding success.

For those of dubious mathematical skills, the first Festival was held on the 700th anniversary of Llywelyn the Last in 1982 in the grim, soul-destroying 80s. A time of low hearts, dodgy back-permed hairstyles and naff thin ties. A time when defeat was snatched from the jaws of success. The grey post-79 eighties, when the establishment of S4C was the only ray of warm light and hope to creep under the damp, dark, heavy clouds. A time when politics had failed and the Celts fled to the hills to reassemble and reassess and fight a guerrilla campaign through culture and the medium of television.

Their court was not an auspicious one. The draughty, shaky halls of the various Mountain Peoples could not compete with the gold-gilded charms of London or Cannes. Their emissaries were rich by comparison to their folk back home, but their trousers were worn and their gifts humble in comparison to the silk-stockinged celluloid-rich company ambassadors who descended annually on the golden shores of southern France from the spacious offices of NY, LA or W12.

Back in 82 establishing the Celtic Festival was a testament to political will. But was it an economic and media reality? Was the Celtic Festival just the latest, most elaborate mirage in an industry of make-believe and story telling? Was the Celtic Festival the Tir Na nOg of film festivals, where the Celtic nations had not grown up to the reality that there was no longer a Welsh nation, that there was no such thing as a modern Irish-speaking community, that Scots Gaelic was a perverse infliction on innocent children and Breton a language, like Kurdish, which did not officially exist? Was winning at the Celtic Festival the same as winning the beauty contest in the hills of the Appalachians?

The doubts stuck there like an irritating pebble in their shiny new shoes and made them walk in an awkward limp just as they'd decided to chat up the beautiful dark-haired foreign maidens. Always there, always nagging and irritating.

The Welsh were way ahead in Celtic-language broadcasting - a pigmy in platform shoes. Questions were raised behind froths of creamy Guinness and in editing suites. What was the Celtic Festival for? Why go to such a small and poor court? When the non-historic peoples of the East, their languages sounding deep and mysterious and like records played backwards, raised their voice against the Soviet Empire, some Celts sought their alliance, or why not the honourary Celts of Galicia or the orphaned Basques? Would it not be better to have strength in numbers?

But then after a decade of miserable rain, slowly the sun came from behind the clouds. Its warm rays were felt on the backs of Scotland's Gaels, who would be given a body to oversee and co-ordinate broadcasting in their language.

After years of campaigning, broken promises, insult and disappointments, the Irish-speakers were given their voice and Teilifis na Gaelige was formed. And most miraculously of all Breton, Europe's most insulted and neglected language, was heard and seen on TV Breizh with other development in the pipeline. Suddenly, it wasn't such a joke.

At Aberystwyth, in the land of Ceredig, son of Cunedda, who, with the fall of Pax Romana, came from Edinburgh in the Old North to fight the invading Irish, the festival celebrated her twenty-first birthday. With a budget of almost a quarter of a million pounds, holding sixty events ranging from short films in Breton and Irish to words of wisdom by eminent guest speakers such as the linguist Professor David Crystal and the historian Norman Davies, the Celtic Film and Television Festival came of age.

But not quite.

John Cale, the Garnant boy who fled the narrow Amman valley for New York and formed the psychedelic 1960s group Velvet Underground, returned to perform. The man who fled Wales was hailed a hero, whilst the awkward squad who stood and fought applauded him. I don't remember John Cale marching through a rainy Port Talbot in support of S4C in 1981 though; funny that. The real heroes for me are the cagoule wearers in horrible C&A slacks, not the mid-Atlantic druggies.

Solomon a Gaenor, the cynical Jewish vote-grabbing film for the Academy Awards, was screened to a full house. I'm glad it got to the finals of the Oscars, but thank God it didn't win. The film that says you should turn your back on your own traditions is best described by that excellent Yiddish word, *schmaltz*. Can we stop making these passionate, irony-free films?

Yes, and the nervous new chairman of the Wales Tourist Board spoke of 'passion'. Bugger passion. Passion is for people without political clout. Passion is for losers and people who sing for tourists but don't sign treaties. The Celts need 'passion' like a soldier needs a handbag.

No, the resounding success of the Celtic Festival wasn't the programmes or the speeches or the awards – though they were good. The resounding successes were the delegate bags that were well packed and trendy. It was the Festival brochure that was well-designed and easy to read in Welsh, English and French. It was the excellent catering by *Blas ar Gymru*/A Taste of Wales. It was the stickers in pubs and restaurants of Aberystwyth that welcomed the delegates in seven languages. It was the crisp, informative website. It was the way the University and the people and institutions of the Welsh state cooperated like a team to put on a great show. The resounding strength of the twenty-first Celtic Film and Television Festival was its organisation. Say that word again, let it roll off your tongue like Irish dew in a naff whiskey advert. Organisation. 'Celtic' and 'Organisation'. Two familiar words unfamiliar in the same sentence – an oxymoron, some would say. Passionate peoples win awards, organised people sponsor them. Let the English and Germans be 'passionate' if they like; the Celts should gladly stick to 'organised'.

Over macaronic Celtic meals, then, let's toast '*iechyd da*' and '*sláinte*' to the warriors of the past in their cagoules and to the organisers of the Festival of today. Without the Celtic Festival there would be no Gaelic service in Scotland, no TnaG (or, as it has now been shrewdly rebranded, TG4) and no service in Breton. Yes, the programmes and films are the raw ingredients for the meals, but without the organisation and presentation you may as well eat them from a trough. So, *iechyd da* to the Celtic Festival and to Pax Cambria and long may it continue.

Cambria, vol. 3, no. 4, Summer 2000

Celtic Film Festival II:
Cardiff 2005

Well, I haven't felt so optimistic in a long time. The beginning was pretty unpromising, though. This year's annual Celtic Film and Television Festival was held in Cardiff, or rather, at the Holland House hotel on Newport Road, one of sixty-five MacDonald hotels in the UK, on one of the most unedifying roads in Cardiff. Hence the 'is-this-it?' feeling one had when crossing the threshold to one of the premiere events of the Celtic calendar. It's not that I expected (nor wanted) bearded blokes in saggy Arran sweaters fiddling 'Celtic' tunes as well as expenses. But stepping into the crashing uniformity of Corporate City gave a sense of anti-climax which only hotel lifts can achieve. And that, on a drizzly April morning, was my first impression of the Festival at this Biedermeier city still celebrating a Grand Slam victory which will patronise us for the next twenty-eight years.

However, following signing in and picking up the angina-inducing rucksack stuffed full with festival freebies (the best was the S4C overnight kit), I began to enjoy myself. One of the joys of living in Aberystwyth is that going to Cardiff brings on a childish anticipation of visiting the big city. And whilst a former colleague complained about seeing the same old faces on the Welsh media circuit, I was genuinely excited and impressed by the level of debate and conversation. Which, I suppose, only goes to confirm that I'm now a fully paid-up yokel, only one step up from gaping with an idiot's dropped jaw at the wonders of automatic doors.

For those not in the know, the Celtic Film and Television Festival is something of a misnomer. It doesn't show much film, because none of the Celtic countries are either big enough – or rich enough – to have a film industry (though all

TV people have an Oedipus complex towards film-making); neither is it much of a festival. Punters can't just walk in off the street and see the latest Celtic film (although some old Welsh films were shown at the Chapter Arts Centre during the festival). It's a back-slapping occasion for Celtic film- ... erm ... television producers. It also has a section for radio programmes that isn't included in the title. 'Celtic Media Festival' would be a more honest description.

You may well have read about the winners of the various categories, but one of the films which most impressed me was the Cornish *Myghternestow Kung Fu Pot-Tin Kernow O-Region*. Made on a budget of about £1.20, it cleverly got round the problem of casting actors who could speak Cornish. The tongue-in-cheek story of the three sisters saving Cornwall gets ten out of ten for ingenuity and graft from me. However, the definition of Celtic material at the Festival could be, shall we say, broadly 'inclusive'. I particularly enjoyed the Estonian-language documentary *Brothers of the Forest*, about the brothers Ulo and Aivar Voitka, who hid in the woods from the Soviet forces to avoid conscription in 1987, and were still in hiding from the police of the free Estonia until 2000 when they gave themselves up. But, mindful of being accused of Baltophobia, shouldn't the film have been shown at the Finno-Uguric Film Festival?

An unkind description of the Festival might possibly be 'pygmies in stilettos', or, a festival of whingeing (or even sadder, wanna-be) Celts. But that would be unfair. The importance of the 'Celtic' is that it normalises Celtic cultures in an Anglo-centric world. It's difficult to imagine that the seven-year old TG4 Irish-language television station, or the Scots Gaelic service, would have seen the light of day without such a festival bringing people together and creating a Celtic sensibility. The Festival offers a rare opportunity for hearing voices rarely heard: how the political impasse of the

Northern Irish Peace Process is hampering Irish language broadcasting; how the Scottish Parliament is letting a crucial report collect dust whilst the Gaelic language television service is frozen at £9 million and not linked to inflation.

You meet different people as well – people like Aodan from Belfast who described himself, without a trace of irony, as an 'Irish-language activist' (a breath of fresh air in such a self-conscious industry). There was something quite bizarre about knowing you're the only two people in the whole of Cardiff ever to have discussed the finer points of Irish-language newspaper subscription. His doubting-Thomas questioning of the the actual number of copies sold by the new daily Irish newspaper, *Lá*, should also give the campaign for a Welsh-language daily, *Y Byd*, food for thought.

However, I'm most grateful to the organisers for setting up the discussion on Thursday morning on the future of broadcasting in the Celtic languages. I was most impressed by the balanced but firm eloquence of Bob Collins, former Director-General of the Irish State broadcaster, RTE. Unfortunately, Bob's eloquence meant there was less time for the other two speakers, who included Dafydd Elis Thomas. Dafydd El's contribution (it wasn't a speech) was the shortest and most provocative. He argued that the forthcoming new licence given to the BBC would be the last time the Corporation would have a monopoly to bid for such a licence and that S4C's budget should be moved from London to the Assembly. He posed a number of questions but gave very few answers.

Dafydd Elis Thomas's contribution got me thinking about the future of broadcasting in Wales. Despite the 2005 General Election looming on the horizon, however, broadcasting wasn't on the political agenda at all. Not surprising perhaps, but then again maybe it is. Considering that the average Welsh voter is more likely to watch television than catch MRSI in a dodgy hospital ward or meet an illegal Iraqi immigrant, then why is this so? Don't people have an interest in the future of Derek the Weatherman, *Pobol y Cwm*, or Iolo Williams's legs? All four main political parties gave the media only a fleeting mention. This, despite the fact that political decisions over the next year could affect both our viewing habits and our wallets.

So, in the spirit of Dafydd El's contribution, I've drawn-up my own media manifesto for Wales (yes, in good time for the next Assembly election).

The first point to make is that Welsh broadcasting currently comes under the Westminster remit. So, should it move to the Assembly? Do I trust anti-Welsh redneck AMs to be responsible for S4C? No. Do I trust politicians not to start influencing the content of S4C? Following the free karaoke session given to the party-in-government during the recent Grand Slam celebrations – no. So, keep S4C under London rule, until the whole of broadcasting comes over to Wales with all the other powers recommended by the Richard Report. The baby comes with the hostage.

For media jobs in Wales, advertisements should appear only in the Welsh press. This would be done, not to keep non-Welsh persons from applying, but to strengthen the revenue of existing – or hopefully, new – Welsh-language publications. And, after all, if you're interested in working in Wales shouldn't you be reading the Welsh press in any case? Such revenue could also lead to the creation of a media magazine which would be an important contribution to civic society here in Wales.

A second Welsh-language radio station to be created. Having just one state-run broadcaster in their language is something most nations left behind in the 1960s. Are we actually saying that in a digital age, with literally hundreds of radio stations across the UK, that in five years time we'll still have only one full-time national Welsh-language station? In broadcasting terms, radio is as cheap as chips, so let's sort it out. Radio Cymru II (let's call it Hwyl FM for fun) would be more pop-orientated, leaving Radio Cymru I to broadcast programming similar to some of the excellent grey-matter stuff on Radio Wales. It would have DJs rather than presenters and needn't be expensive – in fact, the raw energy of new DJs could actually be its saving grace. If BBC won't do it, then what about freeing some of the digital space on S4C to do the job?

We need a Welsh-language local radio station for the south-east. No, not a Radio 4 in Welsh, but a regular local radio station. A music-led station for fifteen to 35-year-olds with the usual local and traffic news, competitions and chat – i.e. the kind of programme people want to, rather than 'should', listen to. If Radio Ceredigion can run on an annual budget of £150k then this is a serious option. This doesn't need the support of any political party, only the vision and dedication of the type of Cardiff people who set-up Clwb Ifor Bach in the 1980s. I don't hold much hope – young professional Welsh-speakers in the city are too post-nationalist to be this creative and get their hands dirty. Let's just hope there are enough people who've learnt Welsh as adults to do the job! S4C, of course, could invest in a network of local radio stations to boost their brand and cross-advertise their programmes. The annual cost of running a local music-orientated radio station would be as little as an average six-part series on television.

I'd like to see a set-up grant for a Welsh Independent Radio Network news bulletin service, either to complement or dislodge the current UK-wide service that is broadcast on our local and community radio stations. The service would include Welsh and sports news, in addition to UK and world. The time spent on raising awareness of the Assembly government's work would be better served this way, and go a long way towards informing Welsh tax-payers of how their money is spent in addition to raising the level of debate and voter participation.

Publishers, be they print-, television-, radio- or web-based in Wales, with their headquarters here and a remit primarily to service the Welsh public, should pay no corporation tax. Our culture and one of our languages are already under pressure. Our government shouldn't tax and punish those entrepreneurs who are fighting for that culture. Doesn't our culture, in either Welsh or English, have enough competition from Anglo-America already? This is another strong argument for the National Assembly to be given powers over taxation.

Wales needs to adopt the .cymru cultural URL to promote awareness of Wales as a tourism, business and cultural entity.

These are my suggestions. Hopefully, by the next election the parties will have given a bit more consideration to the media and less to frightening people with wars on terror or unshaven asylum seekers. Possibly, by the next time the Celtic Film and Television Festival visits Wales, many of these ideas will have been implemented ... well, a man can dream. But, despite the smart but bland surroundings of Holland House hotel, the coming of the Celts to Cardiff during a period of phoney-war on Welsh identity and culture, made one Welshman dream and feel a little more positive for the future.

Cambria, vol. 7, no. 3, May-June 2005

Post-script – since publishing this article, S4C became a 'vassal state' to the BBC. If the BBC Wales's second-class service to Welsh on their online service is anything to go by, this will be bad news.

S4C:
Hands Across the Channel

This article was written in 2005 when there was some debate about the future of S4C, the Welsh- language television channel. Nothing came of it, and I and everyone else forgot about it until 2010 and 2011, when part of a spat between the channel and the new Conservative-LibDem Westminster government saw S4C's budget slashed by up to 40 per cent – several times higher than any other sector – and the channel was to be swallowed by the BBC.

The mishandling of the process by S4C (in particular the then Chief Executive, Iona Jones, who had haughtily neglected to court politicians or Welsh society) will have deep consequences on Welsh society. S4C became, in the word of one BBC journalist, a 'vassal state' to the BBC.

This is bad news for Welsh broadcasting – the BBC have never been as pro-Welsh as they like to tell us they are. The BBC Wales news policy has consistently failed to develop a Welsh narrative to world news, giving us a re-heated translation of whatever comes out of London.

For S4C and the wider Welsh-language civic society the debacle proved one thing. There is a need for our institutions, like S4C, Radio Cymru, the Welsh Language Commissioner and others, to lead and participate in the creation of a broad and deep Welsh-language society, the society which will nurture and develop Welsh culture. S4C's mistake, and Iona Jones's mistake in particular, was to think itself above the little people, the unfashionable language activists, the ones stuck in their boring little villages and market towns. And so, when the attack on S4C came, there were precious few people to support the channel – except the usual duffle-coat-wearers from Cymdeithas yr Iaith Gymraeg – the very people the well-paid executives at S4C or in the language industry had belittled or ignored for the previous decade.

We're in this together. The leaders of Welsh-language society have to realise that the continuation of Welshness and the Welsh language means a life-time of activism for the language. That does not mean protesting against or agreeing to every demand, but it does ask for recognition that the state has to engage meaningfully with grass-roots society in Wales and activists and voice their concerns. Together we can create a vibrant, interesting, diverse culture (or, rather, cultures), which will strengthen Welsh institutions like S4C.

Funny how careless one can become. One minute you've forgotten the nephew's birthday and the next you've lost a television channel. Odd, isn't it, that Wales is in the process of witnessing the incredible disappearing act which is (or was) HTV Wales, and it could now see the end of S4C as well. What did Marx say: losing one television channel is a tragedy, but losing two is a farce?

Not a lot of people seem to have realised that HTV/ITV 1 Wales is, in essence, being air-brushed from the screen in a new shake-up which will see fewer but larger independent TV channels. In fairness, the Labour AM Leighton Andrews is flagging up the threat to ITV1 Wales. The difficulty is that following years of producing programmes starved of a decent budget, which seem deliberately to be created with the cheapest-looking graphics and tinniest theme-tunes available, ITV Wales appears to have lost the will to live years ago. Nobody seems to have noticed, or for that matter, cared. That's an unfortunate situation in a country like Wales, where lack of access to news and programmes from Wales by Welsh media (of any sort) is a serious hindrance to the development of robust, mature and informed political debate.

The other channel which could join the other dead channels in the sky is S4C. In the recently published Ofcom report into the future of the media, three options were outlined, which included closing down S4C as an independent authority and its being taken over by the BBC. Surprisingly, this threat to the future independence of S4C has largely gone unnoticed by the press or the public in Wales, and BBC Wales news (which also supplies the news to S4C) seems in no mood to run a decent item about what must be, after all, one of the biggest media stories of the year.

The BBC's take-over of S4C seems to be a popular course for many politicians in government, though no final decision has been taken yet. Leighton Andrews is also a former Head of Public Affairs at the BBC and has come out in favour of the BBC take-over of S4C. The BBC take-over view is also shared by Labour's Rhondda MP, Chris Bryant (former Head of European Affairs at the BBC). Bryant also happens to be Wales's sole representative on the all-important Westminster media committee. In a debate in the House of Commons on 27 May 2004, he said, 'S4C in its digital future will have to discover a new identity. It will no longer be good enough simply to be a channel for Welsh-speaking Wales ... Wales's growing bilingualism is an important contribution to a stronger society. I want S4C to play a role in encouraging that bilingualism, and not just encouraging Welsh'. This is a bizarre statement which defies all logic. So, let's see. You run-down a Welsh-medium channel (which already has English subtitles for the vast majority of its programmes) in order to create a more bilingual Wales? Is this the same bilingual strategy which sees the compliant destruction of Welsh-speaking communities (the only communities in Wales which actually do speak two languages) so as to create a bilingual Wales? Nobody speaks 'bilingualish'. To promote Welsh is to promote bilingualism.

Of course, here in 2005, television is no more in black and white than are the arguments surrounding it. S4C is in a hole. Like all television channels, its viewing figures have fallen, competition (due to the explosion in digital channels and the competition from the web and the playsation) has increased. Its revenue for spending on digital programmes has not increased in three years (at a time when it was expected to produce an extra 12 hours of digital television a day). It shows both how poor the economy is – and aspirations are – in Wales, that S4C is seen as a milch-cow when Welsh-language programmes cost on average a fifth of those for UK network programmes.

There is also the case of English-language broadcasting from Wales. Non-Welsh-speakers (and of course the Welsh-speakers who also want to watch English-language programmes from Wales) have been hard-done-by.

One can understand the argument of those who believe that, in an increasingly piranha-infested digital world, S4C is simply too small to be able to stand alone. The argument goes that an S4C under the wing of BBC Wales could strengthen its programming through economies of scale, and that the savings could be invested in English-language output.

It is highly unfortunate that debates in Wales about increasing TV output in English are all too often brought down to a level of 'them' (Welsh-speakers) and 'us' (non-Welsh-speakers). After all, as I've pointed out before, Saunders Lewis, the devil-incarnate for so many, called for a bilingual national service in Wales way back in 1935. At the height of the campaign for S4C, the Welsh Language Society was also calling for an English-language channel for Wales. Let's hope the politicians of today won't revert to crass jingoism and words (open to multifarious definition) like 'bilingualism' to promote English-language services to the detriment of S4C, as they make up for the failings of successive governments to develop broadcasting from Wales. One thing is quite clear. If there wasn't an S4C there wouldn't be a single extra hour of broadcasting in English from Wales; indeed there could possibly be even less.

But, like our emotional attachment to old chapel buildings in which nobody worships but everyone wants to save, we should, maybe, take a more pragmatic and less-emotional view of the service. It isn't the name 'S4C' that's important but the very concept of broadcasting through the medium of Welsh. If that service can be achieved by another channel or set-up, why get worked up about a name? Ofcom offers another option whereby S4C, or, rather, a Welsh service, could be run as a franchise with companies bidding to run the whole show in much the same way as ITV Wales is presently handled. This would be a high-risk option, but it could equally be the most exciting one, giving the chance of a new start with a new agenda and new ideas. But then it could also lead to Rupert Murdoch running Welsh television. The third option is maintenance of the status quo, which, one presumes, S4C would want to keep and, when one considers the irrelevance of Wales to the London agenda, could be the default approach if nothing else. After all, the whole tenor of the report has been so Anglocentric as to test the patience of some of the most British establishment figures in Welsh political life.

Whatever the outcome, S4C has to change. The channel is in an unenviable plight, being stuck in the 1950s concept of a 'single national channel'. S4C needs only to screen a single programme of hymn-singing and the surfing viewer is sure to label the station a comfort zone for coffin-dodgers. The demography of Welsh-speakers is both a marketing nightmare and an absolute logistical maze: there are so many contradictions, of age, class, interest, local prejudice and (what so many don't appreciate) varying capabilities of actually speaking Welsh. In many respects it would be easier marketing a channel to the diverse and dispassionate multi-ethnic melting-pot which is metropolitan London than to the broad Welsh-speaking audience. Yet S4C has to do it all.

Let the poets sing about inspiration – S4C needs to be aspirational for the language. In an age where rural communities are transient whilst urban ones are sustainable as well as dynamic, S4C needs to be brave. It's not easy. In fact, it's bloody hard. Sure, mistakes have been made – the channel may have invested too heavily in new digital programmes to the detriment of its overall output. With S4C's Chief Executive Huw Jones retiring later this year, and the post of Chair of the Authority also up for grabs in 2006, now is the time for S4C to take the plunge. To steal a cliché, it needs to become 'New S4C'.

There is much S4C can do in this pivotal year, but allowing the channel to be gobbled up by the BBC shouldn't be one of the choices made on its behalf by the politicians. It is ironic that broadcasting, which has played such a pivotal and controversial part in Welsh political and cultural life, now has such a low priority for the politically active. But it's what happens when a National Movement becomes just a left-wing pressure group. All those irrelevant and inconsequential marches against the war in Iraq have, as usual, taken the minds – and the energy – of many active Welsh people away from the future of the Welsh language and Welsh-language broadcasting. Yet this is a subject which is far more important to Wales, and over which we actually have more control than foreign adventurist wars. In an age of media proliferation, with technology becoming cheaper and more user-friendly, it is, I believe, a sorry sign of the complacent nature of Welsh society that there hasn't been a campaign for a second Welsh-language channel, or a second, youth-orientated Radio Cymru. Nor has there been a campaign to save ITV Wales.

A Welsh-lite S4C as 'part' of the BBC is not an option. The Beeb is an important part of Welsh life with many excellent, dedicated members of staff. But there's no need to get carried away by its propaganda either. When push comes to shove the Welsh language will always lose out to Auntie: you need only compare BBC Wales's online services in Welsh with the far better resourced English one to see that.

As many – right across the political spectrum – have pointed out, the BBC needs to devolve, and S4C needs to remain an independent broadcaster. The next twelve months will see a legislative window at Westminster which can be used to review not only the BBC's Charter but also the structure of broadcasting in the UK. The BBC is already under pressure from many Labour backbenchers to devolve production from London. Rather than eyeing up S4C, campaigners and politicians for increased English-language production from Wales should channel their energy to transferring scheduling power from London to Cardiff – and that 5 per cent (that's Wales' percentage of the UK population) should be commissioned from Wales. Basically we're talking about a federal BBC. There have been momentous changes within the BBC over the last two years and more is to come. Centrally, the BBC is open to change. In fact it has very little choice. As one insider told me, 'They're not moving up to Manchester to line the pockets of the best restaurants in Cheshire – they're moving up there because they have to'.

Ofcom was founded under the Government's 2003 Communications Act. Its remit is to promote an agenda of 'plurality' and 'cultural diversity' in the media and communications. Forgive my cynicism when I see those words, but these are the very words that have been used actually to undermine Welsh-language culture over the last few years. Even in the cynical political world of Westminster and Cardiff Bay, there is a lot to play for. For those interested in the media, in culture in its wider sense, and in a truly bilingual Wales, 2005 should be about Trimsaran, not Tikrit. In 2005 the revolution should be about television.

Cambria, vol. 7, no. 1, January-February 2005

dotCYMRU:
World Wide Wales

I'm a member of an extensive group of people – the failed politicians. Those who thought for a fleeting moment in their youth that they'd like to be an AM or MP. During quiet moments I'm sure some feel bitter that they had no opportunity to 'serve our country'.

For me, however, my failure became a liberation. From feeling a failure I now felt relief: I could be myself, my true self. I didn't have to attend monotonous committees in which you'd lose the will to live; to be ridiculed by some know-all in the pub for not knowing an obscure piece of legislation; to be harangued in the supermarket for not being able to 'do something' about an issue you know full well you can't 'do' anything about. No, thanks. I walked away.

I'd always admired and felt jealous of brickies. They build walls. They can drive around the locality and point to walls and houses they've built with their own hands. Proper jobs, things you can point at. I decided to be a brickie of ideas. I calculated that as a member of Aberystwyth Town Council I had probably spent some 100 hours in the year in meetings and council-related events – the vast majority of them with no concrete outcome. Why not bank those 100 hours to an activity which had something concrete, a 'wall', at the end? That, and the birth of my three wonderful children, meant that it became very difficult for me to attend regular meetings. I would not join any choir or society which could take away my spare time. The dotCYM bid (which we later had to change to dotCYMRU because of a change in ICANN's rules) was to be my 'free time'.

In late 2005 I read that the Catalans had managed to win the .cat domain for themselves. I was involved with the internet in the Welsh language; in fact in 2002 my then wife Siwan

Gwyndaf and I had set up a Welsh-language discussion forum for parents, dimcwsg.com (nosleep.com!). Through my work at the National Library I was also aware of the difficulty of cataloguing websites from Wales because there wasn't a Welsh top level domain.

I began the campaign, drawing in my brother-in-law Maredudd ap Gwyndaf, without whose support, expertise and business experience the campaign couldn't have happened. Our expectation was that the Welsh government would adopt the idea and set up their own board and professional bid and by doing so, allowing us to 'retire' from the campaign. How wrong I was! A campaign I began in January 2006 and which I expected would last some eighteen months didn't conclusively come to an end until January 2012.

Along the way we had the support of several board members, including Aran Jones, Sharanne Basham-Pyke and Tom Brooks, with special thanks to John Wyn Owen, whose level-headed and wise advice was invaluable. There was also support from many politicians, especially Peter Black AM of the LibDems, Plaid Cymru AM Bethan Jenkins, and Ieuan Wyn Jones, who was Economy Minister from 2007 to 2011. But behind us was the support of thousands of individuals and hundreds of Welsh societies and businesses.

Against us was a particularly useless and lazy civil servant in Cardiff who embodied the institutional anti-Welsh sentiment of a significant part of the civil service in our country. She was backed up by a dire report from the Cardiff Business School in Cardiff that saw no need for a Welsh web address. But along the way we made great friends with people from other similar bids in Scotland, Brittany, the Basque Country and Galicia, as well as benefiting from the ready advice of the Catalans, especially the charismatic Amadeu Abril i Abril and his Swiss business partner, Werner Staub.

The whole campaign was a very stressful affair. It came to a head in 2011 when Edwina Hart, the Economy Minister in the new Labour Government in Cardiff, was at best agnostic to the whole idea of a Welsh domain – incredible. In an answer to a question from my local Plaid AM Elin Jones, the First Minister, Carwyn Jones, said that he would not support a .cymru domain – only a .wales one. I exploded. How dare a man who was the First Minister of my country tell me that the only official name for my country on the internet would be our slave name – 'wales'?

Again, we enlisted the support and lobbying of Welsh society. This was invaluable – people had to show their colours. What also made a difference was a piece of public research by the domain name registrars, Nominet, who wanted to run our Welsh domain. They found, to the obvious surprise of the English Pale in Wales, that most Welsh people across the board preferred .cymru to .wales (with the exception of businesses that traded outside Wales). It proved how out of touch the Labour government was and how useless were the 'experts' they keep hiring. Carwyn Jones backed down and Nominet went on to submit the bid for a .wales and .cymru domain in 2012.

It was half a victory, but it taught me the importance of generating support across Welsh society, of getting those people and instutions to show their colours and lobby government. It again highlighted that any report written by 'experts' probably comes with an in-built anti-Welsh institutional perspective.

The bid taught me that for the sake of Welsh dignity, even when one had to persuade a Welsh government – yes, a Welsh government – of the point of a Welsh web address, you never gave up.

In 2013 we will have .cymru and .wales. Wales will be a recognised internet nation.

Maybe we'll have the Arabs to thank for the future

flourishing of Europe's many languages and cultures. And not just the Arabs but the Chinese too. Could it be that the demographic and cultural challenge of the Arab and Islamic world, coupled with the economic challenge that a resurgent China presents to the West, will actually strengthen language minnows like Welsh, rather than threaten them?

Some readers may be aware that I'm one of the people behind the dotCYM bid for a top level domain for the Welsh linguistic and cultural community. In shorthand, this means, if we are successful, then websites that are in Welsh, partly in Welsh or in English (or another language), but of Welsh interest, would have the choice to use .cym at the end of their web address rather than say .com, .org or .uk. It will make a valuable contribution to developing Welsh online and also a civic non-ethnic worldwide Welshness in both Welsh and English. The dotCYM bid (www.dotcym.org) has been inspired by the success of the puntCAT bid for the Catalan linguistic and cultural community and is part of a wave of bids across Europe; puntoGAL for Galician and pointBZH for Breton being two others. And take note – it's for the community and not the country – that's a significant difference which I'll come to later.

The unlikely effect of Islam and China on dotCYM's bid became apparent at a meeting I attended in Prague in September 2006 on behalf of the campaign. Among the many discussions at the conference sponsored by the Internet's governing body ICANN was the underlying realisation that the Internet needed to accommodate and not begrudge different languages, and, more pertinently, alphabets and characters. As one delegate confided, at the dawn of the Internet in the 1990s, American pioneers, if they thought of languages at all, expected the Internet to work on a similar protocol to air-traffic controls: English would be the common language for international discussion.

English will always be the prime language on the Internet, and it could be argued with very little effort that the Internet has confirmed English in that position. But there's been a wake-up call in the last year or so. English isn't the only language. In this respect the Internet is like that other great technological breakthrough, the printing press, which did so much to legitimise the various languages across Europe.

To the frustration of millions of users, Americans developed the Internet. Nothing the matter with that, but Americans speak English, which is probably the only European language (except, maybe, Dutch) which uses no diacritics (marked accents on letters), and so the Americans had no concept of their worth. From a Welsh-language point of view it would have been better had the new technology been developed by the French, who at least use a circumflex on some of their vowels – if only Napoleon hadn't sold Louisiana in 1804! Armies of computer experts have been assigned to make the Internet compatible with the towering number of languages.

Welsh orthography is only belatedly tackling the technology, or an Anglocentric application of it, and not for the first time either. As the Welsh Humanists of the sixteenth and seventeenth centuries wrote and translated works into Welsh, the Welsh they had in mind made use of the letter 'x' for the 'ch' sound (as is the case in Greek), the letter k for today's 'c' and v for 'f'. Unfortunately for them, there were no printing presses in Wales and those in London had letters designed for English-language use. There simply weren't enough xs, ks nor vs to use on the page. Had these Humanists had their way, then those honest angular letters would have been the norm rather than the more slippery curvilinear ones, and I'd be part of the dotKYM campaign.

One of the driving forces behind the need for dotCYM is that it would normalise Welsh on the Internet and with information technology in general, confirming it as a default language rather than a contentious issue. Which brings me to the Arabs and Chinese. As the Internet broadens beyond the intelligentsia and mercantile class of the Third World and Asia, users in Arab-speaking lands are asking why they have to use the Latin alphabet for their URL – their web address. Why should an Internet chat room from Egypt, say, or a local site from Pakistan, have to transliterate the original Arabic or Urdu name into the Latin script – especially if their members don't write or possibly can't even read that alphabet?

In a sign of the growing assertiveness of the east, Arab and Chinese (as well as Korean and Russian) Internet users and governments are beginning to question the American and Anglocentric view of the governance of the Internet. The governing body ICANN (based in Washington DC) is reacting to the demand for URLs in different alphabets and characters. Of course, were this campaign to have been led by, say, Armenia (which has its own excellent 38-letter alphabet, codified in 405AD, and far more supple than our straight-jacketed Latin), one wonders just how much impact it would have. However, since the two biggest challengers to Western/American domination, the Arab world and China, have different ways of writing their languages, and, in addition, make up almost a third of the world's population, ICANN has had to sit up and take notice of linguistic politics.

In this new context of language politics, the Welsh bid for dotCYM seems much less contentious than some would have imagined two years ago. The success of the puntCAT bid also gives us a precedent and a successful one at that. And in a way, the sheer cleverness of the puntCAT campaign, inspired by the vision of the generous and intelligent Catalan lawyer Amadeu Abril i Abril, points the way to what may be the future of politics in Europe, and, possibly the world.

The puntCAT bid was based on the concept of language and culture and not on Catalan nationality or statehood. By doing so it avoided the sterile debate about what 'a nation' actually is, and side-stepped diplomatic machismo. Amadeu Abril i Abril successfully debated that if .aero (for the aerospace industry) could be called a 'community' then there was something ridiculous in not recognising a linguistic group as a community too. The Catalan linguistic and cultural community embraces people in the Catalan territories but also across the world, so that a two-letter country code wouldn't quite be appropriate. To some extent the definition is academic, as the majority of .cat sites are based in Catalan-speaking territories, and so .cat is a country code de facto if not *de jure*. But there is a fundamental shift here of what identities people wish to assume to themselves.

Though for those large and multi-state languages such as English, Spanish and French it would be too generic, for many other languages the 'linguistic and cultural community' classification could actually make more sense than the two-letter country code (.de, .nl). Besides, state departments apart, might not a linguistic code make more sense for, say, speakers of German – lets say .deu – which would include any sites in the German-speaking countries and its historic communities in Eastern Europe? The same could be said for smaller languages with official status in more than one country, Dutch, Hungarian or Swedish, for instance. In the Balkans, if the ex-Yugoslavs could decide on a different definition of what used to be called Serbo-Croat, would not a .yug span the linguistic continuum from Montenegro, Serbia, Bosnia to Croatia, leaving the two-letter codes for the national domains? With the final status of Kosovo still in the balance, a .squ or .alb linguistic and cultural domain for the Albanian-speaking community would make sense, avoiding difficulties with a country code for Kosovo and the Albanian-speaking parts of Macedonia. What of stateless and nationless peoples such as the Romanies? .rom would suffice here; and why not one for the Yiddish community – though perhaps avoiding .yid for all its unfortunate and unkind connotations in the English language?

This is dangerous territory, of course, because for many linguistic and cultural communities the two-letter country code is still the most prestigious one. And after all, why should the Kosovans or Flemish not strive for their own two-letter code if the French or Slovenes won't give theirs up first? But the puntCAT and dotCYM bids do offer another window, and are a recognition of existing and legitimate communities that need their own domains – not so much as flags to wave but as mediums to legitimise and increase the use of their language on-line. Since .cat went on line in April this year, there has been a 33 per cent increase in the number of pages in Catalan and a similar increase in the number of new web-users.

Europe's morality is in its asymmetric borders, and its maturity reflected in the mosaic of independent states within the landmass. The more independent states there are in Europe, the more democracy there will be; the expansion of democracy goes hand in hand with the spread of self-government and national emancipation. The puntCAT debate held a mirror to a changing European sense of itself and its history. The Second World War knocked the stuffing out of the self-confidence of European culture and has cast a lasting emotional shadow over the continent. The First World War, however, laid more lasting political roots. The newly-independent states created in the aftermath of the Great War re-emerged after the hiatus of the Comintern and the Cold War. These new states, with Prague the capital of one of them, all had their Woodrow Wilson Avenue in grateful thanks to the American President whose 'Fourteen Points' recognised their new independence. These submerged nations all outlived the 1930s dictators.

Until recently at least, these funny-sounding states with their diacritics and dictators were a source of fun for Western European sophisticates, but their existence confirms Europe's moral maturity. Some feel that the path towards dotCYM will lead to 'fragmentation' and 'balkanisation' with a multitude of 'Ruritanian' communities and domains. But this attitude represents the tail-end of the 200-year-old deterministic movement which gave birth to totalitarianism, both Right and Left. In his seminal (but rather misleadingly-titled) book *The Breakdown of Nations*, Leopold Kohr, writing in 1957, dealt with these prejudices head on.

The Cambrocentric Austrian philosopher cheekily asked, 'What's wrong with Ruritania in any case?' in the shadow of the towering torsos of the two Cold War superpowers. How many peoples and cultures, he questioned, have been killed off by 'Ruritanian' states as opposed to 'super' or 'great' ones? Likewise, the spreading out of Top Level Domains would be a further democratisation of the Internet as well as a practical way of promoting the diversity of Europe in fairer and non-threatening ways. Because the Internet as a medium is so much cheaper to use, and to publish material on than conventional print publishing or television, for smaller language communities it is a godsend. There is therefore, I would suggest, a clear moral argument for dotCYM, puntCAT and other 'Ruritanian' communities.

Europe is worn out. It's a continent in retirement, both demographically and intellectually. It's a continent emotionally and physically drained by wars over territory, ideology and belief, at least for a generation. There is a parallel here with the situation in Europe at the end of the Thirty Years' War – the last great war fought in the name of religion, and a war in which the German population fell by a third. That's not to say that there was no religious fighting and prejudice after 1648, but religion never achieved such terrible potency, and the Treaty of Westphalia underpinned international diplomacy for the 300 years since. Maybe people woke up to the fact that differences between Christians weren't so great after all and were certainly not worth the bloodletting and disruption the war had caused. The war's conclusion brought about a more ecumenical Europe that tolerated the varying degrees of Christianity. And maybe that's what has happened in today's Europe – a growing ecumenism, not this time of religion but, in the wake of the First World, Second World and Cold Wars, of language and culture.

Up to this growing cultural ecumenism steps the moral, intellectual and demographic challenge of the Muslim states. Likewise does not the on-coming tsunami of Chinese economic hegemony also shake European ideals to their core and undermine Europe's confidence?

Between these two massive movements, Europe is advancing into a geopolity which, as Leopold Kohr suggested, is more similar to the patchwork of states of the medieval age. Eastern Europe, with the exception of the Kosovan question, has probably already democratised and devolved to its most legitimate level. Not all states will have sovereignty and certainly not all will have the same political and cultural clout, but in a global age when we're all sipping cappuccinos and watching American films, dubbed or not, the differences between the European cultures have never been smaller. The consequence of this is more – not fewer – nation-states, because nation-states are the most effective way of defending your people from what which is not already in the domain of the global cultural and economic market. In the same way, your own Internet domain, country or community is the most effective way of elbowing out a cultural space on the web. And if there are a dozen or so new states or domains, is that really such a problem for the Europe of the twenty-first century? My guess is it won't be.

The way the Internet develops could determine the identity politics of the coming century. Maybe in this century it won't be so much nations and states as linguistic and cultural communities that will define our identity. A small change in emphasis, perhaps, but a significant one. This may help create a space where smaller nations and linguistic communities like Wales will benefit. After all, when the European states were strong, countries like Wales and Catalonia were weak. Yes, dotCYM is an idea whose time has come.

Cambria, vol. 8, no. 5 December–January 2006/7

Places

Scotland:
the Thistle and the Dragon

This article attracted some reaction in Cambria. Some mistakenly believed I didn't understand the linguistic situation in Scotland. I do understand the situation, and it was that very difference to which I was alluding in the article. Scotland is different to Wales in the way that I believe many Scots find the Welsh concept of identity different to theirs. This is not to disparage my Scottish nationalist friends, only to point it out.

As this book goes to press I have no idea if Scotland will vote Yes in the independence referendum in 2014. I hope with all my heart that they do. I would go so far as to say that their Yes vote is the only chance for any meaningful future for the Welsh language, as it will break up the United Kingdom, and in so doing give Wales – and the Welsh language – more status.

Of course, if Scotland was to vote Yes, there is no guarantee that Wales would also join the family of nation states. There is a strong current in Welsh life which would be happy with what the political scientists Alan Sandry and Syd Morgan call the 'new Elizabethan state': that is, the English state of the Tudor Queen of England, Elizabeth I, a state in which Wales was but a part of England.

It's surprising to hear so many in the media and society talk of 'nationwide' policies or bodies when they are referring to what they believe to be UK structures: the 'National' Union of Teachers, 'National' Farmers Union, GSCE school exams, the police force – structures which only exist on the England and Wales basis (and occasionally, Northern Ireland). There is a state called Englandandwales that many in the Labour, Tory and LibDem parties would be very happy to be a part of.

If Scotland and Catalonia are like the Baltic states pioneering the way towards independence, then Wales, I'm afraid, could be like Belarus: a mumbling, fumbling nation that could gain independence by default, and yet be run by a governing class and pliant population which may be against any meaningful national project, forever harking back to the Great Patriotic War and class jingoism.

We'll see.

I don't quite get Scotland. I don't quite get its national identity. That's not to say I'm against Scottish independence – far from it, I'm a great advocate of it. It's just that because language isn't a central tenet of its national identity I don't quite understand how Scotland ticks and what makes its call for independence so strong.

There's no denying Scotland's historic 'legitimacy' for independence – if that is a consideration at all for independence. I'd argue that those cultures which have least historic precedent for independence are the ones that most need it to defend their culture, society and language. As neither Gaelic nor Scots seem to have the same central position for Scottish identity as Welsh does for Welsh identity, and if the defence and promotion of a unique language isn't the driving force for independence, then what is?

Is it to retain an accent – as beautiful as it is? But with English now undoubtedly a Scottish language, do the Scots, including Scottish nationalists, feel glad or threatened by the global march of English? Do they have the same concern as Welsh nationalists have about, say, Kurdish, Breton or Tibetan language rights? Nationalism is there to defend institutions as well as culture – but would one argue that Scottish institutions are under threat?

So, yes, Scotland, to me, seems very different to Wales, and that difference affects our relationship and understanding of one another. In fact, the most striking thing about the relationship between our two countries seems to be that there is so little of it! There are some thirty Welsh towns twinned with Breton towns and strong linguistic links between the two countries, but precious little between Wales and Scotland, or Welsh and Gaelic. Ireland has played a pivotal role in the development of Welsh political and cultural nationalism, but Scotland, beyond 'me-too-ism' and being a convenient big brother to watch over Wales, very little.

Of course, Welsh-speakers know of the historic lost Welsh-speaking kingdoms of Rhedeg (Galloway and Cumbria) and Gododdin (Edinburgh), which were lost to the Anglo-Saxons in 635 and 638. Names of places from the era of wattle and battle, nursery rhymes and war crimes live on in the poetry of Aneirin and Taliesin. Yes, the earliest Welsh poetry is from what is today northern England and southern Scotland, composed 1400 years ago. Strathclyde (*Ystrad Clyd* in Welsh) lived on for longer, and pockets of Brythonic/Welsh names still live on in place names such as Partick (from Brythonic, *Peartoc* – Welsh *perth*, 'bush or thicket') and Dumbarton, meaning 'fort of the Britons'.

In the tenth century, Gildas wrote of the Welsh, Scots, Irish, Manx and Vikings uniting to push the English back to the Isle of Thanet and back 'home' across the North Sea to Germany.

Inadvertently, Wales's biggest contribution to Scotland was to be a usefully distracting punch-bag for the English crown. Edward I's colonial wars against Llywelyn nearly bankrupted the English kingdom as he spent around £240,000 on his anti-Welsh crusade – £80,000 was spent on building his Iron Ring of castles. The campaigns cost so much that Edward was forced to borrow £122,000 from the Riccardi banking family of Lucca in Italy. By doing so he inadvertently initiated international capitalism and was forced to make concessions to Parliament. English democracy was built with the stones of Welsh castles.

As John Davies, in his magisterial *History of Wales*, notes, a weakened Edward, bloodied by the Welsh, gave the Scots some breathing space. The Scottish ability to withstand English conquest was by implication a significant factor in Welsh history. It allowed the Scots time and space to develop such national strength that it was able to withstand all efforts to be totally incorporated into England, and so later ensured that the British state would never be a totally uniform centralised state, as France became.

But the Scots and Welsh have never been great allies. As was common in a semi-pastoral society that had months of relative inactivity, seasonal wars were a common source of income and, no doubt, adventure. Incredibly 10,500 of Edward's 12,500 foot soldiers at the Battle of Falkirk in 1298 were Welsh, and there were 5,000 Welsh soldiers at Bannockburn in 1312.

Until the advent of modern nationalism in the twentieth century there was very little formal interaction at all between Welsh and Scots. One unfortunate category of Scot that did become common in Wales was the keeper at the big estate. On account of them undertaking an unpopular (not to say despised) job in the rural economy, the Scots hardly endeared themselves to the Welsh population. But the English language was also a barrier in what would have been essentially monolingual Welsh communities. Up until the early twentieth century to be Welsh meant Welsh-speaking; all non-Welsh-speakers were simply 'Saeson' – a term more in keeping with the word 'Anglophone' than 'English' – and this was a quandary for Welsh people. What *were* the Scots?

One interesting glimpse on inter-ethnic attitudes is a short letter by John Couper (a Scot), the newly-appointed vicar of Roath in Cardiff in 1815. In his letter to the first Marquis of Bute (also a Scot), Couper registers surprise that many of his parishioners spoke no English.

The differences between Wales and Scotland are still great. It's difficult to imagine two nations within such a small state which could be so different. Whereas the Basques and Catalans and Galicians have their different tempos within the Spanish state, there is a symmetry of discourse that links and benefits all three. The obvious case is the call for linguistic parity for the indigenous languages within Spain, but constitutional change is also very high. Whilst the Basques can look to Catalonia for linguistic inspiration, the Welsh can't look to Scotland – although there is now more interaction than before. It heartens me to see the flowering of Gaelic-language culture since devolution, which has, in some small way, been helped by the Welsh experience. There should be more.

However, Scotland's different linguistic history has meant that for most of our history we've been left fighting a linguistic battle within the British state with only one flank. It was always so, it seems. As Robert Phillipson, the author of *Linguistic Imperialism*, noted in passing in his article 'Macaulay Alive and Kicking', some 2,600 books were printed in Welsh in the eighteenth century, whilst only around seventy were published in Gaelic before 1800, and even less in Scots/Lallands. And this really gets to the heart of the difference of what it is to be Welsh and to be Scottish, for their sense of nationality derives from two different concepts – each as legitimate as the other.

Whilst the Scots can claim to have been a recognised historic sovereign nation, which, like the Catalans, just took an unfortunate wrong turning in the eighteenth century, the Welsh are the archetypal non-historic 'stateless nation'. The Scots can boast of civic nationality (a posh way of saying your chosen ethnic and linguistic identity is the dominant culture), whilst the Welsh are a colonised people. The Scots talk of regaining their nationality; we have to create it.

Scotland feels very different and maybe this is a lesson for linguistic nationalists like myself. A nation can be based on something other than a linguistic community.

The architecture of Scotland is different; its diet is different – and I'm not talking of the infamous 'deep fried Mars bars' but rather the everyday 'peasant' food: haggis with chips, 'neeps and tatties' and Irn Bru; the way they wrap their chip suppers with the paper folded beneath the chips rather than above it; the beer; the music – there are *ceilidh* bars in Scottish cities, where we in Wales have naff Irish pubs; they have proper grown-up media and press; their banks and laws and, yes, the kilts and whisky.

What do we have? Strip away the language and what do we have to show a Welsh civic sensibility, a Welsh palate, a Welsh popular culture? That's not a stick to beat the Welsh language – it's a call to arms for us to create something interesting here inclusive of and beyond the language. In fact a notable undercurrent of the last twenty years or so has been the conscious Caledonianisation of Welsh identity. People, maybe not Welsh-speaking but keen to assert their Welshness, have adopted and adapted Scottish icons – Welsh whisky, Welsh kilts, Welsh bagpipes (though Brittany is just as influential in that case), elevating Wenglish to a vernacular like Scots. In short, using the successful Scottish template to will a nationality which isn't defined by the Welsh language.

Scotland's recent cultural and political confidence, like that of the Basques or Haka dance of the New Zealand rugby team today, or the Czechs in the late nineteenth century, is that they've embraced what the International Left euphemistically call the 'rural' and 'traditional' (by which they meant 'narrow-minded', 'backward' and 'ethnic') into their 'city' and the 'urban' (read 'modern', 'cosmopolitan' and 'progressive'). The *'teuchters'* (Scottish Highlanders) have taken over the 'burgh'. Their folk music has been mainstreamed; their languages, Scots and Gaelic, gradually given status; their cuisine no longer ridiculed; the highland bagpipes ubiquitous; and kilts worn at city and Lowland weddings. Until Wales embraces its rural, traditional, peasant self into its cities, we'll never be confident.

And then there's the space. So much of it. The kind of space you can shout your head off and no NIMBY will hear you. The kind of space you only find in Europe above the 55th parallel. It's a big country.

Driving about Scotland seems like driving through Powys … every day! Outside the central belt, there's no ribbon conurbation. The towns are well defined and in their own space, like in medieval Europe – like they should be. Not bumper to bumper villages.

Edinburgh is a proper European capital city. It feels and looks like Prague. It's more impressive than Oslo or Helsinki. Cardiff looks like a second division English provincial city – Nottingham, Reading – and acts like one. It has less international traction than Reykjavik, which is a slightly bigger version of Carmarthen.

And then there is the historic diversity. Scotland always feels to me like a commonwealth, not a simple nation-state. There's a wealth of cultures and linguistic heritage – Lowland Scots, Norse, Gaelic. I've always thought of it as a northern version of that proud Caucasian state, Georgia. Both countries have a beautiful, historic capital, a tradition of indigenous royalty, a similar population and size and a collection of different cultures – a mini-empire. Of course, the Abkhaz, I now know, are not some variation of the Georgians, but a nation in their own right; but there is a variation of people and culture in Scotland which Wales lacks.

In fact, Scotland's patchwork culture places it in two traditions. The Gaelic and Brythonic (ancient Welsh) substratum is evidently Celtic, though the jury is still out on the Picts!

On the eastern seaboard of mainland Scotland and later across the southern hip, Scots, a Germanic language developed. A language of high prestige in the late Middle Ages. Had the Bible been translated into Scots (Lallands) in 1588, then, who knows if Scotland today may be as Scots-speaking as Catalonia is Catalan-speaking? Alas, it wasn't to be.

But again, it raises the question of Scotland's place in the world. For its mercantile history and its Scots language, Scotland seems to tilt east towards the Germanic Hanseatic culture which stretches across the cold North Sea.

Since regaining independence in 1991 the Estonians have tried branding themselves as a Nordic country, as they throw away the unreassuring attribute of an 'ex-Soviet state'. They've even played around with changing their horizontal national tricolour flag into a rather classy Scandinavian cross as a visual demonstration of their new orientation. With independence beckoning, would the Scots consider branding themselves as a Nordic country too? In fact, the Shetland Isles already sport a Scandinavian flag based on the white cross on a blue field of the Scottish saltire. In terms of its size, its politics, its economy and population, it would certainly fit the bill as a Nordic country, and 'Nordic' has more positive connotations in terms of design, urban planning and cuisine than does 'Britishness'.

So, if Scotland regains independence and snuggles up between Saudi Arabia and Senegal at the UN, where would that leave Wales? We'd be a tiny minority of forty MPs in a Westminster parliament of 600. In fact, we'd have reverted to the situation we were in between the death of Llywelyn in 1282 and the Act of Union of 1707. Wales would be a kind of Montenegro in the rump Yugoslavia – a UKslavia, perhaps.

In that respect and in light of my melancholic

temperament I'll allow myself an idle thought. What if the Archduke Ferdinand had not taken the world's worst-ever right-hand turn in a sunny Sarajevo, and the Government of Ireland Act had been implemented in 1914? Would we have seen a self-governing, peaceful Ireland? And with that would there have been 'home rule all round' in, say, 1922? After all, the contemplative space behind our National Museum, where the National War Memorial and gardens now stand, was kept with a National Senedd in mind. And if so, would Wales and Scotland have benefited more with Ireland a devolved part of the UK, like the nations of Iberia do from Catalonia, than with Ireland outside? Would Wales and Scotland have got their parliaments two generations earlier? Three Celtic countries pissing 'inside the tent', rather than one pissing out and two cross-legged and constipated? Of course, the rude awakening of the ethnic Great War and self-governing Eire put paid to the Welsh and Scottish 'entryist' strategy of home rule and led directly to the founding of Plaid Cymru and the SNP. But with Ireland and Scotland out of the Union then Wales would have to either become again a part of the Realm of England or become independent. There is no halfway house.

Wales has already lost out from not having in Scotland a northern flank campaigning for linguistic rights. Were Scotland to become independent we could lose that one strong motor as we try and gain constitutional rights too. Will Wales be weaker if Scotland gains independence? Could Scotland become independent 'too soon' for Wales?

Scotland and Wales are different. We are not Scots – but nor are we English either. Not to follow Scotland's constitutional lead will make us English with a funny accent.

It's time we got to know the Scots better.

Cambria, vol. 13, no. 1, December 2011–January 2012

News from a Small Country:
the Censorship of a Basque Newspaper

'Wastad yn mynd i Lydaw, byth yn mynd i Ffrainc;
wastad yn mynd i Wlad y Basg, byth yn mynd i Sbaen'

is a couplet from a well-known song by the Welsh alternative group,
Datblygu. *Translated it means 'always going to Brittany, never to
France; always going to the Basque Country, never to Spain'.*

Datblygu *were part of the 'underground' counter-culture
Welsh Rock scene of the late 1980s and early 1990s – the best,
the only positive thing about 1980s Wales, in my view. They
were part of the angry young men and women singing in spiky
hair, brown suede shoes and earrings, railing against the boring
middle-of-the-road Welsh-language music played on Radio
Cymru and S4C. It was part, albeit through the medium of
Welsh, of the alternative scene in Margaret Thatcher's Britain. I
was a great fan of Datblygu and still keep the correspondence
from my late teens between myself and the band's enigmatic,
charismatic and clever lyricist, the lead singer and composer,
David R. Edwards from Cardigan. On the wall of my angst-filled
room during my first year at university I'd posted hand-written
cuttings of my favourite lines from his songs.*

*The lines about Brittany and the Basque Country come from
Datblygu's excellent satirical 1991 song, 'Cân i Gymru'. They
are a dig at the middle-class nationalists who keep banging on
about the 'small countries' and can't be normal like everyone else
and just go to France and Spain. A dig at the kind of people
who'd go on holiday to Brittany rather than Disneyland Paris,
or correct you for saying you'd gone on holiday to the 'Spanish'
Costa Brava, pointing out that it is actually in Catalonia. It's a
dig at a Welsh nationalist world-view. It's a clever, humorous
observation by David – they always were.*

Of course, I'd always felt a little uncomfortable with the lines. After all, they are a dig at people like me. But I took the same view as those supporters of the Eliezer Ben-Yehuda did when they learnt that his grave had been desecrated by anti-Zionist graffiti. After realising that the graffiti was in Hebrew they imagined that old Ben-Yehuda would be very happy in the knowledge that even those who hated him and all he stood for expressed their hatred of him in the language he'd given his life to revive. Welsh is a wide community and it's big enough to accept and celebrate different views in its various cultures.

And then, over a decade later, the Basque-language daily newspaper (the only one), Egunkaria was closed down by the Spanish state. As I heard of the state closure, arrest on dodgy charges, harassment and torture conducted by the Spanish state against the editorial board of Egunkaria I was shocked by the silence and ignorance of the Welsh political class, especially the British left wing, I recalled another favourite line by David R. Edwards: 'dyna gyd rwy'n gweld o feddyliau pobl, yw y geiriau maent yn atal' (that's all I see of other people are the words they don't say'). That is, their silence betrayed a deliberate political view. Their silence was political; their silence cost the dignity, freedom and health of journalists in a supposedly democratic European state.

With this in mind, David's clever put-down of a nationalist world view that included Bretons, Basques and, yes, Catalans and all the other obscure 'not-proper' nations doesn't seem quite so innocent. I'd go as far as to say that the sentiment projected in Datblygu's song actually allowed (in its own little way) the Spanish state to get away with torture. They are lines in celebration of ignorance of faraway lands of which we know little. They articulate a counter British (or Spanish) nationalism.

This lack of knowledge about, respect for, and interest in places like the Basque Country has allowed the media and politicians to mostly ignore it. After all, if a country doesn't exist then violations against that country and its culture doesn't exist either – do they?

The 'words that they don't say' by the international British socialists in Wales were deafening. But then, to support or show interest in Basque affairs would mean accepting a world-view which went counter to theirs. It would mean recognising that stateless nations had linguistic and political rights as nations. That was too problematic. After all, where would it end – recognising that Wales wasn't better off together in Britain? Better stick to 'easy-to-read' international politics, like supporting Nelson Mandela or Palestinian rights.

This deliberate ignorance and mocking by the media and political class in Wales and Britain means they are unable to appreciate what is going on today in the Spanish state. As the Basques and Catalans demand the political independence denied to them by past Spanish military conquest and threats, our politicians and media are, by and large, unable to explain to the public why the map of Europe is being re-drawn.

On my innocent student-room wall in 1986 I had two other posters. One was a map by the Catalan organisation, CIEMEN, of the stateless nations and linguistic communities of Europe. It included nations in Eastern Europe, which, at the time, were air-brushed from 'proper' maps and were destined to be kept in the dustbin of history, from Estonia in the north to Slovenia in the south. In the west were the Celts and minoritised nations of Spain and the patchwork of peoples in the southern Alps. Nobody expected (least of all the so-called experts at the Department of International Studies, where I was a student) that these forgotten East European people would, within five short years, re-emerge into history. They were ignorant of them. We'll see if the experts will be a little less ignorant as the last bricks to fall from the Berlin Wall will be independence movements of the 'Brittany and Basque lands'.

Oh, and in case you're wondering about the other poster I had on my student wall in Neuadd Pantycelyn, it was of the lead singer of 'Blondie', Debbie Harry. I wasn't a total odd-ball, honest!

Ten members of the board of a daily newspaper, including a former and the current editor are thrown in jail and tortured. The newspaper is closed down on dubious charges by the full force of the state.

Iraq? Turkey? China? No, Spain, or more correctly, the Basque Country, that cone-shaped country in the armpit of the Bay of Biscay.

On 20 February 2003, *Egunkaria*, the Basque-language daily paper (the only one) was closed down, as members of the Guardia Civil ransacked their offices and arrested ten leading members of the paper's board (and three members of Ikestolen Federazioa, the Basque school's movement and staff of the *Jakin* magazine), and drove them blind to Madrid to interrogate and torture. The charge? Collaboration with the Basque terrorist organisation, ETA. A wholly groundless charge which is the political equivalent of accusing an innocent person of rape – no matter that the allegations are false, the suspicion will linger for ever. The word 'terrorist' likewise predictably closes down any chance of level-headed discussion and in one stroke politically tarnishes the accused.

A few years ago I visited the Basque Country with Simon Brooks, staying with Begotxu Olaizola, a Welsh-speaking Basque aquaintance in the efficient sea-side town of Zarautz. We munched our way around the tasty *pintxo* bars from elegant Donostia to the proud but grimy Bilbao, where the political graffiti is more interesting than the art in the coffee-table culture of the Guggenheim. During our stay, our guest arranged for us to visit the offices of *Egunkaria* in Andoain.

The offices looked like any other newspaper's – the usual melange of empty plastic coffee cups, nasty strip lighting and intense faces, in fact, surprisingly similar in size and ambience to the news offices of BBC Wales. I'd also met the current *Egunkaria* editor, Martxello Otamendi ('tx' in Basque is pronounced 'ch' as in church and 'x' is 'sh') at a conference for publishing in minority languages in Lampeter. He was one of the ten arrested and tortured. One accusation levelled against him was that he'd conducted an interview with an ETA commando – an accusation which would lead to an award ceremony and prize for investigative journalism in most countries. A few months ago *Egunkaria*'s website began producing a daily English summary of the news – a service I logged on to regularly until the screen went blank on 20 February.

The closure of *Egunkaria* brought tens of thousands of people onto the streets of a rainy Donosita (San Sebastian) and within days a surrogate newspaper, *Egunero*, was on sale, thanks to the co-operation of the other daily newspapers in the Basque Country.

Egunkaria is the only paper in the Basque language, is non-politically affiliated, and sells some 17,000 copies daily. It was launched in 1990 following donations by thousands of people across the Basque Country. The newspaper has achieved an iconic status as a badge of a resurgent Basque language – a language which was banned by the fascist regime of Franco. *Egunkaria* also has an iconic status among a small group of people outside Euskadi. Among them are many Welsh-speakers who dream of establishing a Welsh-language newspaper, and also some Irish speakers who will soon be launching the Irish language daily, *Lá*, using many business strategies similar to Egunkaria's.

Following the arrests, the editors of several Welsh publications, *Barn*, *Golwg*, *Y Cymro* and *Yr Herald* sent a letter of support to the *Egunkaria* staff. Cymdeithas yr Iaith Gymraeg (the Welsh Language Society) put up a petition on its website and both the Welsh- and English-language branches of the Academi literary organisation passed a motion voicing their concern to the Spanish Embassy in Chesham Place in London. Several Plaid Cymru members of Parliament and Assembly also spoke out deploring the fact that a newspaper editor could have a plastic bag placed over his head and kept for a week in detention in an European Union member state.

The closure of *Egunkaria* (the name means simply 'the daily') has touched many people, including Ned Thomas, the founder of *Planet* magazine and a much-respected writer on Welsh and international political and cultural affairs. He's been at the vanguard of creating a Welsh-medium daily, and has been a thoughtful advocate of Welsh print media in both Welsh and English. Eighteen months ago, Ned and the Aberystwyth-based Mercator Institute for Media, Languages and Culture began a study into the feasibility of publishing a Welsh-language daily. They point out that linguistic communities with a much smaller population than the Welsh-speaking one can sustain newspapers on a very small circulation. The 300,000 Swedish community in Finland publishes ten daily newspapers and the Slovene daily of the Trieste and Gorica provinces in Italy, *Primorski dnevnik*, sells about 10,000. But these are all communities which have the strength of a sovereign state behind them. That's not the case for the Basques or the Welsh, which is why *Egunkaria* was so important, both as a possible template and as a source of inspiration.

Egunkaria went a long way to normalising the Basque language. But for the ruling Partido Popular party in Spain, any Basque expression which isn't rustic or kitsch is suspicious. The thinking goes like this: ETA are a terrorist group which believes in an independent united Basque state. Many of the readership of *Egunkaria* believe in an independent united Basque state: ergo, *Egunkaria* is a terrorist front. Following this quack interpretation, the daily *Irish News* in Belfast should be closed because, one presumes that a publication whose readership is mostly of the Catholic community also has strong support to the notion of a united and independent Ireland – as does the IRA, of course. Thankfully, the Wales isn't governed by such people as the Spanish Prime Minister, Jose María Aznar, who was a leading member of Franco's Falange movement in his youth and campaigned against the new democratic constitution following the dictator's death, nor either the President of Aznar's ruling Partido Popular, Fraga Iribarne, who was Franco's Interior Minister.

The closing down of *Egunkaria* also raises questions here in Wales. *Egunkaria* was closed because of supposed terrorist links (that old 'rapist' accusation again), ergo it is a terrorist front, ergo, any person writing about *Egunkaria* in *Cambria*, *Barn* or the *Western Mail* is a supporter of terrorism. Is this line of thought gnawing away in Wales? I believe, so. MPs from the British parties at the House of Commons refused to back a motion by the Plaid Cymru MP Simon Thomas, expressing concern at the action of the Spanish state (it's the Basque's misfortune not to be Palestinians, it seems, and for Aznar to be Tony Blair's new best friend).

I believe *Egunkaria*, or the son of *Egunkaria*, will be fine. The Spanish Government's heavy-handed strategy has backfired. Support for the paper has come from all walks of life from the Prime Minister of the Basque Country down, and 110 support groups are already up and running and raising money. But the same can't be said of Wales. We still haven't managed to produce a daily newspaper in Welsh, although Ned Thomas's work may change that. The situation is barely better in the English language. Whereas the Basques have five daily papers published in Spanish, the majority language, in their country we have one and a half (the *Western Mail*, with its geographically-challenged title, and the culturally schizophrenic *Daily Post*). To put it another way, the Basques, with a similar population, have almost 1,000 more professionals employed in journalism than we do, and imagine what that does to the political and cultural debate of a nation and its self-esteem. Which makes you grateful that Henry Jones Davies had the courage to set up *Cambria*, which is a rare and valuable independent platform for Welsh opinion.

Back in the early 1980s following the Cullodenesque defeat of the '79 Referendum, a long-forgotten essay I've ransacked my shelves to find was written on the reasons for the defeat of Welsh Devolution. One of the conclusions of the piece was the need for Welsh-based media which could inform Welsh public opinion beyond the Kinnockite scaremongering which can flourish only in a retarded political climate. The author suggested the imperative of an English-language Welsh newspaper. He put forward different options for creating such a creature, from working within the existing *Western Mail* and Thomson House publishing group to creating a spanking new newspaper set-up. He reckoned it would cost about £2m, with possible support from the Welsh Office or Whitehall. The sum was deemed too high by many who disliked the notion of the state supporting/subsidising the print media.

It goes to show how we've been short-changed, and how short-sighted we've been towards the print media in Wales. And don't let's get too concerned about the virginal qualities of our non-state sponsored newspapers – isn't the money S4C, ELWa, the WDA etc spend on adverts and promotions in the *Western Mail* and *Daily Post* another form of state subsidy?

Yes, the closing of *Egunkaria* makes for very interesting and important reading for us Welsh – the closing down of a newspaper is very disturbing news indeed. But then, at least the Basques have a newspaper to close down in the first place. More pity the Welsh I say. How useless are we?

Cambria, vol. 5, no. 4, Spring 2003

The Border:
a Daily Plebiscite

In 1993 I took a cruise along the Danube from Austria to Bratislava, the capital of the newly independent Slovakia. It was a pleasurable hour-long journey along the brown (rather than blue) Danube. On arriving I changed my Austrian Schillings for Slovak Crowns. The Slovak Crowns were exactly the same as the Czechoslovak Crowns, the state which ceased to exist a few months earlier –they'd just stuck a label with the Slovak double cross on it.

The differences between Vienna and Bratislava were obvious – the wealth of the Austrian capital against the poverty and grime of the Slovak. However, I enjoyed my brief stay in Bratislava and felt very at home; maybe I identified with the people, who'd always played second fiddle to Hungary, Austria or the Czechs. My most enduring memory was the obviousness of the border. Within an hour on a boat – a journey of less than an hour by car – one was transposed to a very different country. Different language, architecture, human faces and history. It's the kind of definite border one didn't encounter in Western Europe, and certainly not between Wales and England.

It's become very fashionable to celebrate the border people, projecting on to them notions of mutual respect for each other across the 'artificial' border. From my experience, border people can, if anything, be more hostile to the people on the opposite side. There may be low-level jealousy over under-cutting, smuggling or being priced out of the housing market by 'those' wealthier commuters on the other side. It may be, as in Wales' case, that there is very little animosity between people on each side of the border. That's not because of a benevolent embrace of multiculturalism against narrow nationalism, but rather because they are essentially the same people. To put it bluntly,

Wales has become culturally a part of England.

But our border is there, and it is a fact, of some sort. It's also interesting and, thankfully, not hostile nor dangerous. I wish not to close the border nor erect border posts, but I'm glad the border is there.

Borders are good.

They're good because they can allow freedom of thought and development for one community beyond the norms of another. Good because they can defend and strengthen a weak community in relation to a stronger one. Borders promote diversity, plurality and democracy. For a small nation not to possess a border is to be as a non-unionised worker in a sweat-shop, dependent on the grace and whims of the boss.

These, of course, are the reasons the messianic anti-border brigade dislike borders. Borders are an affront to 'modernisation','universality' and 'right-thinking people'. The sans frontier soldier will break other people's border posts to proves how much he believes in their freedom. The sans frontier activist may even be in favour of difference and plurality … as long as that plurality is in their own image.

Those who claim to be against borders lie. What they wish for is for their own moral, linguistic or cultural border to extend. Extend so that it incorporates others. Extend so that there are no impediments to their norms within their extended realm. To defend their extended, imperial border is to defend order. To defend your own border within their realm is to be divisive and reactionary.

And it is within this compass that we look at and define our own border. Wales has only one border, unfortunately. How much better would it have been to have three or four tightly-squeezed neighbours. For our pity was not to be conquered by another nation, but to be conquered by only one. We see ourselves in relation to only one dominant other, and not three or four competing norms.

And so, on to our lonely, only border. We'll never know who got to play God, who was the individual who had the power over millions to draw the border between Wales and England – the ultimate signature by an anonymous hand. Whilst Henry VIII signed the Laws of Wales (what's usually called the Acts of Union) in 1536 and 1542, which set down the border, there must have been a civil servant who made the polite recommendations – there always is. The one who decided, for example, that mostly Welsh-speaking Oswestry (or Ewias) would be in England, not Wales.

What we do know is that this border – handsome, curvaceous even – was the product of the kind of streamlining, a centralising drive for equality, of which many of Wales' British politicians would approve. Unlike the Canada–USA 2,475-mile straight border drawn along the 49th parallel – and no, the Sioux and Blackfoot and Mohawks weren't consulted either – our border is indented with history. If we don't know who actually drew the lines of the map we know some of the milestones in the history of the border which later became border posts.

Since the killing of Prince Llywelyn in 1282 the 'Principality' had been ruled directly from London, with counties created on the English model – Anglesey, Caernarvonshire, Merionethshire, Cardiganshire and Carmarthenshire – and under English law. The rest of the land lay in the hands of local lords – those called the Marcher Lords. They were semi-independent; our native laws, the Laws of Hywel Dda, were used side by side with English law. Following the break with Rome, and with signs that the Catholic Spanish and French could become allies and attack London through the back door of Wales, Henry VIII, modern, centralist king that he was, was keen to tidy up this messy medieval anomaly.

Brigands, spivs, and ne'er-do-wells could play the different laws of Wales and England against each other. One can almost imagine, in a tunic and codpiece version of an American Western, the brigand evading the law in one lordship, and poking his long-socked toe over the border to gain sanctuary in another. Not so much the state line as the *cantref* line.

However, by the 1530s the once powerful and fearsome Marcher Lords had become weaker, and the use of Welsh law was also in decline. The lords were ready to lord it in London. As John Davies said, 'By 1534 most of the old families, descendants of the old original conquistadores, were gone'.

The 'Act of Union', it seems, was written somewhat in haste. Although Thomas Cromwell, Henry's Chief Minister, wouldn't want to leave anything to chance, there wasn't a party of plodding servants trekking on land with great topographical, imperial implements to delineate the border. It was probably drawn on a map in a log-fire heated hall in London. This was, after all, the dawn of modern map-making; there was no need to get one's feet wet. There was, and maybe still is, on a secluded shelf, the map used to plot the border.

So, where to draw the border? There was no Welsh party represented in the signing of the Laws of Wales – there were no MPs from Wales at Westminster until 1536 (their creation was one of the benefits of the Laws for the lords). So, there was no one to plead the Welsh case. The border was drawn by a person looking from the east.

There was certainly a definite feeling of difference between Welsh and English. To be Welsh meant to *speak* Welsh. In fact, even to be able to speak English would have labelled a person as a 'Sais', in everyday parlance. The Welsh weren't an imagined community. The locals would have known full well which villages and towns were Welsh-speaking and which weren't. The politics of diglossia, of one language having social authority over another, would have been well understood by both linguistic communities, as they would have been for the medieval Czech, Slovene or Latvian-speaking peasant in the German-speaking towns in their territory; of Prag, Laibach or Revel. But the Welsh language, or ethnicity if you wish, seems not to be the deciding factor in the delineation of the administrative border, even if the linguistic border had been quite settled for almost a millennium by 1536.

Since the Battle of Chester (615 AD), when the Welsh in Wales were cut off from the Welsh in *Yr Hen Ogledd* (north of England/southern Scotland), and the Battle of Dyrham 577, when we were cut off from the Welsh in present-day south-west England and Cornwall, the Welsh were hemmed into our two peninsulas. In 610 Saint Beuno fled to Gwynedd in distress after hearing the pagan Saxon language spoken for the first time on the banks of the Severn.

The fertile land to the west of the Severn was known as Powys and referred to as 'Paradwys Powys' (paradise) for its fertility. But with the loss of the royal seat at Pengwern (which could have been at Baschurch, Wroxeter, Whittington Castle or Shrewsbury) the Welsh retreated once again leaving behind poems (known as *Canu Cynddylan* and *Canu Heledd* – the poems of Cynddylan and his sister Heledd) lamenting strewn, smouldering hearths, and our toponyms. We left these place-names like linguistic archaeology ... Malvern – '*moel fryn*'– 'bald hill' ... testimony to lands which were once ours. Testimony that we lost the land before the big linguistic shift which saw Brythonic become Old Welsh in the seventh century, and the order of our words change from adjective + noun to noun + adjective as it is today.

And what of Powys? It looks similar to the Spanish and French word for country, *pais/pays*. In fact Powys and '*pais*' are the same words with the vowel dipthonged, as so many words were when Brythonic became Old Welsh (as the Latin month *Martius* becoming the Welsh 'Mawrth' also testifies).

In fact Beuno's pagans would have felt at home in Powys, as they are both at root the same word. From the Indo-European word which gives us 'peg' in English, it was originally used in Latin to signify a land boundary, then the land itself, then by implication the people of the land which became '*pagus*', the country bumpkins. This then became a jibe that the newly-Christianised townies of late Roman period used to mock the less refined, still 'pagan' (yes, that word) yokels of the countryside. Powys – you could hardly choose a better word for a rural unit of land which straddles a border.

If he wished to ignore the linguistic facts on the ground, Thomas Cromwell could use other border pegs. The jurisdiction of the Welsh bishoprics would have been a mostly ready-made border: Llandaf in the south, St Asaph in the north. But the new border is, in parts, to the west of this ecclesiastical border. And of course there are the ancient dykes that he would no doubt have been familiar with. Yes, dykes, plural – there are two.

The first was Wat's Dyke. It was built by Aethelbald, King of Mercia, 716–757AD and extended from the Severn Valley north to the estuary of the Dee. However, the Welsh reclaimed some of the land, which meant that by Offa's time (757–796AD) the border was a little further east. But, recent theories conclude that the dykes, or parts of them, date back to the Roman period and could have been built during the reign of Emperor Severus, 193–211AD.

The linguistic and ethnic border remained a hazy but fairly consistent line for centuries afterwards. Eastern parts of Wales are mentioned in the Domesday Book, which testifies to incursion of Norman-English ways and population, especially in the north-east, but the Welsh language and traditions could also gain ground over English.

During the Middle Ages the jurisdictions along the border developed some of the facts on the ground that would give Cromwell's people some measurements for the new border.

Grahame Davies, in his book *The Dragon and the Crescent – Nine Centuries of Contact with Islam,* makes the interesting point that the Crusades in Palestine gave Wales the essential two centuries to develop and consolidate its own laws, language and polity. Whilst the Welsh could be as passionate as anyone about redeeming the Holy Land, when push came to shove, like a schoolboy making his excuses, very few Welsh nobles actually made it to any of the Crusades. While the English lords and a weakened English crown were saving Christendom, the Welsh had some peace. We've a lot to thank the Muslims for.

There are many 'pan-handles' on the maps of the world – Arkansas, Florida and Namibia's Caprivi Strip. Maelor Saesneg is ours! Shorter, stumpier, more a thumb than a handle, this is the piece of land which juts out unexpectedly east to the plains of Cheshire. It's during this period, the Anarchy of Stephen, 1135–54, that Madog ap Maredudd of Powys captured Maelor Saesneg. It's English-speaking Maelor (Welsh-speaking Maelor, *Maelor Cymraeg,* includes Wrexham), that gives the border this distinctive features.

Like all borders, the England–Wales border saw periods of warfare. Had Glyndŵr been successful, then his Tripartite Indenture agreement with Edmund Mortimer and Henry Percy would have seen the Welsh border stretch to the

Severn and Mersey, with Mortimer taking southern England and Percy the north of England.

The failure of Glyndŵr's rebellion didn't mean that collective memory of the lost lands along the Severn was gone. Maybe in recognition of this, or for convenience, Henry VII set up his Wales and the Marches Council, with its capital at Ludlow (*Llwydlo* in Welsh) in Herefordshire. His son, Henry VIII, had no time for niceties, and so with the break from Rome completed he wanted uniformity across his kingdom: the border was drawn.

Wales 'lost' some nine lordships under Henry VIII's rule – Caus (*Cawrse*) to the south of Shrewsbury; eastern Montgomery; the whole of Clun (*Colonwy*), Ludlow, Wigmor; a part of Llandras; the whole of Huntingdon, Clifford and Ewias in Herefordshire: in all some 700 km sq. (about the size of Anglesey). Some of these lordships – Caus, Ludlow, Huntingdon – would have been solidly English; others were very much Welsh. As John Davies says in his *History of Wales*, the border 'excluded districts such as Oswestry and Ewias, where the Welsh language would continue to be spoken for centuries, districts which it would not be wholly fanciful to consider as *Cambria irredenta*'. In fact, a Welsh-language bookshop was opened in Oswestry in 2012. The cleaving of these territories unintentionally created an outline along the Shropshire border that mimics the actual Welsh coastline, though in a somewhat doughy form, with an over-sized Anglesey and club-footed Dyfed.

The border after Ewias then follows the Monnow and Wye rivers, giving us the Gwent rump, a pert bottom on the map of the country.

Interestingly, the earliest printed map of Wales as a separate country from the rest of Britain, Humphrey Lhuyd's 1563, *Cambriae Typus*, depicts a wide Wales. Made only a generation after Henry's Laws, and a century and a half after

Glyndŵr, Wales extends to the Severn. It shows no counties but rather divides Wales into three provinces: Gwynedd, which stretches to Chester; Powys, which includes everywhere west of the Severn and down the eastern side of the Wye; and Deheubarth, which is Dyfed, Glamorgan, Gwent and Brycheiniog. It's a cultural and historic map, but was Lhuyd, despite being an MP and man of the Establishment, trying to make a political point when he drew it? Did it take a generation for the Welsh to understand what had happened?

And so, on to the Question of Gwent – or Monmouthshire, as it was for centuries: a chunk of our land continually questioned, even though it was for the most part solidly Welsh-speaking at the time of the Laws. With Henry's Laws of 1536 and 1542, Wales had been divided into thirteen English-style counties. In one significant area Wales was treated slightly differently to the other English counties: Wales was divided into circuits for the Great and Quarter Session courts. These circuits correspond somewhat to the 'new' 1974 counties. Essentially: North West (Gwynedd), North East (Clwyd), South West (Dyfed) and Glamorgan, Brecknockshire and Radnorshire. Monmouthshire was lumped into the English Oxford circuit. Though, if Monmouthshire was 'English', then Chester was 'Welsh', as that was the centre for the great session courts of Denbighshire and Flintshire in the north east.

Except in the opinion of the most anglophile, Monmouthshire was always Wales. The rule was that the county was treated 'as one with Wales rather than as a legal part of Wales'. When even the 1847 Report into Education treats Monmouthshire as part of Wales and quotes numerous examples of Welsh-speaking kids, it does call into question why this issue was given such prominence by some quarters. Various laws specific to Wales from the 1880s (in relation to closing public houses on Sunday, Intermediate Education and Cemeteries) saw Monmouth included as a part of Wales.

The historian John Davies's theory is that we have Cardiff's megalomania to thank for ensuring that Monmouthshire is part of Wales. As Edwardian Cardiff grew in the late nineteenth and early twentieth centuries, and aimed to achieve city status, its aldermen eyed the slow, polluted Rhymni river, the border between the two counties (and for some, two countries) which flowed out into an ever-growing Cardiff. Cardiff's city status ambitions were realised in 1905 and with it the city took control of the lower parts of the Rhymni. By doing so, it locked a part of Monmouthshire into Wales.

However, the status of Monmouthshire was still a topic of heated debate well into the twentieth century. It was the subject of a long detailed article by D. J. Davies in a 1936 issue of Plaid Cymru's *Welsh Nation* in which he warned, somewhat melodramatically, that Monmouthshire was 'Wales' Ulster'. Plaid Cymru continued to debate, petition and campaign on the question of the border well into the 1950s, and it wasn't only Plaid. The Labour MP for Abertyleri, Llywelyn Williams, was another voiciferous campaigner for confirmation of the county's Welsh status.

The letter-writing, stunts and MPs' questions succeeded, and by the 1960s, the common-sense view was that Monmouthshire was part of Wales. Whilst we can bemoan the nameless civil servant for drawing the border in the first place, we can also thank the nameless civil servants of Harold Wilson's Welsh Office, established exactly 430 years later in 1966, for bringing Monmouthshire back into the fold. As the long process for reorganising and streamlining Welsh local authorities was pushed from desk to desk in the 1960s, plans were laid for the *bara brith*-like dispersed specks of boroughs across Wales, including those in Monmouthshire to be streamlined and unified.

The definitive Local Government Act of 1972 stated unequivocally: 'In every act passed on or after 1 April 1974 'Wales', subject to any alterations of boundaries' included 'the administrative county of Monmouthshire and the county borough of Newport'. And that was it. Amen.

We can be grateful that we don't face the difficulty of our Breton and Basque friends whose historic territories are divided. The historic capital of Brittany, Naoned (Nantes – Cardiff's twin city), was divided from Brittany by the Nazi Vichy government and has been kept legally separate from the rest of Brittany since. It seems the French are ready to keep Nazi decisions when it suits them. Likewise the historic capital of the Basque lands, Iruña (Pamplona) in Navarre, is not part of the other three Basque provinces in the Spanish state – a legacy partly of Franco's divide and rule policies.

Monmouthshire was once bigger by a few square miles too, until an 1844 Act of Parliament abolished the county's four exclaves in England. One of those was Welsh Bicknor, a parish with the wonderful Welsh name of *Llangystennin Garth Brenni*, which lies on the border of Gloucestershire and Herefordshire. By this abolition Westminster denied us the all-important border dispute incumbent on all newly-independent states when freedom is gained!

Our border was drawn by others. One could almost be thankful that our border isn't further to the west, though Wales does, with the exception of Maelor Saesneg and the Wye Valley, start with the mountains.

But what am I saying! It's not further west because the whole of Wales became 'England' – its whole intention was to integrate Wales into England. It wasn't a national border, only the border between some new 'English' counties. 'The country or dominion of Wales shall stand and continue for ever henceforth incorporated united and annexed to and with this his Realm of England', as the Law says. That's why there is no Welsh badge on the Union flag – we are but a collection of English counties represented by the cross of St George.

But this border still isn't our only line on the map. Our border is still contested. The ecclesiastical border of the Church of Wales differs from the political border, with some parishes opting to stay with England and others joining the new Anglican community. Postcodes make Llanfihangel Genau'r-glyn a suburb of Birmingham, and Llanarmon-yn-Iâl a suburb of Chester. Severn Trent Water Authority takes a huge bite of Powys, gobbling up Welshpool, Llanidloes, Newtown, Llanfyllin, to grab the reservoirs of Clywedog, Fyrnwy and Elan. Many unions and large commercial companies still divide Wales as extensions of English conurbations.

Ours is a border which isn't a defence. The border between Wales and England became internalised. It was drawn as an expression of colonisation. As the French philosopher of Breton heritage, Ernest Renan, wrote of the situation of the former French citizens in Alsace after the territory had been incorporated into the new German Reich in 1870, their identity became a 'daily plebiscite'. Dealing with the new political situation became a daily, personal referendum with one's nationality, language and conscience.

It's this will to conduct the 'daily plebiscite' that has given Wales' border and its outline an iconic status. The image of the territory on the map is central to a nation's political identity. Wales has imagined the border into reality, as do all stateless nations ... and dominant nations don't.

All Welsh people could recognise a silhouetted outline of Wales in any context, just as all Scots, Bretons, Basques or Catalans could recognise their countries. But how many

English people could recognise the outline of England – not Britain, but England, without a shaded Wales to its west and Scotland to the north? How many French could recognise France without Brittany in the outline, or Castilians recognise Spain without Galicia, the Basque Country or Catalonia, or Walloons Belgium without Flanders? How many wish to? Isn't this the Freudian, geo-political slip? While minoritised nations have had to 'image' their country, the only perception the dominant have of their identity includes the dominated. Can there be an English nationalist movement before the English can recognise a silhouetted England-only on a map?

It could be argued that the border today is firmer and clearer than it has ever been. In fact, 1974 was probably the first time in Wales' 2,000-year history that we've had a definite, recognised border, and, since 1999, a functional one. Before then we Welsh occupied both sides of the line, and after Henry VIII's Laws of Wales the border had no constitutional dimension. Wales now exists, and it has no border dispute – a surprisingly rare occurrence in political geography.

The whole point of Henry VIII's Laws of Wales was *not* to create a border between Wales and England. The irony is that through our will he *did*. He created a border where there hadn't been one before.

Borders are good.

Cambria, Autumn 2012
(a summarised version of the article published online only)

Gwlad! Gwlad!:
Can I Love This Land?

The title of the article comes, of course, from the chorus of the Welsh National Anthem. The article tries to tackle my relationship – and I believe many Welsh people's relationship – with Welsh landscape.

There is a melancholy for me in the Welsh landscape – a sadness because its beauty is the cause of it no longer being Welsh. The land has left me. In many respects the fume-belching Port Talbot steelworks is prettier than any mist-defying Snowdon. Port Talbot is a place of honest work, where the accent of the street is my accent, not trendy bandana-wearing mountain cyclists, bearded mountain-climbers or dog-walkers, mutilating our mutations and our mountains. Snowdon – Yr Wyddfa – our national mountain – feels to me like Ararat feels to the Armenians: beyond our control. Like Mount Fujimori would to the Japanese if it were run by the Americans.

There is the sadness that we don't possess our own land – it being in the Crown's possession, or, thanks to the Labour Party, deliberately omitted from the 2006 Government of Wales Act. Wales is a big adventure and holiday playground. It is so different from the self-governing Basque Country whose topography is so similar to ours. There, every valley is bursting with factories and industry, creating wealth, work and sustaining a language and culture – not a place to play in, or to retire to.

With majestic mountains, the romantic valleys and the craggy coastline, a recent newspaper poll concluded that the Welsh landscape was one of the things which made people most proud of being Welsh. Me? Well, I'm not a great fan of landscape and especially so Welsh landscape. Snowdonia and its mountains? They're just geological faults.

There's a cynical voice in my head which says that landscape is for a nation which has nothing better to celebrate – no great cities, universities, literature, high art or science. More often than not, celebrating landscape seems to be celebrating *terra nullius* – empty land – a land empty of culture and language.

My feelings for so-called beautiful landscapes are but a step away from the story of the old boy from Anglesey on a rare trip outside the island. The old farmer was on a coach tour to see the 'sights of Snowdonia'. When his companion asked him of his view of the stunning scenery the old boy turned round and, with a sad, knowing look said, '*tir sâl*' (bad land, or literally, sick land). What was beautiful for tourists was barren land for the old farmer. The purpose of land was to sustain livelihoods. For me, the purpose of Welsh land is to sustain Welsh culture. When it fails in that, then it's just '*tir sâl*'. This is a rather melancholic reaction to my feelings of internal exile. I feel safer in towns and cities – there's less to disappoint.

For all its beauty, Welsh landscape seems only faintly to inspire Welsh-language literature. Our landscape is a yoke – the mountains only '*tir sâl*' for farmers, or 'beautiful' as they attract tourists. Welsh poetry – or poetry in Welsh in any case – if it discusses landscape at all, is concerned with the people who live there and sings in praise of the names of the streams and fields, villages and villagers. With the exception of R. Williams-Parry, the landscape is just a backdrop to the culture. One of the most famous poems which does describe Welsh nature is Gruffudd ab yr Ynad Goch's *marwnad* (lament) to the death of Llywelyn the Last in 1282. But his description of 'oak trees colliding' or the 'the sea engulfing the land' is an Armageddon image of the death of the Last Prince. In art, it's no coincidence that the most popular artists in Wales, the late Kyffin Williams and now Aneurin

Jones, are well-known for painting Welsh people in their Welsh landscapes.

Maybe the appreciation of an object changes with language. The colour *glas* (blue) in Welsh can mean anything from green to grey – slate is blue not grey: *llechen las* (blue slate); cows graze on *porfa las* (blue grass); a folk song sings of the lover knocking on the *gwydr glas* (blue glass) of his girlfriend's window. *Coch* (red) can be anything from dark yellow to brown; *te coch* is black tea, and if drunk from a white china cup it is red; tea is sweetened with *siwgwr coch* (brown sugar).

Maybe in Welsh we see mountains as words, great heaps of legends, poetry, folk and family history layered like a pile of scrabble pieces. When those words, those collections of memories, aren't pronounced or aren't remembered, the mountain is deflated, bereft of the oxygen that kept it standing tall. So many of the mountains of Wales, for me, are deflated, like punctured tyres in a forecourt. Our message then is: love our mountains – love our language.

Maybe this malaise at magnificence is historic. Maybe things happened too fast for us. We missed that generation or two from the mid-nineteenth century who were free of the grinding poverty of rural peasant life but hadn't yet succumbed to the fawning servitude of tourism. A time when we could have possessed, not been oppressed by, our landscape. Not for the Welsh the patriotic hiking clubs so enjoyed by the Young Czechs and Sokol societies. How can *Yr Wyddfa* (Snowdon) be a patriotic icon like Slovenia's Triglav, which appears on their flag, when the most famous poetry it's inspired is *Hogia'r Wyddfa*'s jolly, schoolchild ditty about the '*trên bach*' (the little train)? And in any case, why should we show affection to a landscape which has treated us so badly? Mountains meant poverty. Mountains now mean colonisation. The mountains were our millstones.

And so, as the Baltic nations began their road to self-respect and independence in 1988, it was a great shock for me to learn that Estonia wasn't mountainous and that Latvia possessed no narrow valleys, but were rather flat and forested lands. I had thought all small countries were, by default, mountainous! And then, in 2008, as Wales treads its own Baltic Way, I realised that an appreciation and love of Welsh landscape can unite people, whatever their background. Maybe it's time I stopped sulking about my landscape and started embracing it.

The questions are, of course, which landscape and what kind of landscape? At the Fishguard Eisteddfod of 1986 the late artist Paul Davies made a massive relief of Wales from the very soil of the Eisteddfod field. A powerful, almost playful, grabbing of the very land that he loved. An act of possession and respect for the history and contours of Wales – a land and future there to be moulded. Welsh soil moulded by the hands of a Welsh worker. I dare say Paul was ahead of his time. Our landscape is there to be respected and moulded, as the purpose of Welsh soil (as the old farmer would understand) is to sustain Welsh lives ... and nurture Welsh culture.

What has historically been the weakness of Wales – our small mountainous size is – I now realise, our strength. The twenty-first century will be good for Wales and our landscape – if we possess it. We've inherited (not always in the best of health) a fantastic land and excellent future ... Wales has many challenges but our size and population are pretty much ideal.

The power of Wales' topography is there for all to see, though it is yet to be fully harnessed. We're sitting on a goldfield quite as rich as the black gold which disfigured our valleys. An abundance of rain and a small population is our jackpot. Some 4,500 mm of rain falls each year over Blaenau

Ffestiniog compared with 701.0 mm for Tunbridge Wells. And it's not just Blaenau. Swansea is officially the UK's wettest city, with 1,200 mm per annum. Barcelona, for all its style, has water shortages, and there is more rainfall per person in the Sahara than in East Anglia. We could export water as Arabs export oil.

Forget the old lie that Wales is 'too poor' to be independent. Those in power in Westminster know we're not. It would be comic were it not true, but in an almost nineteenth-century colonial grab, Section 101 of the Labour Party's Government of Wales Act 2006 states which competences the Welsh Assembly should have and which it shouldn't. Powers devolved to the Assembly do not include those which Nigel Johnson, Principal Lecturer in Law at Sheffield Hallam University, concluded are 'incompatible with international obligations or the interests of defence or national security; or might have a serious adverse effect on water resources, water supply or water quality in England'. Welsh water is as important as nuclear submarines.

Forget Scotland's North Sea oil, this is more important and potent. It's important because not only does Wales have a surfeit of wet stuff falling from the sky – it also has a comparatively small population, which means that we can export a vast amount of water. There will be no 'Peak Welsh Water'. If the Senedd was a sovereign parliament would not a Welsh Government vote to drown valleys to build new reservoirs? But this time on our own terms. This year Barcelona came within a month of having to ship drinking water for its citizens. Its water shortage was compounded by the increase of Catalonia's population from 6 to 7 million. England's population is expected to increase from 50 to 68 million by 2050, with south-east England affected most, even though England is already four times more densely population that France. Wales's relatively small population is therefore a comparative advantage – and another reason for developing sustainable population strategies in addition to economically sustainable ones.

Take energy. I can do no better than quote an article by Adam Price MP, published in the Welsh-language weekly, *Golwg*:

> Wales currently produces 8.8 per cent of the UK's electricity and will start exporting to Ireland in 2012 when the new inter-connector is completed. Even the decommissioning of Wylfa's twin turbine 980MW reactor will not dent Wales energy export success as five new power stations with a total generating capacity of well over 4000 MW are due to come on stream.

We have a vast potential for developing renewables. We are, as Paul Allen of the Centre for Alternative Technology has said, the 'Saudi Arabia of renewable energy'. We can boast the world's largest biomass plant and soon the world's largest energy wave converter off the coast of Milford Haven. We are still well placed to create the world's first tidal lagoon. And, then (though personally I have my doubts) there is the Severn Barrage. Add to this the significant potential of offshore-wind and genuine clean coal technologies such as underground coal gasification and coal-bed methane – then Wales looks as if it's won the natural lottery.

But Price makes a point which the flawed Government of Wales Act underlines:

> Energy policy in Wales is sadly not dictated by the needs of Wales. Power stations are being built to plug the English power generation gap rather than as part of a sustainable energy policy for Wales. It's great to

see Wales developing a successful energy sector and we could turn Wales into a renewable energy exporter like Denmark. But why didn't the planning consents for these new power stations insist that their waste heat – in the case of RWEs Pembroke mega-plant, equivalent to half Wales's entire electricity output – was used to heat local homes through combined-heat-and power systems? This is largely because the decision was made in London and was more about powering-up the UK grid than meeting Welsh demand. That has to change if we are to move Wales forward.

It's not about punishing England; it's about making the best of *our* assets. Independence will give us the means to make interdependence work for us.

Utilising our land for energy is just one part of the benefits that await us, and that needs to happen. Why is it that Wales seems to go from one mono industry to another – first coal and then sheep? We have 11 million sheep and yet 3 million people. There is great potential for lamb to be sold abroad but meadows full of sheep aren't a sign of strength. They're a badge of our failure and the sooner there are fewer of them the better. Good land, which only a few generations ago was fields of orchards, wheat or vegetables, is wasted in turning our country into a Sahel of sheep. Lands which could be a patchwork of plants and profits are given over to the high-pasture equivalent of deep-sea trawling, destroying our grasses, flowers and wildlife. We could diversify our produce and also diversify our wildlife. We could repopulate our rivers with beavers, and try to reintroduce the five species of butterfly which died out in Wales during the last century. We could also protect and promote our brown hares, water voles and lapwings, whose numbers have declined disastrously.

But there are aspects of the environmental movement which seem to be in conflict with Welsh interests and Welsh geography. The recent protest by some green activists against the liquid natural gas pipeline from Milford Haven to Gloucester was bizarre. More incredibly: the protest was supported by some nationalists. In other parts of the world countries employ lobbying consultants to build pipelines across their territory. Despite lobbying by the Armenian government, BP's Baku-Tbilisi-Ceyhan pipeline from Azerbaijan's Caspian oilfields, for instance, has been deliberately routed the long way round via Georgia to the Turkish port of Ceyhan so as to avoid benefiting Armenia. Belarus's strongest political card is that it is a pivotal transit route into for the 2,500-mile Druzhba pipeline, which carries one fifth of Russia's oil export to Central Europe. In Wales, some would like to stop this vital asset and income generator.

It's time we followed Paul Davies's example and moulded our landscape in our own image and on our own national terms. That means utilising our *tir sâl* to become *tir da* (good land). It means not resisting every possible development nor selling ourselves cheaply. It means working with our landscape to make it work for us. After all, the purpose of that land is to sustain a varied and unique living Welsh culture as well as an ecoculture. It is our land which will make the twenty-first century the Welsh century.

Cambria, vol. 10, no. 2, July–August 2008

Raise a 'peint' for Europe!

Of course, there's a lot written in the name of Europe.

'Europe' can be used by some as dog-whistling xenophobia against people of different races, Muslims and the USA.

Likewise, to be European for others is to celebrate diversity of culture and languages of the Premiere League, like French or Spanish. That makes you cultured. But if you wish to celebrate smaller languages, like Welsh or Basque, then you're relegated to the lower league of the halitosis-hunched trolls shouting against progress and internationalism.

It's good to celebrate and enjoy European culture as long as we also remember it was European culture that caused genocide and war on this continent and every other continent in the world. Promoting our children to speak another European language is also good but I'd despair if that meant that children of non-European languages, such as Igbo, Punjabi or Somali, were not also counted as valuable cultural and economic assets by our schools and society.

Having said all that, I'm very glad to live in Europe and do feel on some practical level 'European'. The wonder of Europe is that is it so small. One can catch an aeroplane and within 2½ hours – the time it takes to travel from Cardiff to Aberystwyth by car – you could be in up to a dozen different states and countries, speaking different languages, eating different foods, smooching about in different streets and architecture … and hopefully not killing one another for another generation.

On hearing of Cwrw Llŷn's wild goose chase to get the word 'peint' inscribed on their pint glass it seemed to say something about Wales, Britain and Europe. Iechyd da!

Cwrw Llŷn is a cooperative brewery based in the town of Nefyn. A little story about their struggle to get the word '*peint*' engraved on to their pint glasses got me thinking about their (and Wales') relationship with Europe.

One of the founders of the brewery is the entrepreneur Myrddin ap Dafydd, who started the venture not only to quench the thirst of Welsh drinkers but also keep money circulating within Wales rather than flowing out to the bingeing FTSE-listed beer monsters. The company was founded in 2011 and now employs twelve people. In 2012 it decided to produce custom-made pint glasses engraved with the company name and logo to serve their four ales rooted in Llŷn's rich history and present culture: 'Brenin Enlli', 'Seithenyn', 'Cochyn' and 'Y Brawd Houdini. Myrddin told me:

> The glasses arrived and looked very nice. However, also inscribed on the glasses were the English crown and the word 'pint'. We felt that this went against our branding and undermined our selling point as a local Welsh firm that we'd spent time trying to cultivate.

They contacted the glass company and asked if the next stock could include the word '*peint*' rather than 'pint'. The glass company readily agreed to the request if Cwrw Llŷn could produce a letter by the local Trading Officer stating that this was acceptable.

'I thought the whole thing would be over in an afternoon!' Myrddin recalled wistfully.

Little did he expect that such a simple request would take so much time and bring the whole issue of Europe to the little Llŷn peninsula brewery.

Cwrw Llŷn contacted Eifion Huws, of Gwynedd's Trade Standards Department. They were supportive of the request and noted that the UK law said clearly that the word 'pint' should appear, but of course this took no consideration of the different language laws in Wales.

Gwynedd County Council's legal department's response was that there was no specific reference or restriction to the language used, only that the imperial measurement had to be denoted 'in pints'. Gwynedd's interpretation was that it was totally valid to note the measurement in Welsh. However, this interpretation was rejected by the British Trading Standard's head office, and so Cwrw Llŷn contacted the National Measurement Office in London. But the reaction there was also negative. The officer there claimed the directive from the European Union was that 'the word 'pint' or the symbol 'pt' must be used' – although this wasn't the exact wording of the rules. To Myrddin, this seemed like:

> an example of a fabled Eurocrat baddie being used by a Britocrat to defend London's authority and the English language. Furthermore, the Britocrat claimed that recent Welsh language laws in Wales could not be used to undermine an English word – the word 'peint' was evidently a threat to the word 'pint'.

Cwrw Llŷn wouldn't take no for an answer.

The brewery took the matter to the office of the newly-established Welsh Language Commissioner, who then raised the matter with the European Commission. In January 2013 a clear answer was given by the Commission that European rules do not in fact limit the languages which are used when denoting a measurement, and that there was not a ban on the Welsh word, *'peint'*.

The European response was relayed to the National Measurement Office in London, asking them to reassess their position.

In February 2012 the Office changed their reason for being against *'peint'* from blaming Europe to saying that the use of the Welsh *'peint'* could mislead people who didn't understand Welsh.

At the time of writing the matter is still in contention but for Myrddin ap Dafydd the issues raised were clear.

'It's one example of how Europe can open the door for the Welsh language and Welsh culture, whilst London closes it,' mused Myrddin.

Now, Cwrw Llŷn's campaign to get 'peint' inscribed on a pint glass is hardly a heroic battle against nasty English-language oppression. It's neither a Tryweryn nor a Welsh Not and is certainly nothing to compare with the great injustices and suffering in the world. Even Myrddin, who's spent more time on this small issue than it warrants, would probably agree with that.

But Myrddin also refused to view the world through a British paradigm. It's the paradigm which leads the Welshman to shrug his defeated shoulder with a 'well-that's-how-things-are-ism'. Myrddin's petty war of a word throws a small but significant light on the nature of power and politics and where it rests: Wales, London or 'Europe'.

If the issue of inscribing 'peint' was so trivial, then why wouldn't the Britocrat just let it pass? Would anyone, even a drunk tourist in Pwllheli inadvertently empting the lager over his mate as he was baffled by the word 'peint' at the bottom of his glass, not understand that 'peint' meant 'pint'? Why would a Eurocrat – presumably having to take into account the anguish of foreign-speaking Greeks, Finns or Maltese visiting Welsh pubs – be relaxed about the elbowing 'e', but a Britocrat not?

The word 'pint' (and 'peint') itself comes from the Old French 'pinte' (and possibly the Latin 'picta' before that, which means 'painted') denoting a mark made to measure the drink. There was a French 'pinte du roi' and in Quebec 'un pinte' equals a quart. In parts of the Netherlands and France '*une pinte*' is 500ml whilst a '*pintje*' in Flanders is 250ml. The word itself and its meaning then does vary, it has been a word for a measurement of liquid.

But the British were proud of their pint and were concerned at European efforts to bring conformity to the weights and measurements. They didn't want to convert their measurements from imperial to metric. The British campaign to save the imperial system was so deeply felt that it appealed to UNESCO's Agreement to defend Intangible Cultural Heritage. The Eurocrat view, so we're told, was that imperial measurements brought confusion and disharmony and that Europe needed to agree on one simple continent-wide measurements – the metric system.

And this is the irony. The same arguments used by the British state against using '*peint*' (confusion, the need for conformity) were the same ones the British state accused the EU of using against their imperial pints, pounds and miles. The imperial measurements were seen as a badge of British identity and tradition. But surely, couldn't the Welsh language be just as equal to the centrality to Welsh identity? And, whilst we're at it, let's bring back the Welsh mile, which was standardised in Hywel Dda's laws a thousand years ago. The '*milltir*' (a word we see today on our road signs) was in fact a '*mil tir*' (thousand 'land'). A '*tir*' was made of three '*cam*' (stride) which was itself made of three '*troedfedd*' (foot). So, a Welsh mile was 27,000 feet, or, just under four English miles. We lost that to some Anglocrat in the Act of Union!

So, there we are, the word pint became one of national interest and international contention. Europe was being scapegoated for creating awkward laws, when in fact it hadn't. The four letter word showed up two different answers to the problem of Welsh, giving us a European and a British answer. Europe can be seen as a threat to Britishness, but is it a threat to Welshness?

A small nation has to align itself with a power block. It will never have total freedom of movement. The power block the Welsh chose for most of their recent history was Britain.

Since the last Catholic Counter Reformers of the sixteenth century, the Welsh by and large, have seen an English state and later British state as the best and only vehicle of Welsh national interest. The British Empire was so vast and so successful that it was a continent unto itself. Added to that was the Pax Britannica and Europe seemed a troublesome, quarrelsome place full of garlic-eating Catholics and dogmatic revolutionaries.

The Welsh, unlike the Irish, have been unable to imagine another future and identity as a European nation. In 1797 a revolutionary French force landed in Fishguard and the Welsh fought for the English crown. In 1798 a revolutionary French force landed in Wexford and the Irish fought with them against the English crown. The Welsh have been consistently un-heroic.

It's not that the Welsh culture was ever insular. It tickles me, for instance, to think that the minor nobility of medieval Glamorgan could have known of faraway Tibet 100 years before their class peers in England. Thanks to *Ffordd y Brawd Odrig*, a Welsh translation of the popular Latin account of Brother Odoric of Pordenone's journey to China and India between 1318 and 1330, the Welsh *uchelwyr* (gentry) knew of '*y'r vrenhiniaeth a elwir Tubec*' (the kingdom known as Tibet) in their own language.

But, whilst the Welsh were open to the world and even created Welsh communities abroad, they seem never to have imaged Wales as a national community at home. Maybe the radical Baptist and supporter of Thomas Paine and the French revolution, Morgan John Rhys of Llanbradach in Gwent, is the clearest example of what I'm trying to say.

In 1794, just a year after founding *Y cylchgrawn Cyn-*

mraeg ('the Welsh magazine' - Rhys had his own peculiar spelling of 'Cymraeg') to promote his radical ideas, fed-up with living under the Crown, Rhys immigrated to America where he founded a Welsh colony, Cambria, in Pennsylvania. That is, it was easier for Rhys, intellectually and physically, to imagine and create a radical Welsh-speaking homeland at the other side of the world than here in Wales! Despite his intellectual ability and fluent French, he couldn't imagine Wales being a political nation in the way Wolfe Tone could imagine Ireland, as he led the United Irishmen rebellion four years later.

Why is this?

For all its many faults, did Catholicism, married with the radical ideas of the Dissenters, offer the Irish a European connection which Welsh Protestantism on its own never did?

And it's partly through Catholicism that we come to Emrys ap Iwan (1853–1906) one of the earliest Welsh nationalists, to see the emergence of a distinct European Welsh dimension. Although he remained true to his Protestant denomination he believed that Catholicism was a more able vehicle for national sentiment. In his famous book *Breuddwyd Pabydd wrth ei Ewyllys* he even imagines a Catholic Wales in the year 2012.

He was born Robert Ambrose Jones in Abergele and was proud that his great-grandmother was French. He left school at fourteen and worked as a draper in Liverpool and later as a gardener in Bodelwyddan. He believed the Welsh language should have official status and believed in Welsh self-government within a British federation. He even invented a Welsh word for self-government: '*ymreolaeth*'. At eighteen he studied at the Theological College in Bala and then abroad in Lausanne, Bonn and Gießen, where he learnt French and German. His nationalist beliefs led to the Welsh Presbyterian Church initially refusing to ordain him.

In October 1889, at court in Rhuthun, he represented and defended a Welsh farmhand who spoke no English. When asked to plead on the farmhand's behalf, ap Iwan answered '*Cymraeg yng Nghymru, os gwelwch yn dda!*' (Welsh in Wales, please). This was probably the first Welsh-language protest in a law court and created a storm. His European experience placed him and his ideas out of step with his generation, until they were picked up again in the 1920s.

The next Welsh protest in court wasn't until Saunders Lewis spoke Welsh (and was similarly admonished) at the trial of the Penyberth Three in 1937 (he and two others had set fire to some buildings as a protest against a proposed bombing school in Llŷn which had been opposed on all sides, without response from the British authorities). Saunders Lewis had converted to Catholicism and was great admirer of Emrys ap Iwan. Like him also, Lewis saw Wales as a European nation. It was after this stand by Saunders Lewis that in 1942 Welsh was partially allowed to be used in court, almost exactly 400 years after it was banned.

Seeing Wales as an active European nation, as Emrys ap Iwan, then Saunders did, is a powerful vision. It's powerful because it changes the rules of nationality – for the concept of agreeing to a nationality is that you agree to a set rules decided by the majority. The concept of a British nation compels Wales to agree to the rules of the majority of the British nation – a majority who are not Welsh. However, as there is no such thing as a European nation, Wales has greater freedom to see itself as a nation among many.

That's not to say that Europe, or more precisely, the European Union, is an unmitigated good thing. Is there any good in substituting Westminster for Brussels or blindly being 'good Europeans'? I tend to agree with the traditional Conservative view of the European Union that it would have been better to have a wider rather than a deeper union.

The 'Wales in Europe' slogan of the early 1990s was powerful because it gave Wales a new mirror to look at itself. The self-image was new to many Welsh people. Many believed for the first time in the 1990s that a map of Europe, as outlined in Leopold Kohr's *Breakdown of Nations* in 1957, was possible. Indeed this vision is still possible, and more likely now than ever before as the Catalans and Scots discuss independence.

Kohr believed that a Europe based on the historic nations and regions would be a safer and better place. Pointing to the First World War, in which the French and Germans went to battle, he asked would the war have been so bloody if there was no France, Germany or Britain? Would Bretons have gone to war with Bavarians? What fight did the Welsh have with the Swabians, or Czechs with Scots? And, if there was war, what would be most dangerous: a war between a small Austria and Serbia, or a war between an Austrian and Russian empire?

By intention, or law of unforeseen consequences, the concept of Europe has helped promote Welsh identity and the political identity of other historic nations in a similar way to Kohr's ideas. James Wilkie, of the Scottish-UN Committee, for instance, argues that it was the Council of Europe's little recognised Charter of Local Self-Government in the mid-1990s which ultimately forced the new Labour government to go ahead with the referendum on Welsh and Scottish devolution that has now led to a situation where independence is being discussed in Scotland.

The Council, a body independent of the European Union, formed the Congress of Local and Regional Authorities of Europe in January 1994. Its goal was to ensure 'the existence of a solid local and regional democracy in conformity with the principle of subsidiarity included in the (1985) European Charter of Local Self-Government'. Having insisted that the newly-liberated former Soviet states adhere to 'European norms' of democracy and devolution of power from highly centralised states, it was seen as being rather hypocritical if the same logic wasn't applied to the established states of Western Europe – including the UK. This was a charter the UK didn't want to sign.

As Wilkie wrote in an article on NewsnetScotland.com online news site in February 2012:

> In March 1997, a few weeks before the election that brought Tony Blair's Labour government to power, the Council of Europe pointedly spelled out the sanctions that would be applied, in a series of escalating steps, to any European state that did not 'fully and swiftly comply with the basic democratic principles that are at the heart of the European Ideal.'
>
> In plain language, get Scotland, Wales, etc. sorted out or be expelled from the Council of Europe in the most humiliatingly public manner – a step that would have had devastating international consequences, especially just a few weeks before the UK presidency of the European Union.

The rest, as they say, is history.

One can argue that there were other, stronger, political reasons for Labour to go ahead with Scotland and Wales's Devolution Referendum – not least that there were very many people in the Labour party who had campaigned for it! But the mood of optimism and hope which Europe experienced after the fall of the Berlin Wall, and the emergence of new small states, helped change the suspicious Cold War stalemate which had made Devolution seem more of a risk in 1979.

The Springtime of Nations optimism of the 1990s has changed to a more cynical view of Europe today.

Whilst demanding money back from Europe plays well to

the nation of British national interest, from the perspective of a Welsh national interest it can be very damaging. It means, for example, money which has historically come from European Union structural funds not coming to Wales, coupled with UK central government policies that also, due to the Barnett Formula, are not being transferred to Wales. That is, the EU and UK Governments are under-investing in Wales, and our feeble Assembly doesn't have any independent means through taxation or the ability to borrow money to stimulate the Welsh economy. We suffer a double whammy, falling between two stools. And then of course there's the German question to contend with.

Frankly the threat that we would 'all be speaking German' had we lost two world wars, or that Germany is ruling Europe by economic domination, doesn't sound so frightening from a Welsh economic point of view. An economy like Wales which was strong on manufacturing but weak in the finance sector would have been better off as the seventeenth German Land than as a UK region. And in any case, what's wrong with speaking German?

If Germany is 'too big' for the European Union, with her priorities dominating the Euro and the continent today, would it not be an idea for us to heed Günther Grass' words at the time of German unification in 1989? The author of *Tin Drum* was against uniting former Communist East Germany with West Germany, and famously said he liked Germany so much he wanted more than one of them! If there were a few more 'Germanies' (an independent Bavaria and Saxony, for instance), Europe's 'German problem' would cease to be, with no harm done to German language or culture.

But of course, the Germanophobes and Eurosceptics will not promote this idea, because the conclusion of the logic of fragmenting Germany would be to devolve Britain, France and Spain to smaller sizes, and those imperial states will never willingly agree to that.

And so, we Welsh are left with a conundrum. The concept of Europe can, on the one hand, be a great defender and promoter of our small nation – as Cwrw Llŷn's *'peint'* issue proves – but we can also be marginalised by the larger core states with a united Europe.

From a Machiavellian point of view, and to promote our Welsh national interest, Wales needs to see Europe replace the UK as the supra-national arbiter of power and ambition. A small nation such as Wales needs a vehicle for the ambitious, the talented and the egotistical to realise their own personal aggrandisement. It is better for Wales that this personal aggrandisement is on a European stage and that these Napoleons see Europe as this vehicle for power, rather than Westminster. It is better to see a Welsh politician play his part as a Welshman in a European supra-state than, as we saw with Lloyd George, a talented Welsh politician tie in his personal ambition with the national interest of the British state.

Wales therefore needs to seek partners within Europe. This would sometimes mean sharing our sovereignty at a British level and other times with countries of similar size and economy across Europe. It wouldn't mean always defending a unique maximalist Welsh line (like retaining our own unique measurements from Hywel Dda's time) and it would sometimes be similar to a British position. But if it is a British position in Europe, then, like the spelling of *'peint'*, it's right we retain our own unique voice and priorities.

Unpublished article

Politics

Grandparent Yet?:
Demography, the Mother of all Politics

This article is another one filed under 'Too embarrassing and damaging to my career?' (It's a long category, by the way!).

Discussing demography is always awkward. Awkward because it's so easy to offend people. And I have. Not from intention but by default. For those of my many gay or childless friends: this is not a finger-pointing article.

However, not discussing or recognising its underlying effects doesn't make it go away any more than ignoring climate change (which is closely related to it) does.

The media has recently woken up to China's demographic challenge following its one-child policy. Back in little Wales, the number of Welsh-speakers was decreasing even during the baby-boom decades when we had replacement-level births. The turmoil and revolution in the Arabic world is driven by demography. Demography matters. It can't be controlled and all predictions should be treated with scepticism – including those in this article – because, thankfully, people and women are not robots but individuals.

However, I'm convinced that the laissez-faire attitude towards demography that was a particular response to the unique golden years after the Second World War will soon be seen for the peculiar phenomenon it was.

In the Welsh context this manifests itself, for instance, in an education policy which is totally relaxed with up to 50 per cent of our young people leaving Wales to study at university (most not to return), whilst we then 'have to' import young people from outside Wales to work here. At its most dogmatic laissez-faire manifestation the population policy encourages migration to a country whilst a significant section of its society is under employed. By doing so it helps create an underclass happy in the knowledge that motivated people from poorer economies will undertake the menial work. This was the Labour policy of the first decade of the millennium and is the American model.

With world-wide female emancipation and education, the world's population growth is starting to slow down. There will always be movements of people – and thank god for that – but states will be forced to think and plan a little more. Retirement ages will rise and better use will have to be made of existing populations. In an increasing number of states, from South East Asia to Eastern Europe, policies will have to be developed to retain its population and reach replacement levels of childbirth.

For the particular situation of 'small' language communities like Welsh, then we already can't afford to be so ready to see so many of our young people leave after the financial, cultural and linguistic investment we've made in them. But first of all, we have to wake up and be honest: we can't hope to revive Welsh and make Wales a 'bilingual nation' if a below-replacement-level number of children are born here. We need to be clever, humane, understanding, but more than anything, we need to be honest.

For that I make no apology.

Do you take part in Wales and the western world's most popular parlour game? It goes by different titles in different places, but tends to be called 'Are you a grandparent yet?' It's the game played by the over-60s as they fret they may never have the chance to enjoy being a grandparent as their own children lead a childfree life.

Every game has rules, and the rules of 'Are you a grandparent yet?' are simple. Everyone can play it but it won't be discussed by politicians or the media. Sure, the media reports that schools are closing because of lack of pupils, or that there aren't enough workers in one sector or another. But nobody in Wales – neither government, media, quangos, nor educationalists – will actually discuss seriously what is blindingly obvious: that we are facing massive problems because our birth rate is so low. With the exception of *Barn*, the Welsh-language current affairs magazine, no media organ in Wales has commissioned an article or programme about the subject. Our 'intelligentsia' has its collective head in the sand whilst a demographic tsunami is about to hit us.

I should, therefore, not have been at all surprised when I received a phone call not from BBC Cymru/Wales but from BBC Radio 4's 'You and Yours' programme, wanting to discuss an article I'd written for *Barn* on the subject. Yes, someone sitting in London commissioned the first documented and researched item in the media about the effects of a low birth rate on a minority language like Welsh. It was broadcast on Wednesday 6 October 2006.

First let's have some facts. Demographers regularly quote 2.1 or 2.2 children as the average number of children that need to be born per mother if a community is to maintain population numbers. The 2 covers both parents and the 0.1 makes up for those who, for whatever reason, haven't conceived. Any birth rate below that, and a community has to absorb others from outside for it to function and continue. The average birth rate in the UK is 1.7, although, in many parts of rural Wales (coincidentally the most Welsh-speaking parts, Gwynedd, Ceredigion, Môn) the rate is lower.

This fall in the birth rate is still too recent a statistic for demographers to digest its effects fully, but responsible and mature states (amongst which Wales, alas, is not numbered) are already doing sums and preparing for knock-on effects.

There is a feeling among our political elite that discussing the birth rate is somehow beyond the pale. How else can one explain the complete absence of serious discussion about a matter which will affect each and every one of us? What's the point of having a University of Wales when such a body fails to produce either serious research papers or hosts conferences on the perhaps the most significant subject affecting Welsh life?

The media is no better. Is it because so many of our media people are blinded by a left-wing perspective that the subject isn't even on the agenda? We're used to seeing whole programme strands and newspaper articles devoted to the projected effects of climate change on our planet in thirty years time (traditionally a left-wing concern), but what about a series on Wales and the world in thirty years' time if current birth trends continue? As part of its mission statement the Welsh Assembly is committed to an assessment of the environmental impact on all its policies. We discuss 'environmental sustainability' but what about 'population sustainability'? After all, there is very little the Welsh Assembly Government, or any of our politicians, can do about the Amazonian rainforest or Chinese carbon emissions, but there is something they can do about our birth rate.

Of course, for those who believe that there is nothing intrinsically worth passing on in Welsh culture, and for those who do not wish to see the Welsh language flourish in any meaningful way, the fall in the birth rate is something to be welcomed. This can all be done comfortably under the guise of progressive internationalism – keeping the global population down whilst encouraging more people to move into Wales to work – people who, from experience, most probably won't learn Welsh.

Let's be clear. 'Demography,' as one linguist said, 'is the mother of all politics'. The combined effects of a low birth-rate and a movement of people into Wales will change, and has changed Wales. I'll come to this in a moment, but let's first try and work out what's happening. I have no interest in an ethnically pure Wales (isn't it tiresome that I feel I must state that!). Nor do I wish to see women chained to the *Kinder, Kirche, Küche* (children, church, kitchen) rôle so thoughtfully alliterated for us in German. My concern for the low birth rate is motivated by a deep concern for the economic, social and environmental future of Wales and, more pressingly, the future health of the Welsh language. Nothing I have read suggests to me that a minority language (and culture) can flourish under the pressure of the triple effects of immigration, outward migration and low birth rate. Equally, nothing I have read produced by the Welsh Language Board, the Welsh Assembly Government nor Plaid Cymru suggests the issue has been, or is being, discussed at all.

The UK birth rate of 1.7 is, by European standards, comparatively healthy (compare with Greece, Spain and Italy at 1.3). Only the socialist – or corporatist – Scandinavian countries are higher (Denmark and Norway 1.8, and Iceland 2.0). And here's the irony: it's the left-wing that has the best policies to tackle Europe's depleting birth rate as they follow a 'feminist' agenda that recognises economic reality and career aspirations, by promoting child care and longer maternity leave. But it is the right-wing that seems to be raising the low birth rate as a political issue.

However, these figures hide an even grimmer prospect for the Welsh language. The fact is that the birth rate of the Welsh-language community is closer to the euthanasiac East European one, where a very low birth rate is exacerbated by large-scale emigration. Alarm-bells already ring out in the corridors of the Kremlin at their low birth rate, and Estonia has initiated a campaign to make it easier for those who want children to raise them. All this is cause for concern and the subject of serious articles at conferences in respected communities and on discussion sites. The Welsh-speaking community is facing a similar – if not worse – demographic trend than our East European friends, yet the body responsible for the language, and our government itself, have yet to issue a single sentence.

Let's look honestly at the situation. Taking the UK and Wales average of 1.7 children, if we factor in that up to a third of Welsh-speakers don't pass on Welsh to their children, then the true Welsh-language community reproduction rate is something closer to Slovakia, Ukraine and Poland's 1.2. Of course, that's just this generation. The next generation will be starting from a smaller number of potential parents – unless, of course, a large amount of people of child-bearing age move into Wales. But what percentage of them would learn Welsh, or whose children, going though our useless linguistic sieve of a school system, would acquire Welsh? Needless to say, Wales has nothing to say about this, although other nations in similar situations, Taiwan (1.2 children) Hong Kong (1.0), even guilt-ridden Germany (1.3) are mature enough to discuss it.

WAG and the WLB will emphasise support for the Welsh nursery movement, *Mudiad Ysgolion Meithrin*, and *Twf* (growth), an agency which tries to promote parents and prospective parents to raise their children to speak both Welsh and English. The support of both these movements is all very well, cute and cuddly, but totally insufficient. What use are more Welsh-medium nurseries when there are no children to attend them? There are 80,000 fewer children in Wales now than there were ten years ago. 80,000?! What kind of a Government doesn't freeze in fear when it hears a figure like that?

What are the implications? For Welsh they are truly catastrophic. Not only are the numbers of Welsh-speaking hearths decreasing, and so a decrease in the 'normalcy' of

Welsh and the ability to integrate non-Welsh speakers, but the number of potential Welsh-speakers is also decreasing. For a minority language to flourish it needs to hold on to its existing community (which Welsh is doing only by two-thirds), but it also needs to absorb new members. The most effective way of doing this is through the education system, and Welsh-medium education at that. Even so-called 'bilingual schools' are ineffective and sell a false premise to parents of 'proficiency in both languages' (which may be one reason that some politicians support them instead of the Welsh-medium equivalent). Put simply, if the Welsh language is to grow, then the number of Welsh-speaking children from non-Welsh-speaking households also needs to increase. One hopes that a coherent education system and the parents' wish to invest Welsh in their children will lead to growth. Policies to make it easier for those who wish to have more children should be targeted right across the board, irrespective of their language, nationality or ethnicity.

There are other effects of 80,000 fewer children. Who will pay the pensions of an increasingly ageing population? In areas like Gwynedd, Môn, the north Wales coast, and Ceredigion, this is complicated by the phenomenon of older people moving into these areas – creating an extra burden on an already low-birth rate area – the very point Simon Glyn made in 2001, much to the chagrin of the political establishment. The same problem of ageing (but for slightly different reasons) faces the Valleys where school numbers have plummeted, but whose politicians have yet to say a word.

Politically Wales is set to become a more conservative and uninteresting place. A culture dominated by the agenda and tastes of older people is doomed. The Zeitgeist is able to sniff the smell of a crumbling culture a mile away; any attractive young culture will not be Welsh (or in English with a Welsh accent), and will probably not even be western.

Birth rate is everything. In the eastern Baltic during the Soviet occupation, Estonia was more Russified than Lithuania not because of any calculated colonisation plan by Moscow, but because, as the historian Anatol Lieven points out, the birth rate in Lithuania was greater than that of Estonia, so there was less need for Lithuania to import workers. Conversely, the French language gained status in 1960s Quebec because of what is called the 'silent revolution' in that, for a generation, the more traditional, Catholic, French-speaking Quebecois had more children than their English-speaking neighbours. This led to an increase in numbers; and because there were more youths, a youthful and thus attractive and confident French political movement and culture came out on top.

What's so wrong with our own political culture that this subject isn't even being mentioned and discussed? Is it a fear of association – of being pigeonholed with Mussolini's Monty Pythonesque 'Medals for Motherhood'? Is it the Nonconformist burden and the madcap idea that Wales can save the world – that if we have no kids then we'll have done our bit against global over-population? This is one argument I heard from a left-wing Welsh nationalist, an argument which is shocking in its naivete and self-loathing – was he actually saying there were too many Welsh people in the world?

So why has the Welsh and UK birth rate decreased, yet the overall population is increasing? This is partly because of increased longevity, and partly because the state needs a workforce to keep the whole economy going unless people want an economic collapse on the scale of 1990s Russia. If it's not children born in Wales doing the work then it's the children of other people from other countries – the same 'carbon foot-print' but with different people.

What on earth is wrong with Welsh-speakers that such an obvious problem for the Welsh language isn't mentioned in polite society? Nobody's calling for women to have eight kids, and there's no need for the anti-gay sentiment of previous times nor any reason to stigmatise those who can't have or don't want children. Surely we are past that sixth-form period. But this is a debate that affects us all.

The intellectual and moral failure of our leaders is deep-rooted. The Welsh-language movement is largely a child of the 1960s conversing in the politics of a stable sustainable birth rate. It's unable and unwilling to comprehend that it's now a whole new ball game. It asks for one last Herculean heave in status politics whilst the very ground crumbles beneath their feet. They're like a flat-earther ranting against scientific reality. The historiography taught in our schools and universities is similarly locked in a teleological Enlightenment thought-trap. It's moved on from the histories of 'Great Men' to the history of thought and the mundane but is yet to move to the history of demography. Our political class is a collective slave to the market force of votes. The very politicians who tell us we need migrant labour because our workforce is shrinking are the very ones who shout down those who propose that a sustainable increase in the birth rate will solve this very problem.

From Taiwan to Canada, demographic, economic, social, cultural and linguistic imperative towards a sustainable birth rate is now a common-sense debate. Amongst the bribes, gimmicks, smoke and mirrors of our forthcoming National Elections in May 2007, will it also become so in Wales? If it does, it will only be by default. Politicians will feign dismay at closing schools and post offices, talk sagely of the need to look after the elderly, but none will talk about the birth deficit and neither will the subject be raised by our craven press.

I'm not advocating a massive increase in the population of Wales. I'm talking about a sustainable birth rate – around the 2.2 of a few decades ago. Is that extreme? I'd like to see our population stay around the three million mark – that's the intelligent and sustainable demographic of the future. In a resources-rich country like Wales there's a definite advantage in having a comparatively small population in relation to our landmass – which would be one of the advantages of Welsh independence.

The challenge of a below-sustainable birth rate calls for a huge change in attitude, of turning around a cultural supertanker. It's a complicated field, not least because policies need to recognise people's aspirations for balancing having children at the same time as pursuing a career.

But there's also a strong cultural context to birth rate which is difficult to quantify. Will our AMs offer free bus-passes to pregnant women and parents, not just to pensioners?

And what of our media? Now that BBC Radio 4 has, at long last, run an item on Welsh demographics, my hunch is that the Welsh media will reckon it might just be safe enough to peek over the parapet of its prejudices and discuss it as well. As editors and commissioners whose formative years were the 1980s approach middle age – and what was, incidentally, the age of grandparenthood in the past – let's hope some may wake up to the reality which isn't on TV. Let's hope the debate about birth-rates can begin, and let's hope it won't be a childish one.

Cambria, vol. 8, no. 4, October–November 2006

How to Secede:
the Unlikely Story of Keep Wales Tidy

I was at university in Aberystwyth with Tegryn Jones, a good man with a dry sense of humour and a good head for facts, both useful and utterly pointless! It was at one of our few brief get-togethers that he casually mentioned that Keep Wales Tidy were better off financially since leaving the British set-up. This was a pleasant surprise and stuck with me for a few years, until I decided that it was a parable for many other organisations which are part of a wider UK (or, worse, Englandandwales) organisation. I thought that was an interesting article in itself, but I was still baffled at how Keep Wales Tidy left the UK one. After all, other more obviously Welsh organisations, such as the Young Farmers' Clubs, still insist on being a part of the Englandandwales organisation.

I decided to re-read Benedict Anderson's famous book on nationalism, Imagined Communities. *For what it's worth, my view is that Anderson's book is very good at explaining the nationalist movements of what I as a Welsh nationalist would consider as artificial nations – Indonesia, Peru, Columbia or Britain – but not much use in explaining 'organic' nationalities such as Wales. But I found it very useful in explaining how a community of people – those who are by and large of the same background, language and culture as the dominant community – decide to throw their lot with the 'indigenous' community.*

This movement for secession still goes on in Wales, piece by piece. Of course a flashing red warning light should be switched on every time an organisation commissions an 'expert'. They will, almost to a man, tell the Welshies to know their place and play second-fiddle to Big Brother. When one considers that the Welsh government is in favour of creating a 'small, intelligent' nation, then one would expect that all organisations active in

Wales should have their HQ in Wales, which would be a small but significant part in strengthening Welsh society and offering high-quality interesting jobs. The fact that they don't helps to explain why Wales is still comparatively poor economically.

If you're in an organisation which hasn't yet declared UDI, then, now is the time for you to get organised and do it. You won't regret it.

Since 1991 over a dozen new independent states have been created in Europe. During that time dozens of Welsh organisation have also seceded from the UK. Does any one know how many? Of course not, but it's these little histories of secession which interests me.

These little patches of independence create a new terrain. They are the slow, wobbly, cud-chewing, tortoise acts of institutional independence. They may at best get a story in the straight-to-recycle internal newsletter or possibly a write-up with accompanying new logo in the Western Mail. Outside their bubble, they're barely noticed by the public; they are the daily weather reports in the climate change of national history. However, in the soon-to-be-written history of a self-governing Wales, the mostly unwritten history of little acts of secession should be as important as the nail-biting referendum of 1997. For it will be these little acts of secession which will make Wales free before it's independent.

The acts of secession may not be by nationalist staff, nor part of a 'nationalist plot' (in fact, they mostly aren't), though all have involved some form of confrontation and nervousness.

One act of secession from the UK was that of Keep Wales Tidy in 2005. Did you notice it?

Keep Wales Tidy isn't a bastion of rabid Welsh

republicanism by anyone's standards. One can hardly think of a more sensible organisation; diligently keeping itself to the non-political, non-confrontational side of the environmental debate. A sort of unfashionable, vest-wearing environmentalism to the rock 'n' roll of Greenpeace. So, how did it get itself mixed up with those ethnic extremists on a slippery slope to independence?

Tegryn Jones was the Chief Executive of Keep Wales Tidy from 2004 to 2010. He joined the organisation shortly after it had decided to secede (along with Scotland and Northern Ireland) from the main UK body, ably led by the late Chair of the Campaign, Rhiannon Bevan, who died in 2005.

The UK movement itself was formed in the brave Bevanite duty and data world of the 1940s. It was one central UK body until the scruffy, long-haired nationalist revolution led to the formation of the Keep Wales Tidy Campaign in 1972. Even then, it amounted to nothing much more than an office and logo with finance from the Welsh Office. By the late 1990s the Welsh branch was contributing £60,000 annually to the central organisation to pay for literature, technical back-up and support. It was from the head office in Wigan that the majority of the development programmes and projects were made. It was from this, it seems, that disquiet began, aided by an increasing divergence in priorities led by the newly-established Assembly in 1999.

Whilst the UK body wanted to follow a Vertical Integration Model strategy (jargonese for lobbying Government and county councils) to achieve its aims, the Welsh branch wanted to follow a different agenda. Their vision was to develop a stronger grass-roots movement to implement change and also, of course, lobby the Welsh (not Westminster) government.

There was of course a lot of opposition to secession –

there always is. Inevitably the views of 'impartial experts' were canvassed – yes, the 'boffins in the white coats' were wheeled out. Papers and documents by 'experts' which proved beyond all reasonable doubt that little Wales couldn't run its own Keep Wales Tidy Campaign.

After years of wrangling, when secession did take place it was by the most unlikely of scenarios. In an echo of Boris Yeltsin's decision to call for Russian independence from the USSR – a decision which led to the independence of the other fourteen republics – it was England that finally left the UK. The rump UK body (aka England) decided that being legally responsible for four organisations but without control over the budgets of the three Celtic organisations was too much of a legal risk.

'I think it was a very important decision for Wales,' Tegryn mused. 'We had to move from being dependent to being independent. There were issues to do with personnel and production which we now had control over. These services were going to be produced and supplied in Wales and so strengthen the Welsh economy.'

All in all the UK/England body lost some £250,000 in annual income from the secession of Wales, Scotland and Northern Ireland.

Tegryn Jones is adamant that the break was the right move for Keep Wales Tidy. The facts certainly back his confidence. In the six years he was Chief Executive the campaign's income increased from £1m to £3m in 2010. Staffing increased from twenty members of staff to sixty.

Wales now enjoys international recognition as a nation in its own right. It's a proud member of the Foundation for Environmental Education, standing shoulder to shoulder with the other ex-UK countries and states as diverse as China, Iran and Russia. 'We would never have had that status under the old regime,' added Tegryn.

So much for the 'experts'.

So, what can we learn, if anything, from the Keep Wales Tidy experience? Firstly, that we're all part of a larger canvas. Keep Wales Tidy wouldn't have become self-governing were it not for the advent of the Assembly, which dramatically changed the landscape. Secondly, change depends on a determined and charismatic individual – a concept which makes many Welsh nationalists uncomfortable. I have no idea if Rhiannon Bevan was a card-carrying nationalist or not, but it was her determination to get the best for her Welsh organisation and uphold the dignity of her nationality and morality that drove the process forward. And then there's probably the element of simple governance. In KWT's case it became irritation with the increasing irrationality of having UK governance post-devolution.

For KWT, the one continuous flat battery in the mechanics of governance was something as unexciting as taxation. Following the reorganisation in the 1990s for legal reasons to do with VAT, the Keep Wales Tidy board had to include a majority of members from the trustees of the UK board. It was little things like this which became to be seen as an irritant. With the advent of devolution a new common sense was created, and what once would have been accepted was seen as irrational.

Despite the unmitigated success of the secession of Keep Wales Tidy from the UK set-up, I'm still surprised by it: surprised, not that it was a success, but that it happened at all.

Even accounting for Rhiannon Bevan's and then Tegryn Jones' leadership skills, how did an organisation whose membership and remit is not obviously or culturally 'national' choose to take what is effectively a nationalist path?

In his seminal book on nationalism, *Imagined Nations*, Benedict Anderson notes that nineteenth-century 'print capitalism' contributed to the concept of a nation. It was print capitalism – that is, local newspapers and books – with mass literacy which helped create nations based on language and a shared history and discussion. That's all fine, and helps explain the success of the national linguistic movements in Eastern Europe, but doesn't fully explain the current Welsh experience.

From the point of view of a public which actually reads and partakes in a national Welsh print discussion, in either language, then Wales is almost pre-industrial and almost illiterate! One could probably add a greater number, around half the population of Wales, who partake regularly in Welsh 'media capitalism' in some form – watching or listening to Welsh TV and radio.

With this in mind, and with the substantial minority, if not majority, of our senior civil servants, heads of industry, academics, not being Welsh, then I'm at a loss to find the pool of people who would discuss their work and challenges within a Welsh context. Where's the cultural space to create such radical political change?

Without wanting to labour the point, maybe we have in Wales a constituency of people whom Anderson refers to as the 'Creoles' in Latin America. People who were not of the indigenous pre-Columbian population, but rather of outside – Iberian – background. It was these people, Anderson claims, that 'invented' the nationalities of Peru, Venezuela, Argentina – they were the revolutionaries like Simon Bolívar and San Martín.

Though culturally and linguistically the same as the Spanish 'peninsulares' the Creoles were denied vertical promotion. It was this class, then, based on the narrowed, embargoed economic horizon of their South American provinces, discussing within their localised print capitalism, which created a cultural and political space, that invented the new American nations. Is there a Welsh parallel with the American Creole class? Are they the ubiquitous but invisible unhistoric class which plays such a pivotal part in Welsh politics and society?

There is no vertical bar on promotion for any UK subject, and nor is there geographic distance. The two-hour journey from Cardiff to London may be tedious but it doesn't compare to the 6,000 Andean and Atlantic miles between Lima and Madrid. And nor is there, it seems, a Welsh print capitalism – or one which is wide enough to include a substantial constituency of public informers. So, what is it that brings people, the 'Welsh Creole', to coalesce around a nationalist narrative like that which made Keep Wales Tidy secede from the 'peninsulares' of the UK body?

How can we have a 'print capitalism' without there being a 'print' and, heavens, without there hardly being a 'capitalism' in Wales!? And maybe that's it. In a country where capitalism is so weak the state in Wales has stepped in to take the role which merchants and industrialists do in other countries. The state is the capital. What we have in Wales is 'state capitalism', or maybe more precisely, 'third sector' or 'public sector' capitalism.

It was the state, in the form of the then Welsh Office in 1972 and the Assembly from 1999, which helped finance KWT and countless other Welsh bodies. The governing class – be they 'indigenous' or 'Creole' – work within the horizons of the Welsh state capitalism. It's this state capitalism that creates the cultural space to discuss and form a community of interest, and it is this state capitalism that also finances this class. Put simply, it would have been mad for KWT not to secede.

Added to that is a second insight by Anderson to the new nationalism of Latin America – the alignment of people like Bolívar with the ideas of emancipation and revolution. It was these ideas which also influenced and inspired the Creoles to break free of Madrid. Of course, the direct heirs to the French Revolution are the 'progressive' left-wing politics of our own age. Is it too fanciful to say that the legacy of the philosophy of the French Revolution was also a contributing factor in KWT breaking free of the centre? After all, the Welsh organisation wanted to follow a 'progressive' strategy of grass-roots participation, whilst the centre followed a more institutional and conservative approach.

That is, Creoles and indigenous people could coalesce around a national project which included greater personal freedom and responsibility for both groups within their own territory; greater freedom to follow and implement a political philosophy which appealed to Creoles irrespective of their own cultural affinity, and lastly, the common sense of working and optimising their own 'state capitalism'. The 'imagined community' became a vehicle for political and personal ambition.

With this stage of autonomy gained, there may be another question to be posed. The Latin American revolutionaries created and invented nation states in their own image. But for all the efforts at writing a new history this image was very much in the image of their intellectual, and sometimes actual, motherland. With a second, peaceful Bolivarian revolution sweeping across Latin America over the last decade, in Venezuela, Bolivia, Peru and Equador, we're seeing a reassessing and reasserting of the pre-Conquest, pre-Peninsulares languages and culture. A revolution which is not in the image of the distant European norms, language and culture. Since 1991 and especially 1997, many of our institutions in Wales have declared independence from the UK. Will the next step be to create truly functioning Welsh institutions, and not institutions in the image, with minor political nuances, of the 'mother' polities? A second Cambrian revolution, so to speak?

But back to Keep Wales Tidy. Tegryn Jones knows that secession was best for Keep Wales Tidy but there is one thing which still bugs him. During the hours of discussion and politicking, one symbolic clause passed unnoticed – 'intellectual property'.

'When the UK organisation came to an end we should have dissolved the UK company. We didn't, and so the English organisation kept the intellectual rights over the 'Keep Britain Tidy' title. They still use it – although they have no remit outside England!' remembered Tegryn.

But then, maybe, that shouldn't be such a surprise. After the Velvet Divorce, the Czech Republic continued to use the old Czechoslovakia flag, much to the chagrin of the Slovaks: a Freudian slip which only confirmed what many believe to have been the case all along.

Cambria, vol. 13, no. 2, February 2012

Iaith gwaith:
the Economic Benefit of Using
a 'Small' Language

Those of us who live in bilingual countries are well aware of the different benefits to the individual of speaking more than one language. However, whilst much has been written about the benefits of a multilingual workforce I couldn't find any literature of the domestic benefit of a country speaking, and more pertinently using, its own unique language.

Without concrete evidence much of the work would have to be counter-factual. How would a state such as Denmark fare if it was a German Land? How many more magazines, books, newspaper, TV programmes, plays would Ireland produce if Irish was its prime language? How much money spent on these activities would stay within the domestic economy if it used its own language, and how much seeps out?

As one born in Zambia I've always had a special interest in the African continent. That interest has increased as I read the writings of people such as Professor Robert Phillipson, who outlines the continuation of colonial policy post-independence – this time through 'linguistic imperialism'. Instances where the meeting of Commonwealth members at Makerere University in Uganda in 1961 decided that English would be the language of education: by doing this, the Africans, like the Welsh before them, effectively signed the death-warrant of their own languages. They also undermined their efforts to build their own intellectual economy – literature, television and film production, music, publishing. The same arguments are used against using the indigenous languages in Africa as were used in Wales and other European nations. Disheartingly, very often the most dogmatic and evangelical arguments made for forgetting the indigenous languages are made by those who do so in the name of social equality and workers' rights.

The pioneering work undertaken by Prof. Kwesi Kwaa Prah, Director of the Centre for Advanced Studies of African Society (CASAS) in South Africa, aims to create and consolidate closely-related African languages into new standardised written forms, and hopes to counteract this tendency. By creating new unified standardisations of the eighteen or so core languages spoken by 75 per cent of indigenous Africans, they hope to bring knowledge closer to the African masses and also build up expertise, literature and industry within the African continent and not be so dependent on outside help or advice.

After all, if promoting, teaching and using the English language is deemed by the British Council to bring millions of pounds to the UK economy, surely there is also an economic benefit to a state promoting and using its own language too?

'Welsh language is a luxury we can't afford', screamed the Western Mail front page headline on 22 May 2012. Or, 'Welsh-medium education: a £10m luxury schools can't afford' (*Times Education Supplement*, 23 April 2010).

Over the years ... no, decades ... no, centuries, this has been a familiar theme a 'common sense' view used against the Welsh language. The words change but the sentiment doesn't. It's even said by a certain subaltern species of Welsh-speaker.

But it's wrong.

In fact, the Welsh language not only isn't a hindrance to economic development, but is an active positive in creating work and strengthening the Welsh economy.

I'm not saying that a 'small' language community like Welsh, Estonian, Quechua or Wolof shouldn't also be bilingual or trilingual – there's an obvious economic benefit to that too. I'm also not referring to the added personal advantage to a bilingual individual within a bilingual state like Wales or Belgium. No, I believe there is an intrinsic added benefit to a nation or community using its own unique language for its own domestic economy.

This, it seems, goes against the grain of economic orthodoxy for minority languages in western Europe, or in relation to the 'developing states' of Africa. Unfortunately, as far as I can see, probably because the global academic economy is in English, very little research has been done into the economic benefits of a state, like Wales or those in Africa, using its own unique language as opposed to a larger one.

As Robert Phillipson writes in his seminal book *Linguistic Imperialism*:

> The arguments in favour of English are intuitively common-sensical, but only in the Gramscian sense of being based on beliefs which reflect the dominant ideology. Hegemonic ideas tend to be internalised by the dominated, even though they are not objectively in their interest.
>
> However, this economic blind-spot is curious, to say the least, especially as the Western economy over the past thirty years has seen an increase in 'soft' service and communications-based industries.

Look, if a community possesses and uses its own unique language, then that community or nation will need to have those services in that language. These services will include newspapers and magazines, television and radio, theatre, books, websites, music or call centres. These, and more, are services which all developed literate communities use. The questions, then, are, in which language are they serviced, and by whom and where are these services produced?

In a community which has two or more languages, these services will tend mostly to be in the dominant language – in

Wales' case, English. And yes, in Wales' situation, a case can be made that Wales can benefit from producing goods and services in English. But as Wales is competing in this language market with other territories that also speak and use English, Wales can also lose out from this huge market.

The one market Wales can't lose out on is in goods and services produced using the Welsh language.

Let me give you an example.

To prove my point I'll look at two very similar communities in terms of geography, population and location, and see how they fare. There are two big differences between them: one speaks and uses its unique tiny language, and the other has found oil within its territory. Which one is the most economically successful?

The two communities are the Faroe Islands, a self-governing territory within the Danish Kingdom, and the Shetland Islands, part of Scotland and the UK.

They are neighbours in the North Sea. Both are about 1,400 sq km. All people on the Faroe Islands speak Faroese (a Scandinavian language closest to Icelandic), with only 50,000 speakers. Shetland is monolingual English-speaking, having lost its own Norn language – a sister language to Faroese – 200 years ago. It's an integral part of the world-wide community of hundreds of millions of speakers. It's also part of the UK, currently the world's sixth biggest economy.

Advancing 'common sense' dominant language economics propagated by Welsh or world-wide Anglophone universities and British nationalist politicians, then the most successful economy and society must surely be the Shetland Islands. After all, Shetland is part of a bigger economic domestic economy, is English-speaking (the global language), and also has oil.

And this is where it gets interesting.

For although Shetland has oil within its maritime

borders, and the Faroe Islands none, the population of the two archipelagoes suggest that the common sense economic model isn't as obvious as it should be. If population growth is a barometer of a healthy economy, then the Faroe Islands, with 50,000 people, is more economically successful than the Shetland Islands, with 22,000.

The Faroe Islands also started from a much weaker position. Whilst the population of the Shetland Isles in 1801 was 22,000, the population of the Faroes was only 5,000. The population of the Faroe Islands has grown to 50,000 today, despite the fact that the Faroese lost 5,000 people due to a severe economic recession in the 1990s, which saw one of its banks collapse. The Shetlands are on 22,000 – which is itself down from 1991 – despite oil, despite a larger domestic economy, despite English.

So, why has the Faroese population continued to grow while Shetland's is on a relatively downward trail?

The Faroese are striking for being one of the few, if not the only, non-immigrant communities in Europe with an above-replacement birth rate. But that could explain a population not falling but not necessary growing. There is not either, as is the case in the UK, the factor of people moving from the metropolis to remote rural areas to retire or sign on. So, the population does show a resilient economy. There are other economic factors. The Faroe Islands are a part of Denmark but not a part of the EU, and so retain control over their fishing waters, which account for almost the whole of their export economy. But is there something else? They currently receive money from Denmark, but then so would Shetland from the UK exchequer.

With one economic orthodoxy discredited following the bling economics of the banking crisis, isn't it time another economic orthodoxy is also discredited – the orthodoxy against 'small' languages? May I suggest therefore that the

Faroese language is a contributing and overlooked factor in the comparative success of the Faroes in relation to the Shetlands? The Shetland Islands is serviced by one weekly paper, *The Shetland Times*. It also has an hour and a half opt-out radio service, Radio Shetland, which is part of BBC Radio Scotland, and a husband-and-wife team music radio station, SIBC.

However, the unique Faroese linguistic community is serviced by two daily newspapers, *Dimmaeletting* and *Sosialurin*; a business paper, *Vinnuvitan*; and half a dozen other papers and magazines in Faroese. There is a Faroese television service, Kringvarp Forya, funded by license fee, bingo and advertising. There are also three radio services – the radio side of Kringvarp Forya (speech and music), Ras 2 (pop music) and Lindin (a Christian station). Add to that the cultural and academic needs answered in the language: leisure reading, text books for schools, music performed and broadcast in the language. There is also even a very small National University of the Faroe Islands. All these services, because they are in the unique language, are produced in the Faroe Islands.

So, my estimate is that some 500 people are employed directly because of the Faroese language, which wouldn't be the case if the islands were Danish-speaking, and certainly not if they were English-speaking. For a population of 50,000 people, that's a substantial employer. Added to that are the jobs created or retained in the Faroe Islands to govern the largely self-governing state: the kind of jobs and skills, again, which would normally be outsourced to the metropolis. As one book about the Faroe Islands said, like Rome, all roads lead to the Faroese capital, Tórshavn. It isn't just jobs that the unique language creates; it's the quality of jobs too – keeping on the islands the kind of people who would otherwise leave for the metropolis.

But there is another factor. Rather than 'losing jobs', the unique Faroese language creates jobs. Not only are jobs created, but the money spent in the Faroe Islands is also more likely to stay in the islands. A book, newspapers, royalty fees – the kind of expenditure which leaves the Shetland Isles for Edinburgh, London or New York – stay in the Faroe Islands. The language, therefore, is an unintended vehicle for strengthening the domestic economy and retaining expenditure. Less money seeps out of the Faroe Islands because they have their unique language.

One of the few economists who have touched on this subject is the Professor Iñaki Zabelata of the Basque Country. His calculation is that for every €1 invested in the Basque language €3 went into the Basque economy. This is because for every euro invested in the core business (e.g. Basque newspaper), money is then invested in supplementary and then ancillary services.

There's no doubt that the €3 for €1 could be relevant to any local expenditures – such as attending a local sporting event, for instance. However, the use of a unique indigenous language by definition will almost always guarantee that the goods and services will be supplied only by a local service provider, using local manufacturers. It could also be the case that the use of the local language replaces services offered by outside providers, and so keeps money which would otherwise leave the linguistic community or nation's economy.

The experience of the expenditure of Radio Cymru and Radio Wales is instructive. Both the BBC services have a broadly similar mix of speech and music. However, where they differ greatly is in their choice of music. Whilst Radio Wales plays mainstream English-language music from the UK and the USA, Radio Cymru's policy is to play only or predominantly Welsh-language music. Because of Radio

Cymru's policy (a policy which has needless to say been called 'narrow-minded' and even 'linguistic apartheid' in the past) the vast amount of the income from its songs goes to singers, songwriters and recording studios in Wales. By comparison, Radio Wales' English-language policy means money leaves Wales. In fact Radio Cymru probably helps more English-language musicians in Wales than Radio Wales. Radio Wales' music policy, on the other hand, subsidises the economy of London, New York or Nashville.

The same situation would be true of Welsh-medium schools buying books in Welsh – *Sali Mali,* not Disney. Again, more non-Welsh speakers are probably employed indirectly by Welsh-medium schools than by English-medium schools.

In a mirror image of the American projects and British Council, the French created the *Haut Comité pour la Défense et l'Expansio de la Langue Français.* With typical lack of the tact the British Council applies, but no doubt with the same sentiment, the French noted candidly, 'Where they speak French they buy French'. If our English and French friends understand the economic benefit of using their own language, why don't we?

In fact, the more I think about it, the more I'm struck by how obvious and fundamental having, and more importantly using, an indigenous language is to a nation's economy. To play counter-factual history for a minute, do you believe that, let's say, Denmark would employ as many people in the print, media, cultural and service industries, if the nationalist awakening and Grundtvig's *Folkehøjskole* (Folk High Schools) hadn't been successful in the nineteenth century, and Denmark was today German-speaking and the seventeenth Land of the *Bundesrepublik*? Not to use your unique language in a world where the service industries and information technology are so important is the twenty-first century equivalent of being an extractive economy. It's like nineteenth-century India producing cotton, seeing it shipped off to Manchester, and having to buy it back as finished goods. As Phillipson noted, again in *Linguistic Imperialism*, 'Linguistic imperialism dovetails with other types of imperialism and is an integral part of them'.

It's all fine saying how using the global language can bring employment – be it a call centre in India or Bridgend. But, if the company wants to, those English-language call centres can just as easily relocate to another English-speaking territory. However, if the public and state demand a service in the unique indigenous language – Bengali or Welsh – then those jobs are not so transferable. Strong linguistic laws, then, would have a more long-term and sustainable effect of retaining employment than any union regulation or employment law.

The argument of the 'cost' of status and using an indigenous language is always brought up, especially so in the field of education – and consistently over-estimated by public and politicians, according to the Swiss linguistic economist, Francois Grin. His research concludes that the cost of changing education from a previous state (colonial) language to a non-state language (Welsh, Quecha, Breton or Nguni) is only 3 per cent higher. And my guess is that this 3 per cent goes almost entirely back into the domestic economy in paying for material and infrastructure.

Even in a 'First World' economy such as Wales', there is strong anti-colonial argument for using the indigenous language: be it with producing goods and services in Welsh in Wales or Kalenjin in Uganda, the economics are the same.

To continue to use the dominant global language to the detriment of the domestic unique language is the economic equivalent of feeding yourself by buying a McDonald's take-away every night. Yes, it's easier in the short run, may even taste better, and is certainly more glamorous for some than cooking at home. But in the long run, isn't it better initially to invest a slightly larger amount of money in buying good ingredients from your local shop and taking a little time to learn to cook? Is this lack of status and use of the indigenous language one reason that Wales, Africa and South America, in their own ways and context, are not as economically successful as they could be, whilst other states that use their own languages, such as Vietnam and Korea, are?

The Blue Books report said the Welsh language was a detriment to Welsh economy. Hundreds of thousands of Welsh-speakers have turned their back on the language since then, because, as Phillipson says, we internalised our colonialism. English was the language to 'get on in the world'. But it hasn't made us richer, has it?

We were sold a lie. Other nations in Europe from Malta to Estonia to Flanders have retained their language, with no detriment to their economy. The turn to English, then, was a political and colonial decision.

Now, English is here to stay. But in the same way that the ability to use English opens a market for us as a people and individuals, using Welsh can also create and strengthen our domestic market. I'd almost say, if the Welsh language didn't exist, then from an economic point of view it would be worth us inventing it! But let's use it. The more we use the medium of Welsh, the more we'll see it as a medium to create and retain skills, jobs and technologies and our young people. We'll create *'gwaith'* (work) through our *'iaith'* (language).

Too Poor to be Independent?: Just Another Version of 'I'm Not Racist, But ...'

What is it Gandhi said? 'First they ignore you, then they ridicule you, then they fight you, then you win'.

I'd become so used to seeing the 'too poor to be independent' comment that I thought it had probably been used as a default for every single state which has striven to become independent. No doubt, it was said of the Thirteen American Colonies as they became independent. What I hadn't seen was a simple, easy-to-read, cut-out-and-keep article which tried to get some of these knee-jerk reactions in one place.

It seems as if a section of society is pre-programmed to believe that big is better, even when everything around them proves that isn't always the case. Why is this? Is it conservatism? Is it just propaganda by the dominant states? The 'too small to be independent' argument is even used against nations which are blatantly industrious and wealthy, such as Scotland, Catalonia or Flanders, so it's hardly a coherent intellectual argument. Were oil-rich Kuwait to strive for independence today, no doubt someone would sagely say they were 'too poor to be independent'.

It's a Pavlovian reaction. Once one sees the endless examples of the prophets of economic doom reel out the scare-stories against every secessionist movement you begin to switch off and laugh at them.

The doomsayers will also place on the secessionist movement a whole basket of political positions which they secessionists don't subscribe to, but are then forced to disassociate themselves from. They make arguments which are as childish as they are ridiculous. People who are coherent and sensible in every other walk of life become totally irrational and lacking in self-

237

awareness, or blind to their own experiences, when they use arguments against independence. It's as if something has been switched off when they hear the word.

The anti-independence spokesman will accuse the secessionists of wanting to have border posts even though, in the European experience, border posts have mostly ceased to exist.

Arguments are made that the secessionist country can't be self-sufficient, as if the UK is self-sufficient in oranges and bananas or Spain in oil. As if the secessionists wish to be self-sufficient in the first place!

Fears are spread that the new state will stop people watching popular television series, unaware of the reality they experience every day where we now have satellite TV and the internet where people can view what they like.

People who've been on holiday to successful 'small countries' come back and say that their own small country can't afford independence.

Welsh members of the European Parliament who deal with 'small countries' daily still say Wales it 'too small to be independent'.

You can point out that no country has voluntarily decided to reject its own independence and become a province; that big states like Russia or China or India are no guarantee of economic prosperity any more than smaller countries. It makes no difference. These people are in some cult, the cult of the big is better even when their own country, in Wales's case, has become poorer as part of that 'big is better' state. The arguments then are rarely economic; they have more to do with the emotional, the cultural and political.

As Daron Acamoglu and James Robinson, in their seminal book Why Nations Fail, note, it is management of a state, the policies they take, not geography, not topography, not climate, not culture, which determines if a state is successful or not. Size doesn't come into it. Or rather, it does, if the size of the state *makes it easier to implement change, develop the state's strength and generate the support of the population.*

The next time you hear the words 'too poor to be independent' insert the words 'I'm not racist but …' – it's the same mentality.

'An independent Wales would not be economically viable.'

Funny, if Wales was given a penny every time somebody said that, then Wales would certainly pay its way!

This 'can't afford independence' is a common refrain by commentators and politicians alike, and is currently used with great gusto as an argument against Scottish independence. But a quick glance through the articles, editorials and letters pages of the past make it clear that Wales and Scotland haven't been the only European countries that 'can't afford independence'.

Malta was one example. An editorial in *The Times* on 7 January 1959 noted gravely:

> Malta cannot live on its own … the island could pay for only one-fifths of her food and essential imports; well over a quarter of the present labour force would be out of work and the economy of the country would collapse without British Treasury subventions. Talk of full independence for Malta is therefore hopelessly impractical.

The Times published a letter on 21 January 1964 by a Joseph Agius of Ta' Xbiex on Malta fearing 'the folly of giving independence to Malta when we are not economically prepared for it'.

Malta gained independence on 21 September 1964. It is essentially a city state on a barren rock; from a British point of view it was a very large dock. In 2009 its GDP at $23,800 per capita was similar to other former imperial port cities like Liverpool, Newcastle or Marseille.

Norway was another country which 'couldn't afford independence'. Like pre-independence Malta, it had limited self-government, but within Sweden. One of the great bones of contention was that the consular service and tariffs were biased towards the more agrarian Swedish economy rather than the exporting Norwegian one. Calls for greater independence were widely felt across Norway, but there were still some who were afraid of it and its consequences.

On 6 July 1892 *The Times* published a letter by 'R.H.' entitled, 'A Warning from Norway';

> as regards the immediate point of consular representation, the opinion of the commercial class in both kingdoms, as expressed in the chambers of commerce, beginning with the Norwegian capital itself, is decidedly hostile to it ... At the same time it seems scarcely possible that the leaders of the movement can clearly realise the fate they are preparing for the country by what may well be termed a suicidal agitation ... would not be a free national existence but subserviency, not to say bondage to Russia ... [Norway] reduced to conditions of a central Asian khanate.

Norway gained independence on 13 May 1905. It didn't become a 'central Asian khanate'.

In a rare article on Icelandic politics on 23 March 1908 *The Guardian* wrote a sentence which I guess has been used for all former colonies: 'It is very interesting to note that in this connection that Denmark has to pay a heavy price for her nominal possession of Iceland in the form of a large annual subvention to the Budget of the island'.

To bring us closer to our present time, Slovakia gained independence in the famous 'Velvet Divorce' in 1993.

In a generally balanced editorial, *The Independent*, on 31 December 1992 noted: 'there is no shortage of potential disputes. Currency union is doomed, with the Czechs determined to balance their budget and the Slovaks expected to head down the road of deficit financing and inflation.'

The *Guardian*'s report on 3 January 1993, two days after independence, highlighted that 'many people see the split as a failure and others are nervous about proving themselves in an uncertain world.'

What no report on Slovak (Norwegian, Icelandic or Maltese) independence seem to foresee is the subsequent economic success of these countries. (The 2011 GVA per capita figures are: Norway $61,041; Iceland $36,609; Malta $25,428; Slovakia $23,304; and Wales, interestingly, $24,534.)

The general tone of the British mindset varies from a mild scepticism to hostility towards independence, a sceptism which is at times more irrational and unscientific than the 'romantic' nationalists are accused of.

In 2011 there are 192 members of the UN – they can all 'afford independence'. This month the UN will accept its latest member, South Sudan. Yes, even South Sudan can 'afford independence'. There is also another country which is expected to declare independence this summer. It is the one country which in terms of its fractured geography, fractious politics and crippled economy you would expect not to be able to 'afford independence'. That country is Palestine. However, in much the same way that Scotland seems to be uniquely the only oil-producing country in the world which many British left-wingers think would be poorer with independence, Palestine seems uniquely to be the only state whose ability to 'afford independence' is never used as an argument against sovereignty by the British left-wing.

Which leads me to wonder whether there is a deeper reason for the historic reaction which some of our 'progressive' friends have against independence for smaller European nations. In a little-quoted article titled 'The Magyar Struggle' in the *Neue Rheinische Zeitung* on 13 January 1849, the co-founder of Communism, Freidrich Engels, wrote of the 'primitive' and 'counter-revolutionary peoples' of Europe. He names nations such as the Basques, Bretons, Scottish Highlanders and Serbians, whom he patronised for not having even reached the stage of capitalism. He calls them *'Völkerabfälle'* ('ethnic waste/trash' or 'waste peoples').

He says:

> These residual fragments of peoples always become fanatical standard-bearers of counter-revolution and remain so until their complete extirpation or loss of their national character, just as their whole existence in general is itself a protest against a great historical revolution.

Is this the root of the deep vein of left-wing ideological hostility towards independence for some small European nations? Is it that these 'progressives' see the larger nations, in Engels' words, as 'the main vehicle of historical development'? Although, Russia, that then very large nation, is (or was) hardly a good advert for equating 'big' with 'progress'.

But back to July 2011. Of course, South Sudan is hardly an economic inspiration for Welsh independence. Not even the South Sudanese wish to celebrate their current economic fortune. But then, the comparison for all economic scenarios, pre- or post-independence, in the short term at least, is the context of the neighbouring countries.

Let's discuss independence in another frame. Maybe we should view economic independence in the light of it just being another economic transition. The Welsh economy has been through several transitions: the agrarian revolution of the early nineteenth century, then an industrial revolution, and a managed (or badly managed) process of de-industrialisation. Independence would be but another economic transition. No Welsh economist or politican would expect the Welsh economy to be the same in twenty years' time as it is now. There will be change whatever happens, so why not a more fundamental economic change with independence as the vehicle?

There are, of course, those who argue that Wales is 'too poor', and without getting into that statistical war of attrition I'll make a few comments. The Welsh economy has been in historic decline since 1923 when the price of coal peaked. During that time Wales has been through three of the five stages of constitutional states. It's been governed as an integral part of 'the Realm of England' (1536–1959); as a part of English Realm but with some administrative functions – the Welsh Office period (1959–1999); and as a state with some self-government (1999 until the present day). There are two stages left, generally speaking. There is self-government with some taxation powers and then independence with full taxation powers. The first three constitutional settlements have not improved Wales's economic well-being. Why not, from an economic point of view, try the next two economic options?

There are numerous examples that independence is the best way to revive a weak economy.

Just as predictable as the 'Can the turnip-eaters afford

independence?' articles are the post-independence later features in the very same papers, which point how better off, economically and culturally, the independent countries have become.

Look again at that barren rock in the North Atlantic, Iceland – the little country which earlier this year had the courage to tell their bankers where to go. On, 1 December 1938, twenty years and a World War after the *Guardian's* dire assessment, *The Times* wrote a glowing report on Iceland's twentieth anniversary of independence from Denmark. Subtitled with the decidedly modernist, 'Roads and Radio', *The Times* notes succinctly; 'Side by side with the political liberation of the country, developed the gradual economic emancipation of the island.' The article continues by outlining the many benefits gained since independence, especially in the fields of modern communications.

So what of Wales? Wales today is guilty of voting for a set of 'national Gombeenism' economic policies. The Gombeen man is the Irish politician who's only out to get some economic or social gain for his constituency, devoid of a broader political, strategic or philosophical outlook. Wales, by belatedly wanting 'fair funding' from Westminster, sulking over 'unfair cuts', 'demanding' electrification of railways, but shirking responsibility over large energy-generating or taxation policies, is unnecessarily humiliating itself as a Gombeen nation.

In his recent article in the *Harvard Kennedy Review*, 'Small is cute, sexy and successful: Why Independence for Wales and other countries makes Economic Sense', Adam Price makes a compelling case for independence for 'small' nations. He compares the economic fortunes of independent Luxembourg and its neighbour, the German province, Saarland, since the Second World War.

But we needn't look to foreign lands for inspiration or

precedent. In every parish in our land there's a successful case of Wales not being 'too poor to be independent' – the Church in Wales founded in 1922. Like those new east European states such as Finland or Estonia, the Church in Wales could hardly have been formed at a worse time. It had to pay its way in the aftermath of the Great War and in the middle of the Great Depression. The Welsh church became independent during what the Rev D. T. W. Price, in his book on its history, calls 'the locust years'. 'Nonetheless,' as the Rev. Price notes, 'by 1937 it was generally felt, and rightly so, that the financial condition of the Church in Wales was as sound as it had been before disestablishment'.

Independence would force politicians and us voters in Wales to grown up. We would be economically viable because we would have to be. We'd have to learn to swim. Let's look at 'good practice'. After communism, bling-capitalism, imperialism, state socialism, supra-national states or religious statehood, the nation-state and independence is the one political construct that not one state or people has turned its back on. Independence works for Malta, Iceland, Norway and Slovakia – as well as larger states. It's time Wales made independence work for her too.

Cambria, vol. 12, no. 5, August 2011

What's the Point of Britain?:
the Empire has No Clothes

We are all nationalists. Yes, everyone of us, and especially those who claim not to be nationalists.

Many people, including Welsh nationalists, are uneasy when I refer to the Conservatives, Labour or Green parties as 'British nationalist parties'. They'll point out that those parties should not be equated with the racist British National Party. But this only highlights the gnawing lack of self-belief that so many Welsh nationalists, including those elected in Plaid Cymru's name, suffer from.

I'm a Welsh nationalist who believes that in a world of other nation states Wales should also be a nation state. I want Wales to have a seat at the United Nations and European Union. I want her language to have the same status and vitality as other state languages. I'll give up my nationalism when I see Russia, Denmark, France, Australia, give up their national status. If Wales became an independent nation tomorrow, then I would not be known as a nationalist. I would be known only as a Welshman. As the Irish republican and socialist James Connolly said, 'Nationalism has to be created in order to be got rid of'.

If believing in international status for Wales defines me as a Welsh nationalist, then, logically, a person who wishes to retain, and who will fight elections and referenda to keep, international status for Britain is a British nationalist.

It doesn't mean that they are racists, any more than being a Welsh nationalist should mean you're racist – though the Conservative, Labour, LibDem, Greens are on the same constitutional continuum as the BNP, of course. They all believe that Britain is 'the nation' of 'this country' and should be recognised as such internationally. Their flag is the Union Jack.

As a Welsh nationalist, I don't recognise the Union Jack and do not wish for 'Britain' to be an internationally recognised state.

Their definition of Britishness, their attitude towards Welshness and the Welsh language, and a host of other political questions, will vary, but that is true of Welsh nationalism too. However, in the final analysis, they will decide that Britain should have the final word and be the final arbiter. They believe that Wales should back down. I don't.

With the Queen's jubilee, the Olympics and the Scottish referendum debate, 2012 saw the British pan-nationalist front coalesce, as we always knew they would. The British state spent £9bn to host the Olympic games; gross domestic product was estimated to have declined 0.2 per cent between April and June due to the jubilee. These are some of the price-tags readily spent to promote British nationalism.

But there is another price tag. What price has Wales paid to be in the UK? Politically, linguistically, economically? As I see Scotland and Catalonia proudly debate independence, as I look back on the last 100 years and see non-historic nations like the Slovenes, Slovaks and Estonians gain independence; as I see languages which were smaller and even weaker than ours a century ago like Icelandic, Maltese and Hebrew, grow in number of speakers and in international prestige; as I see economies poorer than ours, like Ireland, Norway, Flanders, Switzerland, overtake us, I have to conclude that the twentieth century was a wasted century for Wales. It was wasted why? Because we agreed to be Britishised.

We sold our birthright and our self-respect as Welsh people to believe that by holding a tacky royal street party we were champions, better than lesser breeds. We believed that for the gulp of cheap pop from a wobbly plastic cup we were drinking from the same glass as English royalty.

I'm left thinking that Thomas Babington Macaulay's honest strategy in 1835 was as relevant for Wales as it was for India.

The deliberate strategy was to create 'a class of persons, Indian in blood and colour, but English in taste, in opinion, in morals, and in intellect'.

A really disheartening part of the 'British' ideology is the way it militates against an intelligent critique of the issues facing the Welsh language. It creates a set of political norms which infantilise Wales and the Welsh language. Grown-up scientific discussions on the Welsh language, such as are employed in discussing other causes, are ignored. This is seen clearly whithin large sections of the British labour movement in Wales.

The movement which has been so brave in explaining, taking on and changing society and parliament's attitudes and policies in relation to racism, women's rights or gay rights has mostly refused to do the same to get to the root of the economic, social, political and cultural challenges facing a minoritised language such as Welsh. In relation to Welsh, when compared with their attitudes to racism or feminism, it's as if their attitudes are stuck in the early 1950s.

The answers they too often give to the case of Welsh, if put in the context of combating racism, for instance, would be totally insufficient and offensive. They are of the type: 'Racism is bad, so let's all just be nice to black people, and black people can be like white people and not frighten us, and together we can conquer racism.' Or, in the case of women's emancipation: 'Women have a hard time. Let's all buy Mummy a Mother's Day card and everything will be better.'

In the case of the mammoth issues facing the Welsh language – the first language of many Labour party members – it really is as superficial as that. No effort to tackle the economic or social issues where, all of a sudden, the socialists come over all Thatcherite in their concern not to upset the market or capitalism.

And that's before we account for the 'redneck' element, which is against any recognition of Welsh at all.

So, it's not that people aren't intelligent, or that they can't dissect, discuss and give answers to big social and cultural issues. It's that they won't. And at the heart of this is 'Britishness', which conditions its followers never to seriously question the primary of British capital over Welsh national interests.

The British State is a con. Its existence is the very reason for the demise of our language, our claim to nationality and our poverty. Its very concept undermines, belittles and negates us. It's an intellectual trench the Welsh have to constantly navigate, scale and challenge to get but the minimum of concessions to any meaningful Welshness that isn't kitsch or ethnic.

The British project has left a cancerous legacy of wars, famines, economic imperialism and subjection. It feasts on the one just war it fought, the Second World War against Nazism, but is blinded by its own drunk narcissism to the countless genocidal wars and policies it has waged in Asia, Australasia, Africa and the Americas ... and its pernicious, debilitating legacy in Wales. Its political project is to create in Wales a compliant population which, despite scraps to Welsh sensibilities, will always in the final analysis, expect (and receive) from its ideological followers, that Wales will know its place as a conquered people.

Britishness is a political ideology, as is Communism. It isn't a nation. As the philosopher J. R. Jones said in 1966 in his book, *Prydeindod*, 'There already exists such a thing as a British nationality; it is the English one.'

A Nation consists of three strands; a People, two.

The first strand is what's called in Welsh *'priod iaith'*, for which there is no corresponding term in English. In Spanish and French the term is *'llengua prop'*; it is the indigenous language of that territory, that has defined its being. The second strand is a defined territory, and thirdly, sovereignty over that territory. Wales as a People has two strands – the language and the defined territory; it doesn't as yet hold sovereignty to be recognised truly as a free nation.

The 'British nation', likewise, is not a Nation as it does not have a *priod iaith*. There is no 'British language'. It is not Switzerland, where a new nationality has been agreed, with the constituent '*priod iaith*' being recognised and respected as an organic part of that state. The British nationality is an extension of English nationality. Its *priod iaith* is English – as the name suggests, it is the language of the English people and state.

If Scotland were to vote for independence then 'Britain' would cease to exist, and with it the 'British nation'.

To accept British nationality is to accept English nationality, albeit with some local ethnic flavour that only adds to the feeling of imperial majesty which satisfies the English-as-British ideology. In fact, some minor Celtic diversity and ethnic minority colour is to welcomed by the majority English nationality, because it reinforces the self-image and self-worth of a nationality that has conquered and incorporated lesser peoples into their own.

The London state has succeeded fantastically well in its mission to create a new supplanted British ideology. As it accumulates more peoples it has been able to give its English nationality the image of being multi-ethnic. It can offer an avenue for those who wish to drink from the glory of its fountain or wish to enjoy the applause on a bigger stage through its institutions. This is glory that a small nation can't offer, or must be denied the opportunity of offering to its people. For the British ideology will undermine any effort by the conquered to build and achieve those stages and fountains for themselves; for to create our own fountains and stages will be to undermine the empire's role as an arbiter of thought, taste, and power. The British national ideology must undermine these efforts lest the conquered see that the empire has no clothes.

The skills and tools used by the England-as-British state follow the pattern of the Roman Empire. In 97 AD the Roman historian Tacitus reported how the Roman administrator of Britain successfully assimilated the local elite:

> Agricola trained the sons of the chiefs in the liberal arts ... The result was that in place of distaste for the Latin language came a passion to command it. In the same way, our national dress came in to favour and the toga was everywhere to be seen. And so the Britons were gradually led on to the amenities that make vice agreeable – arcades, baths and sumptuous banquets. They spoke of such novelties as 'civilization' when really they were only features of their enslavement.

As Saunders Lewis said in his revolutionary radio lecture, *Tynged yr Iaith* (Fate of the Language) in 1962:

> Thus the policy laid down as the aim of the English Government in Wales in the measure called the Act of Union of England and Wales in 1536 will at last have succeeded. To give the Government its due, throughout some four centuries of governing Wales, despite every change of circumstance, despite every change in parliamentary method and in the means of government, despite every social revolution, it has never wavered in applying this policy of excluding the Welsh language as a language of administration from office, court and legal writing.

A lawyer said in a court of law in 1773: 'It has always been the policy of the legislature to introduce the English language into Wales.'

Matthew Arnold, an Inspector of Schools, said in his official report in 1852:

> It must always be the desire of a Government to render its dominions, as far as possible, homogeneous ... Sooner or later, the difference of language between Wales and England will probably be effaced ... an event which is socially and politically so desirable.

And, that, my friends is how Wales went from being a majority Welsh-speaking country in less than two generations without a fight. It's a situation the British would never allow to happen to the English language in Wales. This need to be accepted by the British ideology made the Welsh, to use Stalin's description of the communist fellow-travellers, 'useful idiots'. Unlike the countless wars fought 'so that we don't all speak German/French now', no blood was spilt – be it English or Welsh – in the name of Wales or for the Welsh language.

But Welsh blood was spilt for the pernicious British ideology and for the glory, spread and *Lebensraum* for British people and the English language.

As the American author Mike Davies documents in *Late Victorian Holocausts: El Niño Famines and the Making of the Third World* (Verso, 2001), the British Empire caused the failure of the monsoon in the 1870s to become a genocide for the poor of Egypt, India and China. With the other European empires, the USA and Japan, it diverted food to feed itself. Davis calculates that up to 50 million died. And when that wasn't enough, the British Empire swept in and stole the land of the famished and desperate. It's no coincidence that the Zulu war, at which a relative of mine fought, was in 1878, following drought in southern Africa.

The difference between the British Empire and the Nazi

Reich is that the Nazis fought a racial war and the British an indiscriminate class war against the poor. The difference is that the Nazi killing of millions of innocents in Europe was seventy years later than the British atrocities and genocides, and too close to home, and too well covered by the media, to be forgotten. Who today, as William Digby noted in 1901, remembers the 'unnecessary deaths of millions of Indians' in the 1876 Madras famine? – a hunger which became a famine because of British rule.

The Madras Famine; warfare by steel and germs; land disposition; anarchy created by deliberate British policy to destabilise local polities – will we ever know the number total millions killed by the British Reich, as we do the German Third Reich?

And yet, such is the hold of 'cloth and trinkets' of the British ideology that many of the Welsh still wish to discard or subsume their Welsh identity to drink from its fountain. And such is the conceit of the British ideology that the Britishers, their press and politicians, will accuse Welsh nationalists of being extreme and causing division among peoples. You really couldn't make it up! Is it not time, as we approach the next round of British 'bread and circuses' – the commemoration of the First World War – that we learn the dictum of our Irish rebel friends, who saw Britishness for what it was? Should we not, in our hearts and in our actions, proclaim as they proclaimed: 'We serve neither King nor Kaiser but Ireland'?

Should we not, before the enforced British nationalism of the BBC gains a narrative, confront the propaganda before it begins? The British, grasping at straws to keep their state and perks together lest the lesser people see that the heavens won't fall if they proclaim independence, will contrive to say black is white and white is black. They will attempt to turn the First World War, a vicious, pointless ethnic war for the glory of English-as-British nationality, into a sermon against Welsh and Scottish nationalism. The nationality blamed for the carnage won't be the British nationality but a nationalism in whose name nobody fought, except in brigades of subalterns.

The ideology of Britishness, like Communism or the Christianity of the Crusade, beguiled thousands of our forefathers to slaughter or be slaughtered. It was not in Wales' name, nor for language or independence, that they fought, despite it being a war for to save 'little countries'. Wales got nothing in return.

Although rooted in English ethnicity – the language of the English and her institutions – 'Britishness' is not an ethnic nationality. It is a political ideology, and it is as a political ideology that those of us must recognise it, and build our own argument against it, and for an ideological Welsh nationality.

So, let me for the benefit of those unfamiliar with joined-up writing, explain it like this: Wales is a country and a nation; Britain is a state. Catalonia is a country and a nation; Spain is a state. When Catalonia or Scotland become independent they will not be 'new countries', they will be 'new states'. I wish for my nationality only what other nations enjoy.

It is my dream to see the end of the British state.

There is no need for a British state except to keep in power a class of people who believe that Welsh identity should be subservient to English norms and that a Welsh state would undermine their personal vainglory or power.

With the exception of waging war – at which the British state has a special talent – there is nothing the British state can do better than a Welsh state could. There is no need for this state. It has been a disaster for Wales. To fly the Union Jack in Wales is to hoist up the white flag and surrender our Welsh nationality.

The functions in whose name the British state has most appeal – music and popular culture – need no state. However, whilst culture and music know no boundaries, we must also not be ashamed of questioning whether this attractive contemporary culture is undermining or edging out contemporary Welsh culture, be it in Welsh or English. We should not accept as unchallenged forms of expression that displace Welsh people from songs and stories and the language of their own experience. We should not unquestioningly accept a culture if its effect is to alienate Welsh people from their culture, language, accent or aspiration. Such is the debilitating force of Britishness that it can be, and has been, used at the expense of a Welsh expression.

But this is now a cultural argument, and although culture and politics are closely related, or rather more transparently related in a Welsh context than a British one, this is an argument a step aside from the continuation of a British state.

For those parts of the British ideology that are most appealing do not need a unified British state or nationality.

British pop music and comedy does not need a British state any more than Beethoven needed a unified German state, or Don Quixote needed a unified Spanish state, or Shakespeare needed a unified British state. It does not need it, because British culture is, in fact, English culture, and England would (re)exist with the demise of the British state. The British language would not be under any threat as there is no British language.

In fact, as the language of this British nationality is English, it could be argued that a plurality of nationalities would in fact add to its appeal by bringing more distinct voices into its imperium.

For those who enjoy English culture and language, and

I'll include myself as one of those, then the death of Britain, I'm glad to say, will not affect that culture one bit.

As a minoritised language Welsh needs a state to defend and develop it; Britishness doesn't.

So, English-language culture will continue to thrive in all its forms, including in Wales, whether there is a British state or not. If some wish to continue calling it 'British culture' as opposed to English or Scottish or Welsh, then, so be it. It will be an assumed common culture, albeit built on conquest. But it will not be aligned to political nationality any more than enjoying Hollywood movies makes one American, or eating spaghetti makes one Italian.

So, who will oppose this change of state?

No doubt many will. For, after all, Britishness has a great appeal, not least, as it assumes in its lexicon, a generosity of identity, combining the Three Countries of Britain.

There will be many, Welsh-speakers included, who wish to identify with the glory of Britain in a way one supports a successful football team.

There are others who will be afraid that the loss of Britishness will bring to question the inbuilt certainty that the unmentioned but deeply understood primacy of the English language will be threatened. After all, if the British state was ready to go to war to make sure that 'we're not all speaking German now' (or in the Falkland Islands' case, 'Spanish now'), then they will fear that the vouchsafed guarantee of English primacy will not be there.

How Welsh in its pitiful situation can ever be a threat or ever again dream to create a monolingual state is beyond me. For the fact is, the English language is here to stay. And as I would no more wish to cut off my left hand because I am right-handed, I would not wish to lose the ability to speak English. What is not here to stay, I hope, is the arrogance that

'Britishness' gives a person. It's the arrogance that a person can live in Wales and can say without blinking, 'I don't speak Welsh' when they should more honestly say, 'I won't speak Welsh. No, not even, 'diolck yn vawer' for the £5 you've just given me for my measly service'.

There are others, the self-proclaimed progressives possibly, who will protest that a British identity is a cosmopolitan one ... implying that Welsh isn't.

In his excellent article 'Single Nation, Double Logic: Ed Milliband and the Problem with British Multiculturalism', Dr Daniel Gwydion Williams of Swansea quotes the Slovene philosopher, Slavoj Žižek, noting that Žižek claims:

> that the Serbs practice a 'kind of two-level nationalism' in which Serbia is the only nation in Yugoslavia that can sustain an open principle of multicultural and democratic citizenship. This results in a 'double logic', for while Serbs are seen to be fundamentally democratic, modern and evolving, the Slovenes are viewed as an inherently closed, traditional, 'primitive Alpine tribe'.

This, Žižek argues, is often the basis for contemporary racism. 'We should be careful when people emphasize their democratic credentials', warns Žižek, for the key question is whether 'these same people allow the Other to have the same credentials'.

'Cosmopolitan', in the scrabble hand of British politics, is a very high-scoring word. But to the British, 'cosmopolitan' is just a Greek word for 'English'. For many people 'cosmopolitan' = 'not Welsh'. We have Mr Bird of Cardiff for enlightening us of this, when in a meeting called by *Cymru Fydd* in 1896 to create a united Welsh Liberal party at Newport, he proclaimed that 'Throughout South Wales there are many thousands of English people … a cosmopolitan population who will never submit to the domination of Welsh ideas'.

That 'cosmopolitanism' didn't mean more than one language, it meant one. In the same way, 'Britishness' doesn't mean more than one nation, but one.

For Britishness wishes to have it both ways. On the one hand being a united nation, and on the other a family or a collection of three (or maybe four if we consider the Irish) nations. It's all very confusing.

Well, not really, for in the British ideology the differences of Welsh, English and Scottish aren't celebrated because they *are* different, but precisely because they are not and any differences are stepped on. So when a Welsh Britisher will say he is in favour of diversity and, look, his neighbour is English and they get on very well in brotherly love, he is saying two things. He is firstly implying that only through Britishness can one be best of friends and respect other people and that this, by implication, is beyond the ability or wish of the Welsh nationalist. But secondly, he is in such agreement culturally and linguistically with his neighbour, because Britishness has made them effectively the same through a deliberate policy of assimilation of the Welsh.

For Britishness is celebrated not because of its differences, but because there are no differences.

Likewise, one must be aware that 'civic society' in Wales is often used as a 'dog whistle' – a high-pitched sound which only some will hear and so it will not be recognised for its true meaning. For, more often than not, 'civic society' is but the polite way of saying 'English society in Wales'. It implies, again, that it is impossible to have a developed, plural, engaging society in Welsh – despite the examples in this book of activism and philosophy across Wales, in Welsh, by people, many of whom are not ethnically Welsh. It also implies that what activism and discussion does go on in Welsh is somehow ethnic-centric and tribal, not the dispassionate civic, English-language debate. 'Fascism' and 'racism' are terms casually thrown like smoke-bombs in Welsh political debate to confuse and disorientate legitimate concerns. But do not taunts of racism and fascism, if relevant at all, relate more to those who support the British state and the political Britishness than those who oppose them?

The UK is by no means a fascist state but it has shared one faculty with all forms of fascism. That is a policy of forcefully promoting a majority state language to the detriment and discrimination of an indigenous language. However, in the *Alice in Wonderland* world of British world view, it is those who've campaigned to reverse this pernicious supremacist doctrine that are labelled 'fascist' and 'language zealots'; not those who wish to erase, or at the least fatally weaken, the indigenous language!

All fascist states campaigned against language minority rights and the British state in its history of education, the law and civil society against Welsh did the same. Change against this has come gradually but only through campaigns by supporters of Welsh. Even today, the fascistic tendency of some of those who support the British political ideology hasn't totally gone away and its effects are still felt.

How many Welsh-speakers reading this book have been told to stop speaking Welsh in a pub, taxi or shop? How many have been beaten up for speaking Welsh or insulted in a queue for asking in Welsh? These things happen, but the Welsh-speaker has over the years mostly internalised them. They've not reported the incidents to the police. They have taken it as a part of being Welsh. They have learnt their lesson and not spoken Welsh publicly. It's not racism because they can turn off their problem by not speaking Welsh and speaking English instead. This is what accepting the perimeters of Britishness does, and by accepting those perimeters the 'racism' is cured.

Is political Britishness racist? No, because a language can be acquired (or lost) whilst skin colour can't.

But let us to consider another looking-glass scenario.

Imagine that the British state had found a miracle cure which could get rid of prejudice and racism against black people. That cure was a medicine which over years changed skin colour from black to white. By taking the medicine the black person would become white and racism and prejudice against him would cease. He'd still be allowed to call himself 'black' if that suited him (after all, he was proud of his background) and he could even black-up like a minstrel for particular sporting events or concerts. But, by and large, he was now a white man and all was well for the state and for him.

There is no miracle cure to 'treat' skin colour, but there is a miracle for curing the Welsh language and the British state, and its propagators have sold it, pushed it and meted it out to generations of Welsh people. Wales, once a 'black' country is now mostly 'white'. Too many 'black faces' upset the sensibility of the British state. Imagine over the centuries, were the choice given to them, how many black people, under pressure to conform by a powerful state and enforced feeling of inferiority in their being, would have chosen to take this 'cure' and change their skin from black to white?

Of course, race isn't language. We've passed the 'black' Wales stage, and many are now 'mixed' or 'brown' – speaking both languages. But even that pale blackness isn't enough for some Britishers still in power in our county councils or business from Cardiff to Anglesey. They want Wales to be wholly white and reverse to the Better Together policies which worked so well until those pesky civil rights people of Cymdeithas yr Iaith Gymraeg came along in the 1960s. Even to become momentarily 'black' by saying 'diolch' or 'bore da' to a customer is too inferior for some. Others still don't wish their children to be educated in a lesser language which could undermine their supremacist world view.

Some may read this article with a feeling of unease. If that is because you are English, then please don't feel that way. For, despite the tired and clichéd taunt that nationalists believe in 'my country, right or wrong', nothing could be further from the truth.

There is much that is wrong with Wales. If you are content with Wales then you really have given up on any aspiration that Wales can be a nation among world nations, and Welsh a lingua franca across Wales. Your ambition for Wales, as the writer Patrick McGuiness said, 'is barely higher than the kerb'.

Yes, much has changed since Saunders Lewis's challenge in 1962. But that change has come despite Britishness, not because of it. Not all people who've worked for the Welsh language or Welsh national status are Welsh nationalists; some of them may identify themselves as British, some aren't even Welsh or British.

But all people who've stood in the way of rights for Wales or the language have believed themselves to be British.

Change has come because people made choices – many of them you have read about in this book. They decided that the 'enemy' wasn't the English: it was Britishness.

The teachers who humiliated Eluned Morgan and the ones who caned Welsh children for speaking Welsh were, by and large, Welsh themselves. The parents of the children often supported their chastisement.

Why? Because Britishness, like communism, is a political philosophy, not a nationality. It made the Welsh ashamed of themselves, that their language was not of the modern world, that to assume full nationality they had to become English.

But they couldn't become English as they spoke this language, or were of this country, in which Welsh was the *priod iaith*. It was impossible for them to claim English nationality, the nationality to which they aspired, because the Welsh language denied them that. They grew to hate and despise this language, which denied them the opportunity to be 'top dog'. Some blamed it for their poor economic and social situation in life.

But they never stopped to think to step out of the *Truman Show* reality of Britishness and ask, as other European nations did, why can't education, society and commerce be in my language or on Welsh terms?

Eluned Morgan was brave because she committed the double treachery – questioning the assumed ordained primacy of Britishness and the English language in Wales, and secondly, by implication, shaming her own people because of their complicit actions in being a *kapo* in accepting and implementing their own subjection. How many of us take the Pasquale Paoliani rather than the Napoleon route?

How many of us today have the guts of that 15-year-old girl? How many of us today have the tenacity of Myrddin John to carry on for decades to win status for Wales, despite the easier path and glory he could have taken? How many of us can question our own Welsh society, in English or Welsh, as the brave men and women of *Cylch* did?

Wales, of course, can and does live with a British political dimension. Many, probably most, Welsh people are currently happy with this. For many it's the 'best of both worlds', and gives the veneer of offering a more relaxed, nuanced and sophisticated concept of nationality. It's a concept of nationality which isn't rigid and about 'building walls' and 'dividing people', as the clichés go, and suits those on the left who are troubled with rigid concepts of nationality and those on the right who wish to retain a strong UK state. This situation, a devolved Welsh Assembly within a larger British framework, could last indefinitely, and may indeed do so. If it does, it will be because of the political philosophy which believes that ultimately the buck stops with the moral authority of Westminster.

My position is that the buck stops with Wales, and that we should then decide how much of our sovereignty we wish to trade and share with other outside organisations, be that a British meeting of equals, a European framework or a world-wide one from the UN to the IMF. That, for me, recognises the nuances of identity, practicality and commonweal, but doesn't belittle Welsh national interests before the altar of Britishness.

What's the point of Britain?

There is no point to the British state. Its existence is used to deny Wales its rightful place among the nations of the world. If Wales is to survive and thrive in the twenty-first century in any meaningful way, the British state has to come to an end. Either it does, or Wales does. The choice is ours.